The Vintage Culture of
OUTBOARD RACING

The Vintage Culture of
OUTBOARD RACING

by **PETER HUNN**

DEVEREUX BOOKS
Marblehead, Massachusetts

Published by Devereux Books
PO Box 503
Marblehead, MA 01945
Internet address: www.devereuxbooks.com

Library of Congress Cataloging in Publication Data

Hunn, Peter 1953–
    The Vintage Culture of Outboard Racing / Peter Hunn
        cm.
    Includes index
    ISBN 0-928862-06-3
Motorboat racing — History. I. Title.

GV835.9 .H85 2000

797.1'4 — dc21   00-025795

On the cover:
It is August 4, 1946, and these hydros are racing before a little crowd at the Neshaminy Aquadrome. Here, not far from Philadelphia, at the "world's only 1/4 mile outboard speedway," races were held each Sunday at 3:00 PM. The Aquadrome was the brainchild of Hank Bowman who went on to become the most prolific and respected writer to chronicle the sport.

The tin, toy boat and the wonderful assortment of outboard-related memorabilia are examples of highly sought after collectibles. The promotional buttons, lunchbox, jewelry and other goodies evoke the bygone vintage culture of American outboard racing. These items are from the collection of long-time Mercury dealer Bob Grubb. (Photography by Bill Hazard)

Front Cover design by Alyssa Morris.
Back Cover and Interior design by Paige Davis

Dedication . . .

Boat and motor buffs usually aren't cat people. I wasn't, until my wife brought home a tiny shaded silver Persian kitten. We named him Stickley after a brand of mission oak furniture he playfully batted as soon as he figured out he was now home. Despite a few scratches to the dining room table, we grew to be great friends. He didn't have a mean bone in his body and would even purr loudly for total strangers. But paper was his true passion, especially any manuscript page I was working on for this or several other books. An incredibly long-haired editor, the "Fuzzball" spent hours sprawled out less than an inch away from my keyboard, thinking nothing of slapping a furry paw on my research notes for an apparent reminder of his ready assistance. He taught me the ambidextrous art of typing with one hand while scratching under a pet's chin with the other. If not obliged, he'd quickly bite the mouse cord or fold down the laptop screen. Because I usually wrote whenever having a free hour or so before heading off to teach, Stickley listened while I anxiously checked the time and asked him to let me know when exactly fifteen minutes were up. He never did, but I took that as a sign that he liked having me around. Anyway, the whole process made it seem less like talking to one's self. And then, "See ya later, Fuzzball," I'd hurriedly promise while grabbing my jacket and rushing out the door, late for work. He would seem to smile back, letting me know he'd keep an eye on the place.

Our great partnership came to a reluctant end during the last few days of preparing this book. Though only eight years old, Stickley just couldn't beat a cancer that suddenly started consuming him. My wife and I tried everything, but his suffering was obvious. After he was gone, the vet put him in a cardboard box that neither one of us could bear to look in. Nor did I feel much like going back to finish the manuscript. Of course, some closure was needed, so I drove to a peaceful meadow at a neighbor's farm. Someone had left an old, weathered rocking chair out there. The box on my lap, I pointed to the countryside and told my longtime writing companion how beautifully the birds sang in the nearby trees. Happy memories of Stickley flooded me as if he were saying, "My pain is gone; I'm basking in God's presence; I'm at peace; I know you loved me, but it's time to move on. Besides," I imagined him purring, "you can probably wrapup that boat racing project without me now."

A soft summer breeze fluttered through the pines while he was gently buried. Then it was time to finally look up and walk away. "See ya later Fuzzball," I found myself whispering. And whenever pages in this book are turned, I suppose I always shall.

Acknowledgments

"*INBOARD RACING* is all about the expensive boats," someone at the Clayton's 1000 Island Antique Boat Museum's Raceboat Regatta remarked to me, "but outboard racing is really about its people." The comment was shouted by an observant spectator who noticed that even the deafening blast-off of some luxurious, multi-engine, supercharged, mahogany inboard hydroplane failed to break the rhythm of nearby outboarders happily swapping their racing stories. For me, it crystallized my experience of researching this book and its sister work *The Golden Age of the Racing Outboard*. Officially, the journey began via the hospitality of Craig and Shanon Bowman in New Jersey. Their invitation for my stock outboard racing questions, as well as the generous loan of their dad's (Hank Bowman) *Boat Sport* files and publicity photos provided this project with a stable foundation. Along the way, Rich Yost lent additional credence to the research with photocopies of sundry racing ephemera I wouldn't have otherwise found. Willingness on the part of Charlie Strang, Claude Fox, Jon Culver, and Bob Switzer to be interviewed and — in several cases — fill out related questionnaires about their life's work, is also greatly appreciated. Correspondence from Hugh Entrop, Tom Moulder, and Ralph Lambrecht added status to the text, too. Additionally, this volume has been enhanced by dozens of *Antique Outboarder* contributors (like racing historian R. C. Hawie), and from other boat racing scribes (Craig Fjarlie for example) who've advanced the sport's culture over the years. Though often cracking a "maximum page count whip," Devereux Books publisher Stan Grayson gets my thanks for believing in vintage outboard racing enough to shepherd not one, but two volumes on this fascinating topic. As I consider all who have touched this endeavor, I feel especially grateful to God for giving me the time to write *Vintage Culture* — and for having created all the people who've ever raced around in a boat.

Contents

Introduction

BUOYED BY A LATE TWENTIETH-CENTURY COLLECTING MANIA, a book was written solely about metal lunchboxes. This niche topic found an especially good reception among baby boomers who vividly recall those back-to-school shopping rituals that included carefully selecting a box capable of transmitting a palpable piece of the owner's developing personality. Ready to make a statement on behalf of the kid clutching its handle were dozens of traditional sports-related lunchboxes, hundreds connected to popular TV shows, and even a few in the riskier miscellaneous realm. In 1959, one even appeared with an outboard racing theme colorfully printed on its front. The aforementioned book touts American Thermos Product Company's *Boating* as a prime example of lunchbox artistry and thematic expression. Good examples have been snapped up by marine memorabilia collectors for six hundred bucks. It is noted here to show that, for some racing buffs, whether or not ever equipped with such a sandwich container, the joys of fast outboarding often transcend boat and motor.

This is a reality I quickly discovered when preparing a previous work, *The Golden Age of the Racing Outboard.* Because of an amazing plethora of outboard-related racing topics, its rough draft took me several years to research and write, but only a few days to realize that the manuscript's 500 pages and scores of related graphics were far too unwieldy for a single book. Fortunately, though, *Golden Age*'s refocused mission of primarily chronicling competition outboard engines and hulls provided a ready harbor for this sister volume about outboard racing's people, as well as their endeavor's ancillary accoutrements. By the way, the books can best be enjoyed together.

On a writer's version of a busman's holiday, I attended The Antique Boat Museum's Race Boat Regatta. Its grassy, tree-lined backyard served as the event's flea market venue. Among the droves who swarmed sundry vendors at that breezy, upstate New York-based attraction, one particularly enthusiastic buff caught my attention. With contagious zeal, he busily examined dusty stuff on makeshift tables and probed mysterious contents of tattered cardboard cartons, all the while discovering goodies not recognized as significant by previous browsers. After snapping together some plastic pieces picked from a $5 box of dusty junk, he politely thanked the seller for providing him with a minuscule model of Mercury's *KG-7Q Quicksilver* racer; part of some 1950s Kellogg's cereal promotion. The vendor sheepishly replied, "I didn't even know there was such a thing." Then on to other tables the outboarder blithely moved, happily sharing detailed explanations to anyone interested, and connecting each find with tales of the personalities who designed, manufactured, or originally used them. This dynamic collector embodies the spirit that I wish this book to convey.

Divided into four parts, *The Vintage Culture of Outboard Racing* begins with historical overviews. Through pre- and post-World War II sections, they are montages of the epoch pieced together to offer a working version of outboard racing chronology. Once these initial laps are run, coverage further focuses upon Racing People, Places for Races, and Racing Paraphernalia. That means readers will be granted pit passes to topics ranging from well-known outboard racing personalities and marathon courses to nearly forgotten high-speed outboarding toys, magazines, and micro-production competition accessories. Of specific interest to individuals who experienced the sport primarily through mundane craft and a lively imagination is a chapter on cottage racing. There, ordinary motors imbued with a fast reputation are identified for devotees of a boating genre long deserving documentation. Cottage racing engines slipped in under the book's *accessories-only* radar because their mystique is a product of popular culture.

With a few earlier exceptions included for texture, this volume's timeframe runs from the late 1920s enthusiastic public embrace of outboard racing through the sport's mainstream swan song around 1960. Simple math will verify that more than a few of its key practitioners have since died. With each veteran throttle-squeezer's passing, unwritten accounts of their experiences fade like ever-distant engine music disappearing around some pine tree peninsula on a big lake. Hopefully, the tales that did make it will serve to uncover yet more vignettes from readers with tales to tell. The text has been written in a snapshot style, and is by no means comprehensive. To claim otherwise would suggest that outboard motor racing's complete and fragile chronicling has already come to light. History and human nature humble such a notion. Much of the sport was enjoyed for a few long-ago seasons, in small groups at rural, adhoc venues by folks with little thought of preserving its cultural implications. And so, admittedly this documentation of the ephemeral is simply an ongoing task. Or, in this case, a labor of love with an open invitation.

Also considered a work-in-progress is the book's treatment of racing paraphernalia. There is no question that some outboard racing gizmos, which are not mentioned herein, do exist. Rather than cause paranoia, though, the thought of subsequently being confronted with descriptions and photos of outboard competition things that eluded *Vintage Culture*'s net makes me smile. That's because they're catalysts for an author's true benefit — a reader's letter, e-mail, or phone call. Then, before you know it, there's enough material for a revised edition. But for now, my editor's poignant edict, "Manuscripts that never seem to get finished never become books," comes to mind and the checkered flag is being waved. Even so, anyone with the slightest additional detail connected to outboard racing topics is most welcome to contact me through the publisher or through its web page www.devereuxbooks.com. Finally, as I type this project's last paragraphs, it is my sincere desire that all the words, pictures, captions, and listings will satisfy a hunger at least as well as would a lovingly prepared sandwich toted in one of those cool 1959 hydroplane lunchboxes.

Peter Hunn
Fulton, New York
September 2002

Part One

Background

If these congregated boaters and their rigs don't look like sophisticated racers, it's because they're not up to the stringent standards of late 1930s-era APBA-NOA sanctioned alky (alcohol-based fuel) competition. No matter, this locally-organized, Seattle, Washington-based "utility racing class" had loads of fun anyway. The group petitioned APBA-NOA officials to adopt this brand of stock motor/boat event nationwide, but they were rebuffed. However, less than a decade later, stock utility would be enthusiastically accepted in major races like the Albany-to-New York Marathon.

Chapter One

From Putt-Putt to Zoom!

"I have sailed sloops, schooners, yawls, and cat boats, and have raced in
power boats, but never have I felt the thrill that I have in a race with
putt-putts!"
— *A yachtsman-turned-outboard-racing buff quoted in* Power
Boating, *January 1923*

*I*N EARLY SEPTEMBER 1908, a Mr. J. F. Richards sent a letter to the Waterman Marine
Motor Company of Detroit. While it's almost certain the Roslindale, Massachusetts,
boater never suspected he'd be crafting opening lines for a book, his words provide us with
a significant starting point,

"Dear Sirs," Richards cordially began, "With a Waterman Out-Board Motor, I took
first prize in the Labor Day Regatta against boats with two horse power installed [inboard]
engines!"

That boastful note marks one of the very first times outboard racing was chronicled.
The Waterman people thought it important enough news to include in their 1909 catalog.
Company officials figured some folks reading the testimonial might purchase a Waterman
in order to achieve similar victories. Given the gift of retrospect, we know that the
Waterman ad copywriters were on to something. The Richards note helped the pioneer
outboard firm set the stage for a style of racing-related, status-conferral marine marketing — though now by way of glossy color photos — that continues today. Rare is the outboard catalog that doesn't include at least a few action shots of motors making their owners happy by making their boats go fast.

A 1911 fun-on-the-water day in Peewaukee, Wisconsin, did good things for
Waterman's chief rival, Evinrude. There, during what some speculate might be the very
first organized outboards-only race, one of Ole Evinrude's contraptions conquered the
finish line. But the match didn't prove much, as all of the other rowboats were propelled
by that same brand of motor. A year later, Evinrude — possibly at the promotional behest
of some of the fledgling firm's dealers — sanctioned the engraving of several racing regatta trophies. Unfortunately, at least one Evinrude cup was quickly claimed by a Waterman
owner who beat out a field of craft almost exclusively pushed with the sponsor's engines.

Many attempts have been made to definitively pinpoint the precise date of organized outboard racing's official beginning. After spending considerable time in dusty periodicals, on the phone chatting with senior racers, or involved in an ad-hoc symposium on the topic at an antique outboard meet, I have concluded that it would be easier to explain the origin of Adam and Eve's daughters-in-law. Luckily, there's Judge Cohn.

Ohio jurist Aaron B. Cohn found weekend outboard motoring to be an enjoyable way to break the courtroom routine. When other rowboat motor enthusiasts began popping up around his Toledo home waters, he made a case for organizing a little friendly competition. His 1923 *Power Boating* magazine "how-to" series about outboard racing now serves as the topic's seminal literature. There, aficionados were dubbed "put-puters" (spelled "put" as opposed to "putt") or "clamp-on" enthusiasts. The judge knew that pioneer outboard racing had not been the province of a single venue, and so testified that the origins of the endeavor at his (Trolley Stop #43) Toledo Beach were "probably the same as at other summer resorts." Cohn recalled the earliest sanctioned outboard races in 1914 involving about eight entrants. Reportedly, this small legion continued competing there over the next couple of summers until the same old tired boats, motors, and results produced a "been there, done that" malaise that killed off the putt-putt races. No doubt World War I contributed to the infant competition's wane, too. Perhaps in celebration of the conflict's end, Toledo Beach's 1919 Fourth of July and Labor Day events reprised outboard racing. More than 20 competitors crossed the finish line, albeit mostly with pre-war equipment. But Cohn cites 1920 as the sport's pivotal year. That's because some of the 68 craft appearing on Lake Erie for Toledo's 1920 Fourth of July contest had been "specially designed and constructed" for speed. Over the winter, several of the previous year's competitors had taken putt-putt racing seriously enough to expend resources experimenting

with wood and hydrodynamics. And an engine with a bigger cylinder displacement than most of the other putt-putts on one of these new hulls took top honors. Suddenly there were discriminating differences between entrants and their rigs. Someone suggested that it'd be fair to stick to the following rules:

Judge Aaron Cohn — the father of outboard racing — poses (in bowtie, top row, center) with his fellow enthusiasts and their motors. This photo was taken aboard a tugboat Cohn chartered to ferry buffs to an outboard competition at the 1923 Inter-Lake Regatta. Near the bottom left is a gas can that likely contained some "hot" homebrew fuel that Cohn recommended for optimum performance.

The state of the art in early 1920s putt-putt racing rigs is this long, flat-bottom craft with two-person crew (for proper balance), spray rails extending outside the gunwales from bow to center, bottom planks running bow-to-stern, and an extension tiller on the outboard. About 10 mph was then considered pretty exciting stuff!

1. Flat-bottomed rowboats of at least 14 feet.
2. Single-cylindered outboards of no more than 2 hp.
3. No re-bored cylinder.

When several Ohio papers covered the 1920 race, and a newsreel movie of the busy outboarders was filmed, word reached the leading motor manufacturers. They notified Cohn that (at the time) "the event was the biggest of its kind in the history of the putt-putts."

Maybe it was the glorious publicity or the 1920 race's prize cache of victory pennants, silver cups, and money (ranging from $35.00 for the overall winner to $2.00 for the thirty-fifth finisher) that generated a remarkable registration for Toledo's 1921 outboard competition. Whatever the reason, more than a few hopefuls showed up with brand new outboards, as well as custom-constructed "speed rowboats of [only] 1/2-inch and 5/16-inch stock [with] bottom boards running lengthwise" to encounter less water resistance. Racers with a proverbial family fishing tub (with which they'd previously stood a chance) watched the special boats whiz past them, causing this plebian group to summarily lose interest. The negative psychological results of that season's first race have been duplicated for decades whenever a new technology embarrasses those who try competing with their old rigs. Accounts of this condition will appear — in various form — throughout the *Vintage Culture* again and again. In an effort to adjudicate a renewed sense of fairness, Cohn decreed that the next "necessary step in the evolution of putt-putt [racing would have to be] that of classification." When his accommodating group instated the following trio of classes, the old crowd (mostly entering Class "B") quickly returned:

- Class "A" — Single-cylinder powered outboard built-for-speed boat with flat bottoms.
- Class "B" — Single-cylinder powered outboard fishing boats with flat bottoms.

• Class "C" — Free-for-all (any boat, any bottom, any motor single or twin-cylinder).

But the categorization wasn't enough. The judge, often summoned from his putt-putt boat to settle some smoldering racing dispute, concluded that:

> Games and contests always provoke the best and worst in humans. No resort or regatta should book any putt-putt races without formulating rules. Just as the fathers of our Country found it necessary to create a fundamental law of the land at the outset, so likewise you must establish rules for these putt-putt races at the outset or you will have chaos, confusion, bitterness, individual and, therefore, conflicting interpretations of fair play, fair competition, etc.

Sometime in 1922, Judge Cohn used his legal talents to pen "a set of outboard racing rules, which were [subsequently] published in *Power Boating* and which formed the basis for the American Power Boat Association [APBA] outboard racing rules." They are included herein in truncated form:

1. The races shall be managed and supervised by a Race Committee of three. They shall be appointed by the parent organization's President and confirmed by the executive committee. The Race Committee's tenure shall be one year, and its rulings shall be final. It may appoint assistants.

2. **Boat** — Flat bottom, minimum 14 feet, any application of substance to surface for increasing speed is permissible. (Judge Cohn recommended a bottom treatment of: "pot lead, graphite, or bronzing with bronzing liquid and banana oil and then rubbed down with steel wool." Because the open rowboats often filled with wave water, light metal spray rails were also suggested.)

3. **Engine** — Any single-cylinder outboard rated as standard 2 hp. Any parts may be added or subtracted. Boring cylinder prohibited.

4. **Crew** — Minimum 15 years of age, not less than 100 pounds. No competing boat shall contain less than two occupants, the boat or motor owner or a member of his/her family, and one crew member, both amateurs. (An amateur is one who, within the last year, has not been associated with a boat or motor business.)

5. **Course** — Triangular (with any length sides) and not less than six miles total.

6. **Fuel** — Any fuel, any mixture.

7. **Starting** — By air bombs or cannon. Preliminary gun 5 minutes before race. Display cards (with 5, 4, 3, 2, 1, and 1/2-minute designations) shall be shown to competitors.

8. **Other** Rules:

     a. The race shall be run so that boats turn to port.

     b. Lead boat gets right-of-way at turn stakes (buoy) and straightaways.

     c. Touching stake with boats or hands, etc., results in disqualification.

  d. Crossing starting line before final gun causes disqualification.

  e. No occupant of any boat shall touch any other boat or person therein with hands, oars, or other device.

  f. The hulls of competing boats shall have no breaks in the longitudinal continuity of the immersed surface.

  g. Competing boats must display a racing number as assigned by the Race Committee.

  h. Competing boats shall report to the Racing Committee at the starting dock no later than 10-minutes prior to the race and (at a designated area) immediately after crossing the finish line.

  i. Except due to weather, advertised start times won't be altered.

  j. An entry fee (of $5 per season or $2 per race) must accompany every application.

  k. Changes in the rules won't go into effect earlier than five months subsequent to their passage.

A May 1929 article in *Power Boating* noted the above directives were "the first outboard racing rules ever published." Curiously, modern APBA Yearbooks don't mention Cohn, and have only included a brief history that reads: "In 1924 the emergence of outboard motors efficient enough to stimulate racing interest prompted [our Association] to put into print a set of rules for boats propelled by *Outboard Detachable Motors.*" The period's small outboarding fraternity, and the APBA's 1924 chronology, is close enough to Cohn's 1922 rules to likely have been related. The fact that that 1929 *Power Boating* retrospective specifically identifies Judge Aaron B. Cohn as *the* "generally recognized *father of outboard racing,*" earns him kudos here. He legitimized an endeavor that had previously not been taken seriously by powerboat officialdom.

For 1923, Cohn chartered a tugboat to take his compatriots and their racing gear to *Put-in-Bay* for participation in that year's *Inter-Lake* regatta. Their rigs still consisted mostly of rowboats and square-stern canoes or half-canoes powered by forward pointing, single-cylinder Evinrudes, Lockwoods, Sears Motor-Go, or an occasional Caille of similar design. Any of them able to hit ten miles per hour were considered state-of-the-art. His prediction of 13 to 14 miles per hour for 1924 seemed like a pipe dream, but he rightly hypothesized that racing would spawn motors and boats that'd somehow make even greater speed possible. Many of the early rules acknowledged that one-lung kickers were the coin of the realm. And, regatta experience showed that catering to garden variety equipment such as the ubiquitous, single-cylinder, 2-horse Evinrude rowboat motor attracted the most participants. During the World War I era, a few manufacturers such as Admiral, Koban, Swedish Archimedes, and Evinrude offered heavy cast-iron twin-cylinder models that looked like they might break some records. Weighted down by double the old-style components, however, engine speeds were typically limited to around 1000 rpm and so squelched even these pioneer twins' anticipated speed excitement. That curse began to lift when, in late 1921, a pair of much lighter, higher revving twins popped coincidentally onto the outboard scene.

Ole Evinrude's new organization Elto (he'd sold his original Evinrude concern in 1914) and the Johnson Motor Company each introduced smooth-running, aluminum-based two-cylinder models that year. Both found an immediately enthusiastic market, prompting other makers like Caille, and Lockwood to also focus on dual-jug fare. Twins suddenly being recognized as state of the art, though, most motor manufacturers were still pleased to be catering to the fishing (as opposed to racing) crowd. Well into middle age, Ole, for example, was quite satisfied serving customers who simply wanted some dependable rowboat power. His *Ruddertwin* — steered with an attached rudder — represented ELTO's entire product line through 1927. Through the mid-twenties, it was primarily the young-at-heart Johnson Brothers who appeared most interested in squeezing some speed out of their outboarding enterprise. This organization, headed by siblings and other relatives, had its roots in making fast inboard boat and airplane engines. New to the outboard trade, the Johnson family had fun with experiments designed to mix business with pleasure. For 1923, they advertised their Light Twin in a limited edition racing version (though didn't elaborate on its characteristics). The brothers' lively research and development sessions were typically of the "now, let's see what we can get this thing to do!" variety. These outings often led to some speed-breakthrough headlines. During the first nationally prominent regatta in which outboards were included, a Johnson took first in the 2-hp division, with an Elto winning the Free-for-All event. The single lap (2-1/2-mile) course at the July 3-5, 1924 Mississippi Valley Power Boat Association's (Oshkosh, Wisconsin) event, was covered by those two-cylinder mills in 22:36 and 16:23 respectively. Later that summer (August 29 to September 1), the APBA put outboards on its Detroit Gold Cup program. Cohn talked up the big Association's first outboard speed event with enough gusto to even entice famed inboarder Gar Wood Senior, into trying his hand at clamp-on racing. After a remarkable victory there in his *Miss Detroit VII* inboard speedboat, Wood made the putt-putt scene with a trio of 2-horsepower Johnson Light Twin outboards clamped to one rowboat's stern, but was bested by Cohn's craft bearing a lone Evinrude 4-hp twin. Wood didn't blame the Johnsons for the fact that he just couldn't control those three motors with two hands.

By the early 1930s, that Gar Wood stunt was long forgotten, and Johnson's racing record (spurred on by advances at rival Elto) served as a cornerstone of outboard racing itself. Outboard industry pioneers Finn Irgens and Jim Webb presented a paper on outboard history — including racing — to a 1930 gathering of the Society of Automotive Engineers. By that time, the Evinrude, ELTO, and Lockwood brands had been united under the Outboard Motors Corporation or OMC banner. Included on the stage with the

Famed inboard speedboater Gar Wood figured his triple Johnson Waterbug/Light Twin-equipped "racer" would easily best all comers in the APBA's first official outboard race. But difficulties operating the trio allowed boats with just one kicker each to pass him by.

participants was a new OMC Speedy-Bee racer. The prestigious venue offered OMC a public relations opportunity to tout the company's most mechanically notable offerings. Even so, their program gave specific high-speed praise to OMC's biggest competitor, Johnson. The corporate duo noted that outboard travel, before 1925, was pretty slow, and that most people back then might have identified "speedboating" and "outboarding" as antonyms. However, they acknowledged, "in the summer of 1925, a twin-cylinder Johnson motor weighing 90 pounds achieved the unbelievable speed of 15.89 miles per hour. [Johnson publicity actually bragged *16* mph, but, understandably, Irgens and Webb weren't at the SAE luncheon to bolster the competition.] In 1926 another Johnson of the same weight, developing six horsepower performed the impossible and made 22 mph . . . and in 1927 a Class "C" Johnson motor weighing 100 pounds, and developing about 11 hp., made 32 miles per hour." Lighter and freer-moving internal parts allowed these Johnson *Big-Twin* kickers to break 2600 RPM. But these motors alone were not responsible for speed advances begun in 1925. The OMC executives noted that hull builders played a vital role in early outboard racing.

"Prior to 1925, the fastest outboard boat was thought to be the long, slim craft which would slice through water. Such was the fastest type for the [low] power then available. Then came the vee-bottom hydroplane [at that time, a generic term for any fast powerboat], a boat which rode flat on top of the water instead of cutting through it." During the mid-twenties, sleek runabouts with a transversely stepped bottom lifted part of the hull off the water to reduce water surface drag. This function made more efficient use of the motor's faster propeller revolutions. A move from all-wooden to some fabric over framing construction further lessened the load and jumped outboarding speeds. Once certain boats

A beautifully cast trophy for the winner of a mid-1920s outboard race. Because the photo of this prize was found in the Evinrude/Elto advertising archive, one can assume that the tiny Elto Ruddertwin on the trophy boat's transom was there by promotional design.

and motors were being built with record-breaking in mind, a type of critical mass was reached that, coupled with youthful enthusiasm, generated a frenzy to be first over the finish line. Almost every boat and motor company yearned for a product it could advertise as "the fastest" in something.

While Johnson was making performance news, Detroit-based Caille rushed into production what can be considered the first cataloged, factory-built racing outboard motor. (Word of the aforementioned, special racing Light Twins' availability was only carried in a Johnson newsletter.) It was the 1926 *Master Five-Speed in Racing Trim*. This model used Caille's standard 4-1/2-horse opposed-twin-cylinders powerhead, but substituted a knife-like forward-only lower unit and related high-pitched propeller for the company's more complex, five-position feathering-prop gear foot. The racer was also equipped with a long tiller handle "permitting, as Caille's 1926 brochure indicated, "the operator to slide forward to trim the boat for distributing his weight properly for planing." Slightly later versions of the motor allowed for placing the propeller — tractor style — in front of the lower unit.

Johnson's officially labeled racing motors made a 1928 debut in the form of its "R" series KR-40, PR-40, and TR-40. Neither had a particularly sleek foot, but benefited from some powerhead advances, or as in the 50-cubic-inch piston displacement TR-40's case, brute force. Meantime, Caille gave most of its racer line twin carbs and the tractor lower unit. Evinrude and Lockwood waited until 1929 to feature full-fledged competition models in their respective brochures. All of these companies, though, had happily seen some of their standard service outboards get drafted into racing.

The rich man's recreational marine journal, *Yachting* magazine, sent a representative to witness what all of the lower class outboard racing was all about. Imagine the incredulous thoughts of an old-line *Yachting* subscriber, sipping expensive wine on deck, and reading: "The speed, snap, agility, surprising results, and spectacular finishes of the outboards, coupled with the natural verve and exuberance of the youthful drivers, simply cannot be equaled . . . outboards are in a class by themselves." Descendants of that perky Waterman, noted in this chapter's first paragraph, had certainly shifted the pleasure boating paradigm.

The sport and its definition of a "big" outboard grew so fast, that the original, Cohn-inspired American Power Boat Association classifications needed changing. Based upon piston displacement, those elementary 1924 APBA mandates pigeonholed motors into the following classes:

"A" under 12 cubic inches.

"B" 12 to 17 cubic inches.

"C" 17 to 30 cubic inches.

"D" over 30 cubic inches.

These vintage regs lumped in Elto Ruddertwin putt-putts with much more powerful

Johnson Big Twins into "C" class. When the first rules were written, Class "D" motors did-n't exist, meaning the category was to serve as a future catchall zone for giant engines. By 1928, however, several outboard makers had motors well into the "D" class. One compa-ny, Cross, was even pushing a five-cylinder, 73 cube racer, just screaming for a whole new criterion. The APBA's catch up, rule revamp looked like this: (Related, quintessential engines of 1928-1930 are noted after their respective class.)

"A" up to 14 cubic inches. (Lockwood Ace, Caille model 35)

"B" up to 20 cubic inches. (Elto High-Speed Speedster, Lockwood Chief/Racing Chief, Johnson SR, Evinrude Speedibee)

"C" up to 30 cubic inches. (Evinrude Speeditwin, Johnson PR, Caille model 50)

"D" up to 40 cubic inches. (Elto High-Speed Quad, Johnson VR)

"E" up to 50 cubic inches. (1929 Elto Quad)

"F" up to 60 cubic inches. (Evinrude/Elto/Lockwood 4-60)

"G" up to 80 cubic inches. (Cross Radial)

As Irgens and Webb told their 1930 SAE audience, members of the public involved in outboard speed endeavors kept motor and boat makers on their toes. "Racing drivers themselves," the Evinrude reps reported, "have in effect, become an auxiliary corps of engineers. Most of them are youthful, enthusiastic chaps, possessed of considerable mechanical ingenuity. They spend many hours during the week each summer, smooth-ing, polishing, 'souping' their motors, so as to get the last possible inch of them. There are several thousand drivers and among such a number it is only natural that some of them stumble on mighty good ideas. All of these serve to increase outboard efficiency." And, the speakers acknowledged, it was these remarkable speed leaps through "spectacular out-board racing which has done the most to attract public attention to the outboard motor."

Through their local press, by 1930, even most landlubbers had sustained at least casu-al exposure to such competition. Sports sections of most big city dailies prominently car-ried outboard racing results. Likewise, smaller papers, and hometown radio sports pro-grams included accounts of the growing sport. That served to increase the already bur-geoning number of spectators. Reporters especially liked the opportunity to cover stu-dents, whose extracurricular activities included giving their high-speed boats and motors "the old college try." In fact, some of these young people were organized under the ban-ner of the Eastern Intercollegiate Outboard Association. Founded in 1930, the EIOA sanc-tioned races through the warm-weather months, with an annual fall grand finale. Charles Strang joined the group years before ever dreaming he'd become a major outboard indus-try executive (with Mercury and OMC). The end-of-season regatta, he noted "had sepa-rate events for high school and college participants. Some school clubs were composed of single individuals [Yale sometimes only had a one-man squad], but there were a few schools [like Dartmouth, and Rutgers] with enough racers to be able to field teams."

All the growing interest and sophistication in late 1920s/early 1930s racing started highlighting a demarcation line that defined two distinct sides of the sport. While there were those satisfied with tiller steering out-of-the box, stock motors and boats around the buoys for a round of applause or trophy, others with steering wheel-equipped hydroplanes, went to great expense modifying their craft and engines to obtain optimum output so as to successfully chase cash prizes. From about 1927 on, there was no shortage of books and magazine articles teaching such modification or "souping." One do-it-your-self publication, the 1931 *Boat Book,* showed how to make a gas-tank-mounted super-charger for an outboard. The hop-up device was actually a flywheel pulley-driven blow-er fan injecting its windy output into the carburetor through a flexible hose. The writer recommended "shoemakers' twine" for the pulley belt to "positively give additional power to any outboard motor."

Most representatives of this "we'll try anything" period were concoctions of home brew fuel additives. This chemical experimentation had its outboard souping origins in the earliest days of the kicker. In fact, unidentified owners of the first Waterman vertical cylinder mills (like our 1908 example at this chapter's open) experimentally mixed oil with the gasoline in the fuel tank and got good results. Pioneer two-cycle motor manu-facturers hadn't thought of such conglomeration and so mandated that lubrication be placed in gravity feed drip oilers piped to the bearings. Human nature assures us that other interesting liquid additives to the tank soon followed. Alcohol-based or "alky" fuel was not a single inventor's brainstorm; rather, the idea originated in hundreds of kitchen-chemists' minds. Racers hoping for more revs swished stuff like camphor, wood alcohol, benzol, benzolene, products of coal tar distillation, high-octane aviation gas, graphited heavy oil with alcohol added, benzene, naphtha, and/or mothballs and ether into the gas tank.

Lube was typically via castor oil, but a *Popular Mechanics* article about hot kickers reported Vaseline and shaving creme attracted some proponents, too. "Doping the fuel" had countless specific definitions. Doc Schnurmacher, the editor of *Outboard Motorboat* magazine recommended: four gallons of low-test gasoline, five ounces of iodine, a half-gallon of castor oil, one pound of chemically pure ether, and a half-gallon of engine oil. According to Schnurmacher's 1930 recipe, "the iodine is added to make the regular oil and castor oil mix." Otherwise, the brew turns into a motor wrecker. Winning racers were often mercilessly pestered for their secret formula, with one friendship endangered when a buff jokingly gave his buddy a "mystery bottle" actually containing nothing more than colorful Lavoris mouthwash! Even Judge Cohn's early 1920s *Power Boating* articles used considerable copy promising outboard speed bugs "that there is much more you can do than merely mix the gasoline and oil and add to tank." Into their rowboat motors pioneer racers dumped everything from kerosene to a blast furnace chemical engineer's concoc-tion dubbed "dy-na-mite." More than a few of the victim motors blew up.

"On one occasion," *Popular Mechanics* reported, an outboard racer "was leading by a large margin when a rod in his engine let go, bombarding him with steel bearings. Then the rod broke loose and pierced one of the two lifejackets he was wearing." Fortunately, someone in the DuPont chemical organization took a shine to outboard racing around this time. Company chemists were authorized to blend a more predictable and stable brand of racing juice. The result came in five-gallon orange cans with black letters that read: *Dynax*. While not the only "store-bought" alcohol/castor oil-based fuel on the market, Dynax was well on its way to being the genre's leader by 1931. Most old-timers who poured the stuff into their alky-burning

mills remember thinking that the dollar-per-gallon price seemed unbelievably high. No wonder, as their cars could be filled with regular at the Depression-era filling station rate of 10 gallons for a buck.

The advent of commercial fuels coincided with another major change in outboard racing. Lengthy tiller handles gave way to steering wheel and remote throttle controls on a strictly-for-racing hull. While in the experimental stage, some of early wheel to motor connections were made with a variety of clothesline, ropes, or cable. What appeared secure at the dock could prove problematic on the race course. The 1931 *Boat Book* verified that a few drivers "have had their steering cable break and whip around their necks and into their faces, causing painful injuries." It didn't take long for a cloth cord with internal cable reinforcement to become standard fare on the pulley and wheel drum steering system. By 1930, few serious competitors were tiller-controlling their motors anymore. The wheel gave them something to grasp while kneeling facing forward. And drivers who valued their bones and cartilage owned at least one set of cushy-rubber kneepads. This was in addition to a stuffed pillow placed on the boat's floor just aft of the wheel. Bowden cable was the next step in motor speed control. Typically, this cable ran between the motor's throttle butterfly valve to a spring-loaded lever (mounted to the driver's left) pushed forward for acceleration. Spark advance/retard remained the province of a timer lever protruding from the flywheel base.

Each advancement, from special fuels to remote controls, represented another investment and so pushed casual racers out of the picture. Innovation in new motors from about 1927 to 1931 was akin to the frenzied output of the 1990s computer industry. Technology changed so fast that a highly touted, top-of-the-line Model 92BR dual-carb Lockwood Racing Chief of 1929, for example, was passé before the end of the season. It wasn't until 1931-1933 that one could buy a new Johnson KR, SR, or PR (albeit for the price of a pretty nice used car), and be reasonably certain that it'd still be competitive the following year. Due, at least in part, to this expense, and the need to keep current with all

This late 1920s painting shows race drivers still tiller-steering their motors on (probably) single-step hulls built to plane. These craft were a far cry from flat-bottomed ones. Arguably they're variations on the theme of the lighter square stern canoes that gave naval architects context for speedier outboard boat designs.

the updates, racers backed by motor agencies and/or factories became commonplace. Around 1930, one needed such resources and sophistication in order to have a chance of winning the average race. People showing up at an event in their faithful old runabout and tiller-steered Elto Hi-Speed Speedster — a hot mill just a season or two earlier — were wasting their $2.00 entrance fee. That's a reason why the (first) National Outboard Association was formed. Just as Judge Cohn pointed out nearly a decade earlier, NOA organizers (predominantly industry officials) understood that racing wouldn't continue to prosper without a level playing field. It also recognized the need for nationwide racing criteria more specifically outboard oriented than the traditionally yacht-focused American Power Boat Association then provided. "Early in 1929," the new group's 1930 yearbook noted, "it became evident to officials of the NOA that something would have to be done to give the amateur a better chance in outboard regattas. The pilots who were racing for motor dealers, or for commercial gain, were crowding the 'simon-pure' amateurs out and the sport was threatened with commercialization. The average owner of an outboard motor boat has had little chance to compete," the document continued, "with expert pilots who have devoted much of their time to racing for cash prizes [in 1928 and 1929. For these past two years,] his family runabout has been useless compared to the speed king's racing hull. [As of 1930,] this has been changed and the whole racing system has been recast so that the average owner of an outboard can get some real fun out of the regattas staged in his district." NOA's remedy racing rules (effective January 1, 1930) compartmentalized competitors into three categories:

Division I — consisted of relatively **novice amateurs** who started in fewer than 15 races or heats since March 1, 1929.

Division II — were the more **experienced amateurs** with 15 or more races or heats to their credit.

Division III — was a place in which the **professionals** could do their thing. A pro got defined as a driver with any connection to the outboard motor industry. Racing for pay, commercial gain, or competing in events where cash prizes were offered also resulted in reception of this classification.

This categorical trio lasted until 1932, when the system was simplified by placing all amateurs in Division I, and reclassifying pros into a new Division II. NOA rule makers

Though the original National Outboard Association hoped for members who enjoyed water sports like swimming and angling, NOA officials often courted the racing crowd, as evidenced by the top position of the hydro on this 1930 NOA yearbook cover.

tried expanding into four sections later on, but the divisions 1 and 2 deal seemed to be best accepted. Under these rules, amateurs were required to use stock motors, and their craft had to meet a minimum weight (100 pounds for Class "A," 150 for "B" and "C," and 190 for "D and E"). Builders of such boats were under Association mandate to "permanently stamp the weight of each hull, in a dry condition, with steering wheel and motor controls aboard, into the transom of the hull." Regs also said these Division I, just-for-fun weekend warriors could never compete for money. Meanwhile, Division II professionals got the nod to run a highly modified outboard on the back of a featherweight "shingle," and do so for dollars. Chasing cash proved to be a good catalyst for keeping this group active. That's not to postulate pros were greedy; it's just that the green helped pay for the sport and lifestyle these commercially connected campaigners considered crucial. The idea of the separate division system was to provide a haven for casual (those who use regular motors) "stock" racers, while making sure there were still some daring pros doing enough crazy things and making sufficient exhaust noise (with their modified, alcohol-powered mills) to wow the crowds. NOA guidelines barred the philosophically opposed speedsters from meeting on the water, even in a well-intentioned "free-for-all" event. And both group's rigs were subject to inspection before as well as after a race. No matter amateur or pro, racers had to wear lifejackets, and apply foot-high identification numbers to both sides of their craft. Officials understood that the tension between mundane safety and dramatic boat flips attracted spectators, but had no desire to generate grizzly headlines.

During its first National Championship Races at Peoria, Illinois. NOA organizers of the October 12-13, 1929, event were secretly worried that no one would show up. Cosponsoring representatives of the APBA and similarly influential Mississippi Valley Power Boat Association attended, but early on whispered their skepticism of much turnout. Then, slowly at first, dusty cars started pulling into Peoria. "Many came from the Atlantic and Pacific coasts with their little boats strapped to automobiles. [Soon,] the entry blanks mounted up so fast that any fears that the events might not be popular quickly went by the board, and for the first time in the history of outboard regattas, it became necessary to reject those which were late in arriving. One hundred and fifty-two pilots from twenty-six states swarmed the course — all eager to carry home one or more of the beautiful championship trophies. It can be accurately stated," an NOA publication later noted, "that the meet [was] without parallel in the annals of the outboard sport." Winners in the historic "outboards-only" regatta included Douglas Haskins, Class "A" (Lockwood Ace on a Porteus hull); H. G. Ferguson, Class "B" (Elsinore boat and Johnson SR motor); Carl Koeffler, Class "C" (Evinrude Speeditwin); Dick Upsall, Class "D" (Century boat with Johnson VR); and F. E. Ludolph in Class "E" (Elto Quad and Hooton hull). Victorious speeds ranged from 25.19 to 44.65 mph. Potentially faster Class "G" (up to 80 cubic inches), and the trial balloon, over 80 cubes "H" category were void of takers. During the happy hubbub of those premier Nationals, predictions flowed about outboard racing being in the process of truly taking off! After all, there was a place for almost everybody's interest. Motor makers were just as enthusiastic, with plans for even faster models, as well as one for kids or petite women. And, the soon-to-be-issued (as of January, 1930) driver divisions would fence out inequities between amateur and pro, between out-of-the-crate stock motors and the more expensively workshop prepared, souped-up mills. Alas, two weeks later, the stock market crashed. Banks began going sour, jobs thinned out, and the economy started its nearly decade-long sputter on just one "iffy" cylinder. Money got tight enough to choke off the erstwhile Roaring Twenties' ready supply of amateur racers who had the extra dough for equipment and travel.

During the early 1930s, both U.S. coasts and waters in the middle experienced a noticeable decrease of stock racing activity. A Seattle outboarding history concurs "the 1929 stock market crash hurt boat racing [there. Consequently,] during the early '30s, most racers were people who either inherited money or owned their own business [which the activity could promote in some way]." Meets for informal amateur stockers were scarce in those financially lean days. New Jersey-based racer Craig Bowman verified the same thing happened back East. "This tends to be a working-class sport, and it suffers in hard times," he noted. "With the cost of travel — which is a stock outboarder's major expense — there's [bound to be] some attrition." By the time 1933 Chicago World's Fair developers opened an outboard lagoon at their exposition site, they had to promise Pro Division cash-prize racing in order to draw competitors. Otherwise, during uncertain economic times, who could afford to campaign a high-performance boat and motor simply for fun? That is to say, the Great Depression dropped the bottom out of the strictly stock, amateur racing fraternity with one deep plunge of the Dow. The weak economy, however, gave professional, Division II-type outboard racers new resolve and a panache that earned some of them remarkably wide recognition. It also caused advertisers, hungry for public attention, to promote themselves alongside victorious competitors.

By the mid-1930s, the annual Albany-to-New York Marathon had been covered on sufficient occasions to spark all kinds of exciting stories. Through radio, movie newsreel, and massive press coverage, average citizens could conjure up images of tiny boats precariously speeding sideways on a ten foot swell. While the Hudson River course was treacherous, flamboyant reporters and their chattering Smith-Corona's typed-out tales of bucking hydroplanes ejecting drivers high into the air. Charles Lindberg's 1927 solo flight across the Atlantic was still in most memory banks, and folks wanted more of that kind of daring hero.

Famed boat-building family member, Fred Jacoby, Jr., was at his peak during this era. Noticing he won the 1935 Albany-to-New York competition, one large corporation authorized a full-page cartoon strip of his exploits. "FEATURING OUTBOARD CHAMPION FRED JACOBY, Jr!" the headline copy announced. It noted his 51 racing wins of 1935, including the "Greatest Race of the Year . . . The Albany to New York Marathon." There "he kept his tiny craft zooming down the Hudson for 130 miles of THE WORST GOING EVER EXPERIENCED IN THE RACE — only 17 of the 75 starters finished. Now," said the ad, "let's see how he did it." Outboard enthusiasts might be surprised to learn that Jacoby's river conquest had nothing to do with his motor, boat, or driving acumen. Rather, the commercial inferred Fred Junior was the first to hit the Big Apple finish line because he stopped to puff on a helpful Camel cigarette at Poughkeepsie's halfway point dock. The tobacco company was quite willing to handsomely compensate recognized athletes and sports figures for such an endorsement. That ad demonstrates the prominence top outboarders, and outboard racing itself, enjoyed in the thirties. The cigarette-to-the-rescue deal probably also made Jacoby chuckle or his alky-burning Johnson racing engine might have occasionally done so, but he didn't smoke.

Other companies wanting to look hot co-opted an outboard racing theme in their advertising. Shots of bantamweight boats and their buzzing little motors battling angry water linked the advertiser with everything good from the work ethic to determined perseverance. Layouts in various 1937 editions of *Fortune* magazine, for example, included such motifs. The Molybdenum Steel Company featured a half-page drawing of a closed-course race, captioned "Wide Open." Accompanying copy suggested the metals firm was open to helping cut costs and creating sales. KODAK offered an even larger photo image of the opening moments at the May 1937 Albany-to-New York competition, labeling it a "great day for the home movie cameras." Especially photogenic in the outboard world was Loretta Turnbull. A keenly serious racer with a 1,000-watt smile, she opted to compete in what some observers

Len Keller is assisted by his wife who would also help him start an outboard racing accessory manufacturing company after World War II. Typically, a sympathetic spouse represented a racer's (male or female) best chance of being successful in the sport.

might call the real man's outboard category — the robust, 30-cubic-inch Class "C." A good "C" rig could be as challenging as any larger outboard craft. For giving her best during an early zenith of outboard racing, Turnbull captured the public's imagination and served as a great role model for others who'd enter the sport. Women in outboard racing are covered in a subsequent chapter. There, it is hypothesized that the endeavor has no record of gender bias.

More often than not, the economy discriminated against those wanting to campaign a motorboat from race to race. Staying competitive meant considerable travel, a luxury for the average Depression-era individual primarily refocused on food and shelter. The fact that Evinrude/Elto were then offering a minuscule competition model — the 7 1/2-cubic inch, Class "M" *Midget Racer* — for just $125 didn't eradicate the other fiscal barriers (boat, trailer, car with hitch, custom fuel, safety gear, association/entry fees, etc.) that folks of ordinary means found daunting when considering the sport. Amidst the faltering economic picture, outboard makers Caille, Cross, and Lockwood quietly went under by 1935. Each had made racing engines, but neither the publicity nor meager revenue base from fast motors provided much protection from the recoiled economy. And Johnson was on its last independent legs that year, with Evinrude/Elto doing all it could to keep a stiff upper lip.

Once the Depression set in, Johnson's "official" racing department couldn't afford to be very active. Besides, the receivers sent to Waukegan to run the business knew little about regular kickers, let alone niche-market high performance machines. Over at Evinrude/Elto, cutbacks were also the way of survival. Even so, it did retain a small factory racing division. This shop prepared new racing motors for shipment and occasionally "souped-up" a well-to-do customer's outboard. While boating pros needing advice on obtaining more speed from their Evinrude/Elto 4-60, Speeditwin, or Midget were welcomed, most of the traffic came from midget racecar owners seeking a 4-60 for their pint-sized vehicles. In fact, many more of these legendary 60-cube mills were sold to auto people than were purchased by hydro or runabout drivers.

The Evinrude people were able to buy their long-time rival, Johnson, in 1936. Some say, Ralph Evinrude and his business partner Steve Briggs kept the critically ill Johnson out of the morgue through timely infusions of their personal funds. As a live acquisition, the widely known Sea Horse brand was well worth the duo's investment. Among many other assets, Johnson came to them with the external rotary-valve technology that had often made mincemeat of Evinrude Speeditwin Racers in popular Class "C" events. The new owners authorized their designers to incorporate the feature in a new 1938 Speeditwin. Without meaning to incorrectly infer that the Evinrude family was vindictive in any way, that rotary-valve Evinrude racer represented the "spoils of war." After pulling Johnson into the clan, the Evinrude's new company, Outboard Marine and Manufacturing (later OMC), owned about 99.9 percent of the outboard racing market, from small to large. Pit scenes of any such competition could be expected to include glimpses of their Evinrude Midget; Johnson (Class "A") KR; "B" size Johnson SR, Evinrude Speeditwin, or Johnson PR for Class "C;" Evinrude 4-60 in "F;" and an occasional "X" Class (61 cubic inches) Johnson or bored-out 4-60. "D" and "E" engines, although not widely professionally raced by the late 1930s, also belonged to the firm in the form of the then-discontinued Johnson VR, and cottage racing favorite, Evinrude Speedifour. As the second half of the Great Depression decade played out, a single firm held the sport's source for motive power (motors and parts) in it hands.

No such prewar quasi-monopoly existed in the race boat crafting world. To be sure, New Jersey's Jacoby and Dick Neal out of Kansas City built many of the hydroplanes victorious in outboard competition, but scores of other makers (such as Century, Cute-Craft, Fairchild, Flowers, Hooton, Penn Yan, and Pigeon) dotted North America. Especially during the 1920s, numerous speed hull designs, from skiff-like flat bottoms, to vee and semi-vee, were tried. Late 20's Penn Yan and Century hull research contributed greatly to the step bottom. At plane, this step raised a good portion of the bottom a few inches off the water. Many other builders of single-step or "conventional" hydros adopted it. These craft played a role in every major speed record of the thirties. Illinois racer Ray Pregenzer put a new 1930 Elto 4-60 on his Century Hurricane hydroplane, and then amazed the boating world at 50.93 miles per hour. Shortly thereafter, U.K. outboard enthusiast, Charles Harrison, had a 4-60 shipped to England, and got it pushing his hydro 52.09 mph. Harrison was so taken with the sport that he later acquired the British Anzani aircraft engine interests and turned it into an outboard producer. On the Continent in 1931, an Italian quad with the Laros marque bumped Harrison off the top of the list with a 54 mph showing. The 61-cube, Johnson XR four-cylinder mill brought the speed record back to the U.S. later that year when Dick Neal (of Neal hydro fame) used one on his boat to do 55.36 miles per hour. This got nudged to 56.535 as driver Tommy Estlick gave it a go. An unusual four-stroke, six-cylinder Spanish motor, the Soriano, broke the mile-a-minute mark in 1932. Its initial 60.15 mph performance was self-bested to 65.21 by another European run during 1934.

An Oklahoman surpassed that Continental record in 1935. George Coleman nailed 69.383 mph with an enhanced 4-60. The rare "X"-type Elto mill — a 61-cube powerhead possessing four (not just two) rotary valves — drove a tractor lower unit made by Walker-Bauman. Speeds so close to 70 inspired more back and forth. French outboard proponent Jean Dupuy bought the Soriano motor factory and then had one of the small firm's fast engines revamped. He'd been to the US, where his wife, Dorothy Spreckels, had grown up near Seattle. There, some of her family were into outboard racing. Dupuy commissioned American Don Flowers to build a hydro for the 102-hp double-overhead cam outboard. The resulting combo yielded 74.39 mph during the summer of 1936. Americans recaptured the honors the following year. First, a limited edition Draper "X" (61 cubic inches) on a tractor lower unit, made 78.121 with suburban New York's Bedford Davie at the Jacoby hydro helm. Then, the final US outboard speed record of the pre-World War II period was claimed by a Massachusetts racer, Clint Ferguson. He used an experimental, four-cylinder "X" motor, built by Marshall Eldredge using a pair of Johnson PR-65 components and a custom crankcase. It, too, had a tractor lower unit. Ferguson's unique engine and Jacoby hydro zoomed to over 78 miles per hour in 1938. Turmoil was spreading through Europe in 1939 when Jean Dupuy put an enhanced Soriano six-popper on the stern of his Jacoby to whip through a measured course at 79.04 mph. The little boat's design had done the job, but was actually old technology at the time of Dupuy's feat. A new kind of hydroplane, using trapped air to buoy much of the hull just above the surface water, waited for acceptance in the outboard community.

Inboard builder Arno Apel received a patent for his three-point hydro concept. The first one hit the water in 1936. It took three more years, around the time Dupuy hit 79 miles per hour on a conventional Jacoby, for a few three-pointers to get tried with outboard power. Unlike inboard three-pointers bearing heavy erstwhile car engines mount-

Evinrude's 1936 acquisition of Johnson slowed the previously frenetic pace of racing motor development by manufacturers. For this 1939 race in Anacortes, Washington, much of the souping-up was done by individual racers who loved to tinker with fuel, carburetion, ignition, and propellers for extra speed. (Richard Humble collection)

ed amidship, outboard motor versions had a penchant for flipping up and over when the triple points allowed the new kind of craft to become slightly airborne. Clearly, there was a need for refining the new design and better understanding what it would let a racer do.

Johnson helped usher in the 1940 competition season with what could be considered a 10th-anniversary edition of its quintessential Class "A" motor. But, it's unlikely sentimental thoughts went through the mind of the person stamping matching serial numbers on the crankcase and rope sheave plate of the run's final Johnson model KR-10. His hammer taps were, however, signaling the last new factory racer Sea Horse dealers would see for decades. In the 1941 catalog Evinrude offered another edition of the Midget Racer and announced a new competition Speeditwin. The 4-60 had been dropped. Most of the quads in that venerable series hadn't been sold to boaters, anyway, as — before the introduction of the Offenhauser engine — midget car racers were 4-60's biggest buyers. Midget and Speeditwin Racers were placed in the 1941 lineup ostensibly as a nod to the sport that had helped all of outboarding gain positive and widespread public attention. As an Evinrude executive stated for the record, "Most outboard manufacturers [know] there is no money to be made selling racing engines." To the bookkeepers, spending precious company resources hand-building a few of each racing model per year probably seemed more like making a charitable donation.

About twenty miles from where Evinrude motors originated, a new outboard venture — the Kiekhaefer Corporation — struggled to shake off the bankrupt reputation of its predecessor's notoriously crude kickers. For 1940, and with the help of engineer Leo T. Kincannon, E. Carl Kiekhaefer designed a small stable of outboards featuring streamlining, slicker bearings, and lightweight powerheads that typically delivered more horsepower than advertised. Kiekhaefer's fledgling Mercury line produced acceptable initial sales. Even the novice outboard executive knew, however, that some kind of publicity would be needed to generate more interest in his brand. But what kind of public relations stunts or photo opportunities? Even though he entertained a host of innovative attention-getting ideas while preparing Merc's 1941 line, it appears racing never crossed Kiekhaefer's mind.

Skimming atop New Jersey's Raritan River, student Charles Strang was focused on the finish line, and became 1941's Eastern Inter-Collegiate Outboard Association Class "C" champion. During the awards dinner, Strang's joy was tempered by remarks from EIOA head Everett Morris. "As you most likely know, boys," the *Motor Boating* magazine editor and Naval Reserve officer solemnly began, "the world is about to go to hell. Only God knows where each of us will be next year. I'm sorry to have to say I shall be closing down our Association for the duration of the war which is about to explode." A few months later, Evinrude, the era's last maker of racing outboards, quietly ceased production of competition and standard-use models. The government asked that all civilian outboard manufacturing be put on hold. Rumor had it, though, that the company's parent organization had no desire to re-enter the racing market following the hostilities, anyway. Not even the National Outboard Association stayed the course. One day in the early 1940s, it closed its doors and simply disappeared. But few racers had time to notice. By then, most were already caught in the upheaval of World War II.

Chapter Two

The Suburban Stocker Era

"Al Benson is a tough [outboard racing] competitor in the D Stock
  Hydro and DU Stock Runabout classes, but his greatest boating pleasure is helping his [grade school age] boys, Donnie and Jimmy go after
  records in the stock outboard racing mile trials."
  — *from a 1955 Champion Sparkplugs ad that paid tribute to competitive outboarding as a family affair.*

"As a kid, I spent an entire summer bussing tables at a restaurant and
  delivering newspapers to earn $325 for a new 1951 Mercury KG-7Q.
  The next year, someone loaned me an A/B utility so I could enter my
  first race. Even placing 5th made me ecstatic. Those stock racing years
  [1952-58] represent some of the happiest times in my life."
  — *Tom Yost*

AS SOON AS THEY WALKED INTO the restaurant, one of Claude Fox's racing buddies happened to recognize the executive sitting over at the bar. "Hey, Look!" he said to Fox, "It's old man Rayniak from Johnson Motors! What say we drop him another subtle hint?" Fox, a Tennessee marine dealer and erstwhile prewar National Outboard Association official, was in New York with some of his associates to take in the huge 1946 Boat Show. World War II had ended only six months earlier, but the nautical exposition shouted long-term peace and prosperity. Opportunity and the good life seemed to be embodied in every one of the hundreds of hulls on unabashedly commercial display there. Optimism and happy planning, along with reams of colorful manufacturers' literature flowed through the endless sea of small craft skippers who were there to convert their Allied victory into vee-hull tickets for fun on the water. The Fox group had origi-nally spotted OMC vice president (and future CEO) Joseph G. Rayniak in Johnson's elab-orate show booth. What began as chitchat about the motor maker's 1946 line shifted to Fox's suggestion that the firm should quickly get some racing engines into production. Rayniak winced, brushing the recommendation aside. Later, they saw him at Evinrude's display where Fox's enthusiastic congregation again preached the racing motor message.

Around 1945-1946, as veteran racing enthusiasts took their rigs out of mothballs and looked to return to the pre-war schedule. Here, Al Benson gives his old faithful, alky-fired Class "C" Elto a refresher run. Later, he and his family would embrace stock racing.

But it was no use. To Rayniak, these pitches made about as much sense as a screen door on a submarine. The two were simply at cross-purposes. Fox wanted a new batch of competition mills for re-equipping old-line outboard racers who had not able to purchase such a machine in at least half a decade. Meanwhile, the OMC official was having headaches trying to figure out how to meet all the fishing/pleasure-use motor demand just generated at the show. That evening, when Rayniak noticed Fox and company walking toward him in a New York restaurant bar, he ducked. No matter, the outboard official immediately registered on the racers' radar. After receiving a good ol slap on the back and the third beg-a-thon pleading for a fresh crop of Johnson/Evinrude competition outboards, he completely blew a gasket. "Go to Blazes!" the frustrated exec unwound. "Not only will we never make another Evinrude or Johnson racing motor . . . I absolutely guarantee *you*, we'll never even make another racing part! In fact," he concluded, "my company does not care, one way or the other, whether there is ever another outboard race staged!" Fox and compatriots stood there, shell-shocked, then left quietly, pondering the postwar fate of their sport.

It's unlikely Joseph Rayniak gave much thought to another engine maker whose booth he'd brushed by several times at the big boat show. That firm's motors looked interesting, he might have thought for a moment, but the comparatively tiny Kiekhaefer Corporation's outboard catalog didn't even extend beyond six horsepower. Plus, government red tape and materials shortages leftover from the recent war economy were no doubt also hampering the Cedarburg, Wisconsin, outfit's ability to put much of a dent into pent-up consumer demand. Then there were the Western Auto and Disston Saw folks hounding Kiekhaefer for Wizard outboards and chain saw engines, respectively. In 1946, neither OMC's Rayniak nor Carl Kiekhaefer had time to ponder the potential publicity value of racing. They had their hands full with the standard-issue variety of motor. Kiekhaefer, too, simply hoped for an unfettered opportunity to produce his engine line for the traditional fishing motor market. At that point, a Mercury for racing would have seemed ludicrous to Kiekhaefer, Rayniak, or Fox's cohorts.

Charles Strang, whose collegiate outboard racing career had been cut short by an Air Force research stint during the war, trolled around the idea of restarting the old Eastern Intercollegiate Outboard Association, but got no bites. Colleges, around 1946, were filled with returning veterans highly focused upon making up for years lost in the war. Such a student, typically older than traditional 18-to-22 university demographics, often balanced studies, and work, plus a new wife and fussy baby. There was little time, energy, or money, left to expend on racing boats, motors, machine shops, travel, and recreational weekends. The guys Strang could have easily signed before Pearl Harbor now just wanted to "get their degrees and start life anew."

Navy vet Hank Bowman had a different clientele in mind when he decided to give the old college try to revitalizing an interest he'd had before entering the Service. The erstwhile PT skipper spotted a Bucks County, Pennsylvania, gravel pit that seemed like it might make a neat little racing lake. A bit of planning and lots of water later, he and some

Mercury's CEO Carl Kiekhaefer loved pictures like this! One of his little 7-1/2-horse Mercs passes Evinrude's 50-hp giant. During the 1947 Albany-to-New York Marathon, Mercury's 10-horsepower model didn't quite beat the competition's 50s, but clobbered several OMCs of 17 and 22-hp. That was all it took to get Mercury solidly in the stock racing camp. Actually, this particular shot was taken during a photo finish at the 1951 Seattle Sea-Fair race. Merc KG-4 vs. Evinrude Big Four.

associates converted the site into something christened Neshaminy Aquadrome, "the *world's only 1/4 mile outboard speedway.*" Just as Bowman figured, many of the "old-time" Pennsylvania, New Jersey, Long Island, and New York City area alky drivers — most of whom were not engaged in scholastic rigors — dusted off their rigs and circled around his Aquadrome. For a few years, starting June 16, 1946, races were held there at 3 pm every summer Sunday. Spectators parking in the establishment's gravel lot at Frankfort Avenue and Nashaminy Creek in Eddington, Pennsylvania, would make their way past the admission booth and into the wooden grandstand. Official programs were a dime. Bowman filled them with a "Just Among Us Buoys!" racer-profile and news column, previous race results, lists of entrants, an Aquadrome management roster, a list of staff members (from Chief Judge to Pit Stewards), some basic regulations of outboard racing, a "thank you" to the local rescue squad, and the standings of Aquadrome "high point" champs. There were also blanks in which onlookers could note the day's records, and then vote for their favorite driver. Rules were homemade to fit the pond, typically consisting of eight to ten laps in a pair of concocted classes: The program indicated "Class 1 [was] open to outboard hydroplanes powered by outboard motors of 15-cubic-inch displacement or less. Two types of motors [were] driven in this class, 'M,' and 'A.' Class 2 [called for motors] of 15-to-30 cubic inches, including the 16-hp 'B's and the 24-hp 'C's" (all pre-War Johnsons). Such groupings might appear imbalanced, but it seemed to work for the amalgamation of old friends who frequented their compatriot Bowman's waterway. The competitors also came for a little green, as prize money was an Aquadrome staple. A check of vintage photos, however, confirms the grandstand was almost always rather empty. That meant most of the cash awards, Bowman enthusiastically announced on the 'Drome's loudspeaker, came out of his own pocket. When the APBA decided the course was too short for the powerful organization's official sanctioning, Hank Bowman ceased casting bread on those waters, letting his interesting venture seep into outboarding history.

Post-war Beginnings

During the first year or two after the war, amateurs who competed just for fun played only a minor role in outboard racing. The sport's rich past (1930s-40s) was largely the province of professional alky drivers trying to coax some prize money out of the outboard competition circuit, and (like Fox's crew) these folks were first to seek out or help organize contests from the summer of 1945 through about 1947. Cash awards from winning a big weekend event might be $50 to $80, a tidy sum in the mid-1940s eighty-cent per hour employment universe. Stalwarts who frequented the Aquadrome, and/or other local races during the early postwar years, enjoyed their hobby (and did run informally for fun and testing), but liked it better when there were some real fiscal rewards. The old alky guys shifted into seriousness for races involving a decent purse. It could help with groceries and justify the pursuit to a dubious spouse. One of Bowman's best racing buddies grossed about $2,500 yearly (in the late 1940s and early 1950s) from a Monday through Saturday job at the local Sears store. During a good racing season, the fellow could match that by being on the water every Sunday. Of course, there was lots of winter and late night machining work to be done. In the mid-late 1940s, do-it-your-selfing was required, as the basis for alcohol-fueled competition motors didn't come from a dealer's showroom anymore. Johnson and Evinrude were making only standard-service product. Fortunately, many returnees to racing were products of the "make-do and fix" Depression era. Most were self-taught machinists quite comfortable with doing things themselves. A rough casting, some scrounged metal, drill press, lathe, and a mental picture of the desired outcome was considered a pretty good start. At a 1990s Antique Outboard Motor Club meet, a strange-looking kicker appeared. In the depths of hard economic times, it had been largely home-built using plumber's copper tubing, cylinders fashioned out of blocks of steel, parts from a number of different junked outboards, and a vacuum cleaner handle. The story went that the builder spent six months crafting the two-and-a-half horse egg-beater. When asked why that tinkerer didn't save himself time and trouble by simply buying an already operable machine from any 1930s dealer's $15 used motor rack, it was stated that time was something the old guy could manage, an extra fifteen bucks for a luxury item, however, he did not have. That brand of necessity had mothered most of the old pros who awakened outboard racing out of its war years coma. It had also equipped them with some pretty fast motors. But, younger, less dyed-in-the-wool guys wanting to get together a competition motor and try the sport were at a distinct disadvantage.

Evinrude/Johnson's refusal to re-enter racing widened the chasm between experience and novice. When OMC gave California machinist Randolph Hubbell rights to clone its 1930s-style racers, the picture brightened. Even so, his aftermarket parts and complete alky-burning motors were targeted to a technically savvy (and fiscally sound) clientele, not the average teen just hoping for an affordable new motor that might quicken his family's 12-foot utility runabout. Realistically, Hubbell's engines really required a special hull made for short, high-speed lower units. Little interest in clamp-on competition on the part of the general boating public could be generated if the hobby required such equipment and acumen. That placed the future of the world's most famous outboard race in jeopardy. All during the war, a tight circle of metropolitan New York boating enthusiasts were dreaming of the cherished New York-to-Albany Marathon's return. Among the visionaries musing a way to resurrect the contest were *Motor Boating* magazine publisher Charles F. Chapman, outboard man Lou Eppel, speedometer maker, (and former Class "M" champ) Dick McFadyen, Victor Oristano, and Mel Crook. By 1946, the cadre's brainstorming sessions were put into a more concrete form by Chapman's secretary, Ruth Smith, who spent hours organizing their notes. The group targeted the next year's Memorial Day weekend for tentative race dates, then began considering how such an event might be staged in a marketplace void of new racing outboards. Through 1941, the previous 14 Albany-to-New York bouts were typically won by savvy pros using sophisticated customized alky-burning mills. Considering the dearth of specialized motors, the big race's revitalizers unanimously agreed all entrants to their river run would drive standard boats and "service motors." The term "stock outboard" was not then in common usage. Hundreds of optimistic publicity releases went out to North American newspapers and the general boating press. *Motor Boating* wasn't about to keep silent on the opportunity. Neither was the APBA *Newsletter* (later dubbed *Propeller*). Both announced in early 1947 that the renowned race was waking from a six-year sleep, no longer as an alky driver's specialized scene, but for *anybody* with a small seaworthy boat and store-bought outboard. The promos did the trick. Of course, the budding crop of newcomers lured into racing by the ease of obtaining and operating regular "service" equipment sure helped organizers smile. Officials like McFadyen were able to see their idea bear fruit with every new count of the mountainous stack of entry forms.

Anne Jensen was one of this *new* Albany-to-New York Marathon's 150-plus competitors. A reporter from the Albany *Times-Union* learned that she was the only female slated to battle the Hudson on that late spring 1947 morning. The photojournalist spied her getting into a boat, yelled over the two-stroke tunes buzzing by the dock and then motioned for Jensen to wait. After jotting down something for a caption, he asked her to pose with a starter rope wrapped around her Class "C" Evinrude *Speeditwin*. As soon as the guy said "thanks, Mrs. Jensen," the cord did its thing, and the brunette was off.

Six months earlier, somebody in the engineering department of Massachusetts Institute of Technology informed colleague, Charles Strang, that he had a phone call.

"Charlie, this is Dick," announced the fellow via long-distance. Strang, who'd joined the MIT teaching staff following his Air Force work, recognized the voice of Richard McFadyen from their prewar days when they'd both raced alky outboards.

"Listen, Charlie . . . We're going to be doing a new "service" version of the Albany-to-New York Marathon," McFadyen said, "and, I really think this could be something you'd like. How about

By 1947, Dick McFadyen — an official with the Aqua-meter marine instruments firm, and chairman of the APBA's Outboard Racing Commission — realized that sanctioning events in which only stock equipment was raced represented the most logical way to attract average boaters into the sport.

Up early, an Albany Times-Union photographer caught Anne Jensen firing-up her Speeditwin for an 8 a.m. start of the 130-mile Albany-to-New York Marathon of 1947. The 24-year old nurse from Flushing, NY was drawn to the venerable race because — beginning that year — no special motor or boat was required.

rounding up a standard family runabout and "service" motor for a run on the old Hudson?"

"Sounds interesting," Strang nodded. "I'll contact Maury Beckman over in Cleveland to see if he'd like to have a go at it, too."

During his Air Force assignment at an Ohio military lab, Strang bumped into racing enthusiast Maurice Beckman, a pharmacist who owned a number of performance rigs. One, which Strang drove for him in a few, rare, war-era races, was powered by a high-strung "C-Service" Class, Evinrude Speeditwin converted to alcohol fire. Years later, he chuckled remembering what that association eventually led to on May 26, 1947.

"Beckman was a friend of Fred Wiehn, the fellow who ran the Lyman Boat Company," said Strang. "Fred built a special 13-foot Lyman runabout for us with a built-in aluminum gas tank, fuel transfer pump, remote steering and throttle control. Beckman put a 30-cubic-inch Speeditwin together for the boat. Now here was a bit of confusion! The Albany race was for *service motors*, as the term "stock" had not yet been approved. Beckman took the *service* to mean service as used in APBA 'C-Service,' and built a red-hot, ported engine [but decided to try equipping this marathon motor] with muffler and a standard carburetor instead of the Vacturi carb used in 'C-Service.' We went to Albany. The race drew a tremendous number of entries. The favored boats were those powered by those 60-cubic-inch Evinrudes [Big Four] derived from the 'Storm Boat' engines of World War II, which, in turn were derived from the prewar 4-60. In testing on the day before the race, my little [30-cube] Speeditwin literally ran away from the 60-cubic-inch outfits. We had the engine jacked up on the transom so the exhaust outlet was above the water and we were running about 6,000 rpm. The sound was quite different from most of the fleet. During a question-and-answer session at the huge drivers' meeting that night, held in an auditorium, one 60-cubic-inch driver rose to growl that he had an ear for music and he heard one boat out there that day that sure as hell didn't sound '*service*,' and that if that boat beat him to New York, he would *take care* of the driver! The growling giant was a heavyweight contender who was soon to fight [legendary boxer] Joe Louis!"

"Beckman suddenly realized what the race organizers meant by 'service.' They cer-

tainly wouldn't equate it in any way, shape or form with a custom-built "C-Service" powerplant. Once that light went on, the pharmacist and MIT professor tried to shrink under
their auditorium chairs. Anyway, there was no time to buy a new motor, since dealers were
closed for the night and the race was due to begin at eight the next morning. As incon-
spicuously as possible, Strang pulled the starter rope, motivating Beckman's handiwork to
immediately propel the Lyman way out in front of the field. The "special" Evinrude decided to stop a few miles downriver. Strang struggled with the carb, and then dismantled the
thing to discover a glob of gook. Underway again, he quickly caught the boats that had
passed him during repairs. Then, it conked out again. . . . More glop in the carb and fuel
line. Bouncing all over the place, he facilitated a half dozen more fixes, only to have the
gook reinfect the system every several miles. The last time his balky mill slowed to a sputter, he could see the finish line, but was far too fatigued to mess with all those tiny screws
and gaskets anymore. A friendly Coast Guard tug pushed the Lyman and palsied engine
across the final goal, but dozens had already made it. Winning the first major "stock" outboard race with a nonstock engine would not have looked too good on the front page,
anyhow. But what a newsflash a reporter might have scooped had that miffed, 60-cube
prize fighter caught up with Maury Beckman and Charlie Strang. Shortly after that 1947
run, the welder who made the duo's special fuel container probably remembered something; "Now, did I tell those outboard guys," he reflected, "that I might have gotten a little
excess welding flux in the tank? Oh, well." Meanwhile, McFadyen and his associates were
extra happy with their first "service" marathon's success. Even so, at the time, none had
any thought of creating what would eventually become *stock* outboard racing. Neither
was there a plan for racing to attract boat and motor manufacturers.

The man who made Mercury outboards had been drawn to Albany by sheer terror,
and then only at the last minute. When Carl Kiekhaefer (who probably hadn't previously thought two seconds about such an event) heard somebody was going to try one of his
newly released 10-hp KE-7 Lightning in the venerable contest, he implored the Merc customer to take a profit on the motor and forget the race. The thought of getting trampled
by a Hudson River full of Evinrudes and Johnsons made the fledgling industrialist's teeth
chatter. He was inconsolable until the lone Mercury entrant saw the 1947 checkered flag
before any other driver in his class. That sole Lightning victory seemed to flip a switch in
Kiekhaefer's promotional game plan. By midsummer of 1947, his public relations people
were well aware that he now wanted them to use the inferential power of racing in company advertising. Words such as *"Speed and Stamina"* quickly joined the firm's more traditional family/fishing motor ad lingo.

Stock's Appeal Grows
The 1947 Albany-to-New York Stock Marathon publicly demonstrated how people could
enter the sport without having to spend mortgage money on extravagant for-racing-only

equipment. According to Strang, throughout that summer, "this type of racing started to pop up all over the country in marathons, as well as closed course events." When winter 1948 rolled around, many yacht club's "hot stove meetings" had stock outboard racing on the agenda. A whole new crop of young people with family utility hulls and shiny green-top Mercs were waiting for the ice to melt and for someone to invite them to participate in a real race (with some real rules). Most everybody was accommodated. Hopeful competitors in waterside communities void of venerable powerboating organizations concocted their own clubs. All it took was a few enthusiastic families, a little paperwork at the courthouse, a couple of home-brew marker buoys, somebody's beach, and maybe a few $5 trophies. Some of the smaller clubs only promised "certificates suitable for framing" for folks in their winners' circle. Inexperience and modest facilities didn't seem to matter so much to this new crop of outboard racers. The 1948 season proved that the previous year's well-received Hudson River grind had been no fluke, rather it started cranking out a nice trend. Population for the second postwar Albany-to-New York Marathon exploded. There were 191 entries, 181 boats actually participated, and 142 finished.

The Albany-to-New York boom came in loud and clear at the American Power Boating Association. Adding machines at the APBA headquarters clicked through potential numbers. Association officials noted all the stock outboarding activity and figured — for two reasons — that it would be wise to enter the genre. First, adding stockers to APBA membership roles would generate a nice revenue stream for the venerable organization. And, joining up wouldn't be burdensome to the racers at three bucks for annual dues, which included membership, boat/motor registration cards, a rule book, and the assignment of official racing numbers. The actual race-day registration fee was similarly nominal. Second, clubs large or small, running under an APBA sanction would have an instant connection to uniformity, clout, and a safety net offered through national affiliation. Things started shaping up for future stockers during the APBA's January 1949 annual meeting in New York. Its Newsletter noted that, in the Big Apple's swanky Hotel Lexington, a vote was taken to determine whether or not "to adopt Stock Utility Racing as an officially recognized branch of the sport." Anyone happening down the richly carpeted hall that moment would have heard a healthy, unanimous "aye" rush out from a slice of light under the closed door. When the big group's freshly appointed committee sat down to formally craft stock outboarding rules, new 1949 motors in their spotlight included the 7-1/2-hp Mercury KE-4 *Rocket*, a new version of the legendary Mercury Lightning [dubbed KF-7 *Super Ten*], 40-cubic-inch KF-9 Merc *Thunderbolt*, Johnson *PO* with 22 hp, a similarly sized Evinrude *Speeditwin*, 33.4 hp *Speedifour* by Evinrude, and that firm's 50-hp Big Four. Also in focus at those APBA meetings were the specifications of the average family utility hulls then on the market. Racing historian Craig Bowman indicates "the original APBA stock outboarding rules (of 1948-49) were designed with the existing boat builders in mind." Even with all the available boat and motor standardiza-

Here is Charlie Strang cranking his Speeditwin on the morning of May 26, 1947. Because of a misunder-standing, his mill had been modified for "C-Service" alky operation — a far cry from the stock or regular "service" motor that Albany-to-New York officials required. The man with the worried look is Maury Beckman, a Cleveland pharmacist who sponsored Strang's endeavor.

tion, however, the formulation sessions were not without snags. Charlie Strang was in on the planning, remembering, "I was deeply involved in that activity and still [in 1999] have files of correspondence covering our hassles over rules, engine acceptability, etc."

A tiny blurb in the APBA's March-April 1949 *Newsletter* apprised members that the committee appointed to draft a set of racing rules to fit stock utility outboard classes, "spent considerable time and research" in doing so. For a major portion of this background, it had poured through papers documenting requirements set forth by organizers of the successful Albany events. There, boats and motors had to fit into the following classes:

CLASS	Motor Cubic Inch Displacement	Minimum Hull Weight (lbs.)
I	up to and including 12.5	75
II	12.6 to 18.5	150
III	18.6 to 25.5	225
IV	25.6 to 30.5	300
V	30.6 to 50.5	350
VI	50.6+	400

Additionally, the Albany rules stated boats had to be "stock displacement of family type and standard manufacture." Homemade craft were generally OK, too, as long as inspectors felt these hulls had been constructed in the spirit of pleasure (as opposed to specifically racing) use. Each boat could be powered by a single motor built as "a stock service model . . . of standard manufacture . . . as advertised, sold and delivered by the manufacturer, with nothing removed or changed, except: Any propeller, spark plugs or piston rings of standard manufacture may be used; spray shields [lower cowls] may be removed; any type of steering apparatus and spark and throttle control may be used. It will be permissible to add connections to gas tank for auxiliary gas supply, but no special racing fuel or racing parts may be used, [although] cylinder tie rods may be added."

The APBA stock utility formulators discussed the importance of enlisting boat and motor makers to embracing their new classification. Carl Kiekhaefer's post- 1947 Albany-to-New York burst of enthusiasm for such a program was duly noted. Some of the committee members felt providing a stage for the vociferous Kiekhaefer's Mercury line might help make the new stock category fly. For the Merc man, this appeared to offer opportunity indeed, and opened a way to knock the same Evinrude/Johnson that had sworn-off a connection with racing. That's why somebody passed around copies of the *Mercury Messenger* newsletter. Within the issues mailed about the time of the 1948 Albany race, Kiekhaefer made it clear he didn't think stock motor cylinders should be equipped with accessory tie rods (as were often owner-installed on OMC mills). His publication also screamed about the event's inequity in the cubic-inch displacement class structure. It threw the 19.8-cubic inch *Lightning* in with the OMC motors some five cubes heftier. And, for the 1949 Albany contest, Merc's new 39.6 four-cylinder *Thunderbolt* had to race with Evinrudes way up in the 50-cubic-inch zone. APBA stock regulation crafters borrowed a bit from its alky specs, and decided to coin a letter-distinguished class system. Most were rounded off in units of ten. There was "JU" ("U" for Utility), then "AU" up to "FU." In the "BU" and "DU" classes where Mercury had the best chance of reigning supreme, maximum cubic inch limits were fixed just a smidgen above the motors' specs. The stock group's work was approved at a March 3rd APBA Council meeting, with a promise by the rule makers that they'd add a little something here and there before making the new regulations public. After a few revisions, and shakedown over the 1949 season (including their use for the 1949 Albany race), APBA's new Stock Utility Outboard Racing Commission rules had a cornerstone that looked like this, as of October 30, 1949:

Class	Maximum Motor Cubic Inch Displacement	Minimum Hull Weight (lbs.)
JU	10 (Later lowered to 7.5 probably to accommodate the 7.2-cube Mercury 5-hp engine.)	
AU	15	
BU	20	(All Classes: 7 pounds
CU	30	per cubic inch)
DU	40	
EU	50	
FU	60	

Over the years, the APBA interpretation of a "stock" outboard shifted with product availability, but during the genre's peak in the 1950s, it was defined (according to a 1950 APBA newsletter) as one that "is the product of a recognized manufacturer engaged in the production of outboard motors for sale to the general public as service motors. . . . Has been advertised and offered for sale to the public as a service motor. . . . And, if a current model, is available for purchase on the open market through recognized sources of supply." That's one of the reasons why Mercury devoted at least a little catalog space to limited-production motors such as its Quicksilver models. Any boat competing in a stock utility event was required by these rules to have "two or more cross seats." The rear seat could be removable, but all seats needed to measure at least 10-inches in width, and be capable of providing a minimum of 15 inches seat space per potential passenger. Both the spirit and the letter of these early directives had true racing and pleasure boating utility in mind, so seating for at least three people in "JU" hulls, four in "AU" and "BU," and five folks for classes "CU" through "FU" was a must. If a boat didn't look like it could hold a family, judges were allowed to ask the driver to "circle the race course at a fair speed with the required number of passengers" aboard. Kids had to be at least 12 years old to run in "JU" or "AU," and 14-plus to qualify in the other categories. Clearly, though, there was room in stock outboarding for just about anyone with sea legs.

Three hundred and fifteen of those Utility skippers showed up in Albany for the 1949 running of the famous marathon. As Lou Eppel's *Yachting* retrospective beamed, "no outboard regatta of any type had ever [before] attracted so many boats." A few, reportedly through key distributors, had the advantage of having quite recently acquired Mercury motors not readily available to the general public. A select corps of Class "AU" standouts quietly clamped a Kiekhaefer model identified as KE-4HD (Heavy Duty) to their transom, while lucky "BU" stars found specially built KF-7HD (pre-production KG-7) mills available for their boats. *Yachting* magazine hinted that Kiekhaefer's rare HD outboards were "the first *special* motor equipment aimed [specifically] for stock racing." As such, these modified 1949-1/2 Mercs overstepped the definition of "stock." Plus, for the formerly equalized stock enthusiasts, getting outpaced by what was ostensibly a new hand-built (in the Merc factory) engine they couldn't readily buy, HDs caused some bad feelings. "Suddenly," *Yachting* noted, true "stock owners tasted obsolescence in mid-season unless they too acquired the special high power and obviously faster (HD) components for their motors." But, there doesn't seem to be much historical data to show bigwigs made a fuss about the heavy duty powerhead. Reflecting on similar irregularities in the avenue of standards for "stock utility" hulls, an APBA Commissioner indicated "race committees took the attitude that the rules were just too tough to enforce for every motor and hull. No one was anxious to disqualify a boat in these early days of Stock Utility Racing merely because it was an inch short in length, provided everything else was legal." Besides, Mercury HD models were still equipped with a standard "fishing" lower unit (some from the smaller, 5-horse motor), and sure didn't look like blatant racing motors.

Just before the aforementioned (October 30, 1949) revamped rule approval, APBA officials held a "manufacturers' forum" for boat and motor makers. Mercury was there with positive input. The Association's September *Newsletter* confirmed that the "Kiekhaefer Corporation has indicated its approval in a very concrete manner by generously contributing to the support of our [APBA] activities in governing this branch of racing. Kiekhaefer has also sent out four thousand bulletins and [APBA stock racing] membership forms to dealers, distributors and others urging their support of the [stock] program." In those days, Mercury motors were sold by the factory to a web of some twenty to thirty distributors. In turn, these organizations sold the outboards to local dealers, which peddled them motor by motor to individual customers. Owning a distributorship was where a good portion of the big money could be made in outboard sales. Charlie Strang verified that from *Lightning*'s initial 1947 win, "the distributors were all active in promoting racing and encouraging the local dealers to become involved, and it was this Mercury effort that built stock racing to its [eventual 1950s] peak." Wheels, Incorporated in New York City, Bill Bell in Texas, Don Guerin in upstate New York, and Merlyn Culver throughout Ohio were some of the most notable Merc distributors who became major forces in the fledgling sport. Along the way, both Guerin and Culver served as Stock Outboard Vice President, as well as APBA president. In addition to the monetary benefits his Mercury sales organization would realize from a strong association with stock racing, each had another motive, young sons who wanted to race.

The 1950s were heady years for do-it-yourselfers interested in constructing their own watercraft. Most every newsstand or corner store that sold magazines offered at least a few like this Boat Builder's Handbook. Almost without exception, outboard racing hulls were featured on the cover and inside.

While grade schooler Allyn Guerin had to wait a few years after his dad became a Merc distributor to squeeze a throttle, Jon Culver was just old enough to get in on the stock genre's ground floor. When the APBA sponsored another 1949 stock utility rules forum, this time for utility drivers, 15-year-old Culver was one its most seasoned stocker attendees. The red-headed high school student began racing (around 1947) on waterways near his Dayton, Ohio, hometown, and then moved up to a national level competition through the 1948 Albany-to-New York run. That's where his big league reputation started on the first pull, as a June 1948 *Mercury Sales Bulletin* described the youngster pitted against "some of the country's most capable drivers. He studied navigation charts and took an advance trip down the river and hit the starting line with enough knowledge of the course so that he was able to hold his [KE-7 Mercury] motor at open throttle every foot of the way without fear of running aground or fouling on hidden obstructions."

The successful trip to New York gave Culver the zeal to fully participate in stock utility racing's first official season, 1949. That September (27th), his dad's Mercury endeavors also helped make it feasible for him to travel all the way to Lake Alfred, Florida, for the debut APBA Stock Utility Outboard National Championships. Actually, the Utility's card was tacked on to the end of the then more traditionally prominent, alky outboard "Nationals." While a whole weekend, and related Monday for mile-trials was devoted to the pros or alcohol-burning outboarders, the nascent stockers just got scheduled to run (Tuesday and Wednesday) a mile fly-by. Reportedly, however, that was more than enough time for the handful of participants. Dick McFadyen admitted in *Motor Boating* that "since [stock utility outboarding had] only recently been organized, it was not surprising that the event was not without difficulties. Probably the most disappointing was the limited turnout." He was referring to a "lightly sparse" field of "CU" people, two lonely "EU" entries and the goose egg on the "FU" entrant list. A few kids were present for a run at "Junior Utility" (or "JU") glory. Many of the old-time alky drivers stayed to see what the new stockers, and especially the tiny "JU" Mercury *Super 5* mills could do. Floridian, Roy Ridgell made the crowd smile with a five-mile average speed of 20.689 mph that captured that first closed course stock Nationals title. The "JU" mile record went to Bob Terry, also a Florida boy, for hitting 21.480 miles per hour.

In 1949, Nationals "AU" honors went to Paul Wearly. One of the country's finest alky-burners, he'd just stowed away his Johnson SR, related boat, and prize money won in the "B" Hydro professional event. Then the Hoosier hopped into a Merc-powered rowboat to try his throttle hand in the new utility avenue. The veteran knee-padder started the race kneeling, but soon took advantage of the craft's seating arrangements. Wearly won the five mile competition "AU" event sitting down at 28.758 mph. Bob Terry took the "AU" mile trial with a speed of 29.292 miles per hour.

"BU" was Jon Culver's specialty. His Mercury motor/Speedliner boat combo moved around the buoys at 34.201 mph. Somebody complained that the Speedliner's seats were undersized, but inspectors ruled that they were Okay. The Ohio boy also ran fastest in the "BU" mile trials. 27.229 mph wasn't stellar, but since

For folks thinking of buying a stock racing outboard during the 1950s, this was the sign they liked to see. When illuminated, it transmitted beautiful back lighting.

Seasoned alky racer Paul Wearly did well in the professional class (with vintage Johnson-based engines like this one) at the 1949 APBA Outboard Nationals. When he noticed several stock events were included on the schedule, Wearly found a KE-4 Merc and proceeded to try his hand at the small "AU" (utility) class — becoming the category's first nationwide champion.

there were no previous national figures, however, it was fast enough to establish a baseline record. Spectators found most of their "BU" excitement when one of Culver's competitors, whose bucking boat tossed him in the drink. *Motor Boating* chronicled that the driverless craft continued making "erratic circles until it was intercepted" by the patrol squad.

Marylander Charles Wingo, was next in the winner's circle with a 33.088 mph performance in Class "CU." When the figure was posted, scuttlebutt around the pits included wondering why the big 30-cube "C" motor was a mile-an-hour and change slower than Culver's much smaller Merc. Wingo redeemed his class in the mile trial, though, with a slightly faster attainment of 34.738 mph.

Paul Wearly returned to the water in a "DU" boat to compete against a group of other Mercury *25 Thunderbolt* operators. Veteran outboarder, Jack Maypole, of Chicagoland ran his 4-cylinder Merc past everybody to claim the five-mile closed course win at 38.944 mph. Quincy, Illinois' Eddie Palmer gunned his Mercury-power hull to 43.426 mph for the mile straightaway record. During part of the day, Jack Maypole's "DU" honors were in jeopardy. A referee trying to enforce every letter of the new stock law discounted the win based on an arcane measurement. Massachusetts Institute of Technology instructor Charles Strang served as an APBA engine inspector at the event, and came to Maypole's rescue. That's where Carl Kiekhaefer first met Strang, his future right-hand man and major player in stock outboard racing's salad days.

To cap the seminal stock contest, a pair of "EU" boats jogged around the course in the low- to mid-30s range. Antonio Stroscio from New Jersey, and New Yorker Al Zolko were just going through the motions. Though only two are required to tango, APBA rules required a larger field for the establishment of official championship records. Consequently, the first true "E" Utility nationwide figures were the provinces of a subsequent year.

Cradled in nostalgic retrospect, those 1949 Nationals seem so easygoing and idyllic today that it's difficult to imagine the pioneer event was rife with controversy. Inspectors like Al Hart (APBA Utility Outboard Racing Commission Chairman) were going nuts

If enthusiasts couldn't get to a racing-friendly local Mercury dealer, some shop owners just might come to them. This is Al Zeller & Sons' (Green Bay, WI) mobile showroom and Merc parts center. Some of the goodies displayed in the picnic area of a race site, include: Aeromarine 2-cycle oil, KAMINC safety throttles, Handy-Coil rope, gas tanks, sparkplugs, lifejackets, and crash helmets.

trying to determine which boats were or were not "utility" hulls, and what motors technically "stock." The boat definitions gave officials fits. Dick McFadyen, who'd helped draft the division's original rules (and the 1947-48 Albany-to-New York regs), was clearly bothered by what he saw happening to his baby in 1949. "A few years ago, when stock utility racing was in its infancy," he editorialized in *Motor Boating*, "it wasn't too difficult to define a stock boat, as everything available at that time, discounting hydroplanes, probably fitted the category. When the stock-boat owners became speed happy, the builders started to angle their products towards the racing market. Some came right out and called their boats *racers*, which under the strict interpretation of the current rules, would bar their boat. It became quite obvious that, at Lake Alfred [1949 Nationals], many of the boats had been designed for someone no larger than [one of Disney's seven dwarfs], and like the poor penguin who has wings but can't fly, most of the boats had seats that couldn't sit and decks that had as much resemblance to a family runabout as [Titanic] has to a rowboat." This father of stock utility racing was also concerned about the Nationals' stock records going to so many old pros. Like a seasoned Broadway star easily walking away with first prize in a local amateur talent show (much to the disappointment of a kid who'd stuttered while reciting some Shakespearean verse), veteran alky drivers who effortlessly dominated the newly created stock classes bugged McFadyen no end. He was a die-hard family utility proponent hoping both the letter and the spirit of the stocker law might always be obeyed. "It would be healthy for the sport," the former alky burner stated, "if a prohibition was included to ban the competition of drivers in both the senior [professional] division and Utilities during the same racing season." Fluky boats and souped-up motors" were also on his bad list. Touted outboarder and fellow columnist Lou Eppel concurred with McFadyen that pros entering the stock realm could easily discourage novices. "The original intent for the utility classes," he noted in *Motorboat*, "was to give the chaps and gals with restricted purses and a lack of engine savvy a chance to run on a more or less even level with the rest of the competition." Shortly thereafter, the pro drivers bowed out, leaving the true stock utility devotees (as well as thousands of hopefuls) a more equalized environment. Still, though, there was the matter of maintaining consensus about the true definition of "stock." Officials wrestling with questionable entries to the 1949 Nationals had seen only the issue's tip. Human nature was the real iceberg, always bobbing about for an advantage over the other guy. Such is the condition that has, ever since, kept inspectors busy checking to see that victors had come to the race with only as much of. a chance as the person who ended up in last place.

One APBA inspector, that debut stock utility year, was Charlie Strang. While scrutinizing a winning Mercury, he met the man who owned the company that built the motor. A few minutes after the chance encounter, Carl Kiekhaefer recognized honest engineering talent, and mused, "I oughtta hire that guy."

Feedback from editorials like those of McFadyen and Eppel kept the APBA working on ways to ensure its contests were equitable. For the Association, 1949 was an especially notable year, too, with regard to democracy. A change in bylaws gave each of its individual members complete voting rights. Consequently, instead of power resting with the affiliated clubs (where the club size had mattered), anyone who joined the APBA had an equal say in its policy. That provided stock and alky outboarders, the Association's largest interest block, with real clout. Of course, no amount of gerrymandering can make everyone happy. With more voters, greater numbers of lobby pressure points could be exerted on the rules. In the stock utility camp, much of that infuence, in some way, belonged to Mercury and its customers. After all, the company produced the engines that were driving the program. So, what was good for Merc was also tacitly viewed by many stockers as fine for stock outboarding. The Kiekhaefer/APBA connection was a serious relationship that some believe stifled other stock racing motor makers. Others recognize, however, that Kiekhaefer mills were right for the stock racing role. Arguably, even an average example was typically faster and stronger than the best a rival's production line could offer.

The Fifties . . . and Controversy

From the porch of his family's summer place, Dick O'Dea could see the little boats bouncing around Greenwood Lake. These craft were just some of the hundreds typically there that helped earn the popular New York/New Jersey waterway a tongue-in-cheek reputation for marine traffic jams. No matter such congestion, for a kid with his own boat, it

Dick O'Dea, age 16, is out in the Hudson River to try the 1950 Albany-to-New York race. Unfortunately, his new Champion motor had difficulty making the trip

was a mighty exciting place to be. The teen had recently gotten together the money to buy a 10-foot Sid-Craft hull made by some Jersey guys who competed on the Lake. They were part of a group called the Mercury Racing Club of Greenwood Lake (subsequently, Greenwood Lake Racing Club) that, as the original name suggested, had fun comparing the speed of Kiekhaefer products on their favorite pond. O'Dea hung around talking with Sid Urytzski and Mickey Starego, and then ordered one of their Sid-Craft new stock utilities. Securing an appropriate motor would be another matter. On a race day in 1949, the young boat owner co-opted a horse-and-a-half Evinrude from his folks' garage so he could putt-putt the Sid-Craft to the race site. Mickey and Sid chuckled at the sight of the youngster with an eggbeater on the back of one of their specialized competition hulls. Sid was still shaking his head as he popped open the trunk of his car to grab an extra Mercury *Rocket* for the customer's boat. O'Dea was thrilled with the loaner . . . and especially with doing pretty well in an "AU" event. After it was all over, he helped Sid put the Merc back in the car. Reattached, his family's little sputtering Evinrude single couldn't seem to get the kid home fast enough with all the news.

"NOW AVAILABLE," shouted the headline. With that, the Kiekhaefer Corporation was happily announcing its new *high efficiency* lower units for Mercury motors popular in stock utility classes. Staffers who crafted the simple (May 1950) APBA *Newsletter* ad were careful not to identify the offering as a full-fledged *racing* component, as that would be admitting the new *Quicksilver* gear foot wasn't kosher "stock." This component was a major factor in begging the question: Should "stock" mean "regular all-purpose outboard," or simply, "a for-racing-only engine universally available from dealers' stock? Mercs affixed to Quicksilvers also opened the marine equivalent of Pandora's Box.

Anyone not noticing that the "Quickie" and related short driveshaft housing were hardly suitable for a traditional utility hull probably needed a white cane.

When thinking about his competitors, the man who owned Mercury typically saw red. Chalie Strang vividly recalls that "Carl Kiekhaefer considered them all out to get him," and, for the Merc CEO, 1949's double-barrel onslaught introduction of the Champion Hot Rod, plus the Martin "*60*" Hi-Speed was more than sufficient proof. Both engines had powerhead features far in excess of their "fishing" model sisters. While the Champion possessed some extra streamlining in its lower unit, the Martin's foot was obviously for all-out racing. With no room spared for a pump, the Martin wouldn't even support cooling water to the cylinders until traveling at a good clip. Certainly, neither motor embraced the original spirit of the stock utility program Kiekhaefer very early and actively supported. APBA officials (in the September 1949 *Newsletter*) publicly acknowledged that his "cooperation [was] not only most helpful, but [was] greatly appreciated." Consequently, he figured rule makers wouldn't mind if he came up with motors that allowed him to get even with, or maybe a little ahead of the sport's inevitably dynamic curve. Merc's new KG-7 Hurricane was ready for the 1950 Albany-to-New York Marathon. In "fishing motor" stock form it was notably livelier than its Lightning predecessors. But, with the accessory Quicksilver lower unit and/or abbreviated driveshaft housing, the motor completely exited the "family Sunday cruise" realm. This kind of add-on raised some eyebrows the night before the Albany race and almost started a shoving match on the reviewing stand. By the time officials fired the starting gun, though, consensus waved the new lower units through.

Wins with a borrowed Merc KE-4 on his hull gave Dick O'Dea confidence to show his stuff in the 1950 Hudson River event. No matter, the youngster didn't come equipped with a Mercury. His dad, who owned WOV (AM 1280) Radio in New York City got in on the process too, promising Dick a new motor for that Sid-Craft. Somebody in the business suggested Mr. O'Dea contact Earl

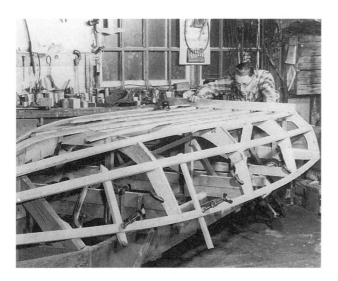

Sid Urytzski of Sid-Craft boats makes sure everything on the framework of his latest stock or utility runabout is on the level. No slightly warped family fishing boat bottom here! By 1950, the most competitive utility craft were ones built with the APBA rulebook in hand. That is to say, the letter of the law became more of a factor than its spirit.

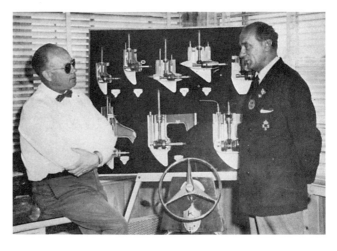

Carl Kiekhaefer (left) explains the finer points of lower unit design to a visiting Mercury distributor. Cutaways of "A/B," and "D" size Quickie gearfeet are center stage on the display board.

DuMonte who ran Champion Outboard Company. Easy negotiations netted the young racer with a 1950 Champion *Hot Rod* for the important run, because DuMonte hoped a win might help Champion in the publicity department. This motor was Okay, O'Dea recalled, but pounding from all that rough water loosened the Sid's special auxiliary fuel tank that fed the mill. When it split open partway down the river, there wasn't much remedy available.

Certainly, other such contests featured persnickety conditions, but Albany-to-New York was a leader in water hazards. One year, (according to APBA *Newsletter* accounts) participants were nervously laughing that it best be renamed "Driftwood Derby" in honor of all the debris, including "a house that went floating down the river" not long before the starting gun sounded. A fellow trying to pilot a small runabout and KE-4 Merc down the wavy route, later suggested that organizers should "arrange to have the wind turned off the day of the race." Blowing and swells coaxed the bottom right out of participant Bill Allard's Evinrude-powered runabout. "Another year, near West Point," he remembered with a deliberate shake of the head, "there were gusts like a wind tunnel!" His *Speeditiwin* gave him fits, too. The spring in the ignition points busted, prompting the 22-horse to quit. Amid all the chop, Allard was able to stretch out the disabled spring, and bring the motor back to life. But that reacquired smooth purr lasted for only a few miles. The spring broke again, and then again, until eventually, there just wasn't enough of it left to work with. It was simply a factor of outboard marathoning's luck of the draw. And, for the lack of a twenty-cent OMC replacement part, Allard had to wait around in the angry chop for a tow in to the docks.

Clerks in the APBA mailroom hadn't had time to sit still on April 11, 1950. That day lengthy "notice[s] went out to all outboard motor manufacturers stating that on and after May 10, 1950, only those motors will be eligible for APBA stock utility racing whose manufacturers have filed with the chief measurer of the APBA those specifications and data required by all parts of . . . the stock utility outboard racing rules for 1950." The letter was endorsed by the Association's president who was hoping to get motor makers to identify what was "stock," and then stick to it for that particular model year. At issue were sudden manufacturing "updates" that left proponents of the genre's original spirit and intent confounded. Die-hard stockers were especially peeved about "dealer service bulletins," often a few arcane paragraphs on a company letterhead announcing some mechanical modification. Mercury seemed to have a printing press that specialized in such ad hoc notices, as well as a delivery system famous for bringing them to the attention of racing commission inspectors at the very last minute. Craig Bowman, whose *Boat Sport* magazine writer father, Hank, fielded all sides of a given controversy, remembered that "in the early fifties, a service bulletin from Mercury made some new [feature on a motor] legal overnight." The well-equipped racers would show up with some very recent development on their Mercs, sometimes just hours after a factory service bulletin would have been filed about it. "This kind of thing," Bowman noted, "created hard feelings [among have-nots as well as officials] and eventually caused [along with other factors like insurance costs] events like the Albany-to-New York Marathon to end."

Without significant premeditation, Evinrude and Johnson muddied stock utility's waters, too. OMC hadn't made racing engines in either brand since 1941, nor put much effort into providing the APBA with complete spec sheets on standard service outboards it did produce soon after the war. When the Johnson *PO*/Evinrude *Speeditwin*, Evinrude *Speedifour*, and *Big Four* became early stock utility favorites in classes "CU, EU, and FU," respectively, some owners altered their motors for a bit more speed. Annoyed by Kiekhaefer's gloating over the Albany-to-New York victory, OMC decided to play a bit of the stock utility game, and so recommended a few modifications OMC owners could try. But the APBA wouldn't approve them all. Officials simply felt the changes took the Evinrude/Johnson mills too far afield "from the original concept of stock." Big-water racers who felt the most offended by the Association's thumbs-down were typically from either Long Island or coastal California. They argued that the need for souped-up "CU," "EU," and "FU" mills stemmed from regional traditions forged by the use of hefty hulls and a penchant for machine shop skills. Their case was staked to the fact that the 30, 50, and 60-cubic inch Johnson and Evinrude motors they used were largely prewar design relics, no longer actively supported by the manufacturers. Furthermore, OMC had new alternate-firing, full-gearshift models on its mind, and already planned to deep-six the last of the anachronistic line of opposed-twins and quads (the likes of *Speeditwin*, *SpeediFour*, and *Big Four*) by 1951. A year later, racing officials agreed that this factor placed the future of "CU," "EU," and "FU" classes in jeopardy, but still felt uncomfortable calling owner-altered engines "stock."

By early 1952, APBA executives announced (in the February 1952 edition of *Propeller*) they'd hit upon a compromise. In an effort to be reunited with outboarders who for "the past two seasons [have been] racing outside the jurisdiction of the American Power Boat Association," three new classes were authorized on a probationary basis. With the nod from officials, modified stock "CU," "EU," and "FU" engines were re-branded into "CM,"

The driver in boat F-200 at this NOA alky race is probably thinking his motor has too much acceleration capability! And maybe the owner of racing runabout Y-66 is considering where his neighbor's vertical craft is going to land? These kinds of experiences can make or break a racing career. Many veteran competitors confirm that once you loose your nerve, you should get out of the sport. An old west coast "B" stock hydro competitor recalled the day he decided to sell his gear; "Right near the finish of an especially crowded race, some nuts in an overloaded rowboat strayed near the course and laid down a huge, jagged wake that suddenly scared the wits out me. I remember backing off the throttle just long enough to collect my thoughts and saw a teenage girl in one of the buzzing hydros beside me glance my way with steely determination and go flying right over the big waves. Something immediately told me I'd lost my nerve and it wouldn't be coming back!"

"EM," and "FM" nooks, respectively. As desired, the rule change quickly skyrocketed sanctioned racing participation in the populated Long Island area. One event, held as a fundraiser for the Glen Cove, Long Island, Community Chest, bulged with modified (as well as stock) boat entries, and attracted 10,000 spectators. In addition to seeing the modified stockers, that legion got a glimpse of non-OMC branded engines.

Pushing many of APBA membership's 686 registered stock utility boats as of early 1950, the motors listed in the accompanying graphic might have been at a typical race, as each of the following enjoyed the Association's stock approved status

Favorite Stock Motors

<u>JU</u>

Mercury: KF-5

<u>AU</u>

Champion: 4K, 4KS, 4L-HD, 4LS.

Martin: "60" CHS.

Mercury: KE-4, KE-4HD, KG-4*.

<u>BU</u>

Mercury: KE-7, KF-7*, KF-7HD*, KG-7*.

<u>DU</u>

Mercury: KF-9*, KF-9HD*, KG-9*

---

*Sometimes dubbed a "Q Motor" as equipped with a long (upper and lower cavitation plates) Quicksilver racing lower unit.

In the meantime, some APBA officials — siding with purists — were already describing (through the September 1950 *Newsletter*) their 1950-era Stock Utility Division with words like "ailing" and "disintegrate[d]." They even declined "an offer of financial assistance" from an unspecified motor maker. The Association's head argued "if the manufacturers mean what they've preached that Utility racing is *for the kids*, instead of for the sole purposes of advertising motors, there is no place in this class for the professional" or royal amateur knighted by the factory, latest stock upgrade, and related service bulletin. One Association leader was quoted as saying he had "serious doubts whether some of the manufacturers actually want the Utility racing program to succeed." He never specified which ones, but any company making changes primarily for the sole purpose of racing (as opposed to a design modification that simply adds greater standard-use reliability to a regular service model) really struck a nerve with most of the Association's leadership. Each change could discourage thousands of casual racing buffs who were not able afford annual equipment updates.

Motor makers weren't alone in generating this frustration. Boat builders had been placed on the Association's most wanted list first. *Yachting* observed that the initial "departure from the intent of the [Stock Utility] rules was brought about by the appearance on the market of racing utilities, which were merely cut down models of regular production line boats, with the weight brought down from the absolute minimum and the freeboard and deck all but eliminated." Armed with a copy of the rules and interpretive brainstorming, even the smallest boat-building enterprises were in a position to take the next step. Fledgling firms like Sid-Craft and Switzer "began turning out custom-built Utility racing boats which were far from utility in intent and performance." Old alky driver and all around boat racing enthusiast Lou Eppel admired the ingenuity of such enterprises, but said in that January 1953 *Yachting* piece "they were defeating all of the plans for having classes of outboards, which could be raced as well as be used for other purposes." He admitted that "these early *racing* Utility boats offered much in increased speed and in many cases they were better handling and somewhat safer in competition, nevertheless they were designed and built for racing and not for general use." With that, Eppel figuratively saw the ideal of *fishing in the family boat on Saturday and then racing it on Sunday* get tossed off the dock.

Around 1951, traditionalists running on that "Hurrah for racing general-use boats and motors!" platform recognized they were being outnumbered by an emerging force wielding specialized green-top Mercs and 1/4-inch plywood. Stock's original concept image of a multi-purpose, truly five passenger lapstrake Lyman family runabout and 33.4 horse Evinrude was quickly fading from the Stock Utility scene. Actually, though, its replacement by lightweight 10-foot hulls and *Super Tens* was more of a plebian revolution than APBA rule conservatives originally recognized. Soon, the cheaper little (primarily for racing) boats and affordable Mercury stock *racing* motors, especially exemplified in

"AU/BU" competition, were viewed by most newcomers as the reason for the "out-of-the-box" racing's growth within the ever-increasing middle class. This seemed especially true in families that had teenagers who were into boating. And the growing number of boating families impacted racing schedules. For example, 1951's respectable card of 81 APBA sanctioned stock *utility* outboard regattas got dwarfed by 131 such events in 1952. Few of the contests that year saw the entry of true, dual-purpose hulls.

By the time Eisenhower was on the political campaign trail, officials who, in the late 1940s, had voted stock utility into existence, allowed the word "utility" (as in the aforementioned Lyman *utility* craft) to be dropped in favor of the truer, monosyllabic term "stock" outboard racing. Once the runabout hull-style issue appeared to be settled, factions seeking APBA blessings for further change were freed up to lobby elsewhere. Some pushed for extra latitude in modifying their motors, a few hoped rules regarding cash prizes might be dumped, most pledged to guard the stock genre's "store-bought" universality, and one led the fight for hydroplanes.

Hydros

It's a mystery whether or not most 1950s speed buffs who sent for one of Joe Swift's boat catalogs made sense out of its logo. In reality, literature from the Mount Dora, Florida-based Swift Woodcraft, Inc., arrived more in the form of inexpensively printed, 8 1/2 inch by 14 inch flyer sheets. On the bottom was a stylized depiction of Swift's chief manufacturing endeavor, the clothespin. No matter, the company advertising was especially interesting to folks with hang ups about thrift. During the late 1940s and early 1950s, a new Neal or Jacoby hydroplane, complete with brass screws and planked mahogany construction would set you back $400. Swift, whose shop was into clothespins and rustic furniture, introduced a small line of hydros that retailed for only about $160 apiece. His secret ingredients were plywood, clinch nails and lots of glue. At first, old-timers snickered that these lightweight, cheap boats would soon fall apart, but Swift's hulls gained a quick reputation for holding up well and for representing a very good value.

MOUNT DORA, FLORIDA

Boat maker Joe Swift produced fast, featherweight runabouts, but is best remembered for his popular line of stock hydros.

Pen Yan Heavy Composite Construction
Model CZT Swift
(Steering gear and backs are extras.)

PENN YAN BOATS
INCORPORATED
PENN YAN, N.Y.

Another classic craft of the 1950s is the Penn Yan Swift. The boat had no relationship to Joe Swift's competition hulls, and was most at home winning cottage-racing contests. With brightly varnished wood, brilliantly colored outer hull canvas, and a rich cedar green Merc, these boats were real attention getters.

Rather than being sold direct from the Florida factory, this new breed of hydro (as well as a "BU" runabout) was marketed through local boat shops. "SEE YOUR DEALER" was imprinted near the bottom of most Swift brochures. Because leftover wood strips were in great supply at the shop, Swift made the wise decision to use some to open-crate each boat produced. He did this in such a way as to provide an easily "stackable" package that dealers could pile three or four boats high, while yielding potential customers access to the craft on the showroom floor. Many were sold through the Mercury dealership organization. This, of course, was a natural since Merc was already pushing motors, stock racing, and fun. Even in the most bucolic water-side hamlet, a person interested in the sport could do one-stop shopping for a reliable Swift hydro, Merc KG-4H, KG-7H, or Mark 20H *Hurricane*, and accessories. Plus, to go along with the reasonably priced rig, there'd be details about the next local races, an APBA membership application, and some friendly instruction by the dealer's resident racing-nut mechanic.

Hahn & Walters was one of those favorite spots for high-performance Kiekhaefer nuts in the 1950s Milwaukee, Wisconsin area. "They always had a supply of used stock out-board boats and motors for sale," remembered Chris Wilde, an erstwhile racer who got his start there. "The place was the magnetic center for drivers in the Badger State Outboard Association. Nate Walters, one of the owners and an "A" Stock Hydro competitor, acted as mentor and friend to the drivers who congregated there." Especially during the winter months, when there was more time for folks at a marine dealership to muse and host an informal gathering, old-timers might stop by to encourage the youngsters. "When my brother and I [dreamed of being stock outboard stars] and were getting started," the Milwaukeean smiled, "we were fortunate enough to have several, more experienced racers take pity on us and give us technical and moral support. Chief among these was Carl Stippich, a well-liked competitor often specializing in "DU" activity, who sold us one of his boats at a reasonable price, helped us tune our KG-4H, and lent us propellers." Happily, there were more than a few such father figures or big brothers willing to bring up novices throughout stock outboarding's 1950s heyday.

The convenient availability of ready-to-race stock combos at local marine outlets sold lots of product. Dealers also understood that a fast-looking Merc and brightly painted Swift out front even attracted those who were thinking only of buying a five-hp fishing motor and pram. Similarly, lots of mundane station wagons were bought by people who noticed the red Corvette convertible nicely featured in their local Chevy agency's window.

In early 1951, APBA brass wanted to see whether hydroplanes could be viable in its stock program. The evolution from dual-purpose (or utility) runabouts to stock (or primarily for racing) runabouts had discouraged some of the former genre's original proponents. But with the stock legion, who quickly got used to the idea of employing craft built "for racing only," the concept of stock hydros (in which no one expected a family cruise or fishing outing) seemed reasonable. A special February meeting was called in Cincinnati, Ohio, to tackle such a proposal, resulting in the creation of Classes "A," "B," and "D" (subsequently dubbed "ASH," "BSH," and "DSH") Stock Hydro. Engine cylinder displacement followed those of the "regular" stock (utility) specs, but hydro hull weight maximums were pegged at 100, 100, and 150 pounds respectively. On March 4th, the Sun Dance regatta, sponsored by West Palm Beach's Propeller and Sail Club, offered to make racing history by placing a Stock Hydro schedule on the card. Unfortunately, the water was rough, causing the cancellation of the "ASH" run. With winds still somewhat strong, only five starters answered the gun in the Class "B" bracket. Jeff Tobin, of Madeira Beach, Florida, who won both heats for the Class "BSH," thus goes down in APBA history as the initial winner of a Stock Hydroplane race staged under the jurisdiction of the APBA.

By now, dozens of racers had bought and registered their hydro equipment for competition. Officially, they were only participating in a "probationary" class, with a formal two-thirds majority vote by stock and alky membership needed the following year to make it permanent. Adoption arrived in a 1952 landslide. For a while, it seemed that hydros — a pre-World War II Hudson River crowd pleaser — would rush back into the spotlight of the famed Albany-to-New York Marathon. Event organizers stopped the APBA presses in time to get a front page flash on the Association's March 1951 newsletter, which had recently been renamed *Propeller*. The blurb heralded "a major change in policy regarding the running of the 1951 Marathon [in that] competition [was to] be limited to Racing [alky] "F" hydroplanes and to Stock Hydroplanes in Classes A, B, and D." Hydros had not been allowed in the event since the early 1940s. Runabout pilots responded quickly.

While most stock utility (by then simply referred to a "stock runabout") drivers had more than enough events to keep them busy elsewhere, being denied the opportunity to run in this "super bowl" of outboard contests made some pretty unhappy. To the diplomatic, it seemed only fair to let hydros have a shot at the Hudson. In April the proposed hydroplane lineup was expanded to include all popular alky classes. That made the runabout gossip louder, causing the Stock Outboard Racing Association of Long Island to seek an APBA sanction for its own runabout race — to be held on a day separate from the hydros — down the rough river. Everything appeared copacetic until the Long Islanders mentioned inviting mechanically oriented OMC "CU," "EU," and "FU" drivers who'd modified their mills outside of APBA guidelines. (The Association wouldn't sanction these modifications until 1952.) This sore spot, as well as fracases among the hydro group (on several arcane points) reached such a crescendo that, as reported in the June 1951 *Propeller*, the "Association decided, with great reluctance, to cancel the [Albany-to-New York] event."

Upheaval

Identifying 1951 as a "challenging year" for APBA leadership is an exercise in euphemistic understatement. Not long after that Albany race collapsed, the Association's capstone stock/alky outboard "Nationals" ended in a controversy (see Chapter Five). There were also frequent jabs from those pushing for departures from a hundred different APBA rules, like mandates requiring purely stock motors in "Stock Outboarding." Rumblings that all of this upheaval was on the horizon may have been the reason why APBA president Jack Horsley and Stock Utility vice president Doctor Harter embarked upon a fact finding trip during the spring of 1951. They started in Florida, headed to New York and through the Midwest to make sure the Association's real power base, stockers, were understood. Along the way, "several hundred" representatives of this legion chatted with the brass about hopes for the genre's future. Additionally, officials received input from the "major manufacturers of outboard engines" they visited. Charlie Strang's June 1951 *Motor Boating* column (*With the Outboarders*) reported that their on-the-road survey showed membership's overwhelming desire to have the APBA "maintain [stock] classes in an *unhopped-up* state despite the somewhat vague wording of the Stock Utility rules [of that period]."

A major flash-point issue among stock outboard rules revolved around the practice and definition of engine part polishing. Even staunch proponents of polishing admitted that it could be taken to an unreasonable extreme. But, with what boundaries might the general racing community be satisfied? Anyone even mildly mechanical understands that it's possible to polish something enough to have essentially changed it into something else. To fast-traveling gases, highly polished internal outboard parts, smoothed by racers for better fuel flow, provide much more efficient passageways than do the rougher inside surfaces normally associated with (and perfectly acceptable for) an assembly line motor. Such improvements offer the potential to yield the extra mile per hour needed to exert a distinct advantage over a driver not savvy in the workshop. Since many 1951-era stock outboarders were newcomers, it is logical that they did not favor much motor modification through polishing or other methods. A few weeks before joining Carl Kiekhaefer as a high-level engineer at Mercury, Charlie Strang wrote in the same June 1951 *Motor*

Boating piece that engine inspectors working APBA-sanctioned races would be looking for motors "polished [internally] into a state where it's no longer a stock engine . . . even if still within the limits on the spec sheet." The [clarified] definition went something like: "[Allowable] polishing, as applied to Stock Utility engines, shall be an operation which smoothes or improves the surface finish of a part or passage without altering appreciably the contours or dimensions of a part or passage. Where doubt exists the engine inspector should compare the part in question to a new or unpolished part of the same make and model." At the end of 1953, APBA's Stock Outboard Racing Commission (SORC) came to see that even judicious polishing and balancing of internal reciprocating parts gave those proficient with the practice a leg-up on literal stockers.

By Christmas of 1953, Mercury dealerships (often a haven for racers) provided a calm to this storm in that they heralded the state-of-the-art *Mark 20H* stock-racing outboard. Because these 1954-57 Class "B" Mercs were so well die-cast and balanced during production, SORC officials cited this model's excellence as a reason for nixing polishing and balancing of any stock engine made after January 1, 1954. With the average *20H* and Swift *Big-Bee* hydro, one could possess a rig that needed no improvement. For a while, the little green and gold Mercury returned the genre to an "off-the-rack" culture where driving skills, water conditions, and luck were paramount. Such a democracy, however, was not eagerly embraced by all throttle-squeezers.

While preparing this chapter, I felt mired in all the documented controversy about rule

Lots of families, beach umbrellas, blankets, picnic lunches, and racers turn out for a local Ardmore, Oklahoma, event in 1952. Attendance in the sport stayed remarkably strong until the late 1950s.

modifications, and wondered if early 1950s "stock" outboard racing was actually a myth. However, upon shifting focus to pint-sized regatta articles in hometown weeklies, I learned it was not. Truth is, typical stock enthusiasts involved, *for fun*, in their local racing scene simply paid no attention to most of the big-picture controversy. Reporters for a hundred hometown gazettes covered race days in their respective circulation area with nary a mention of the stock vs. non-stock issues, and so on, and so forth. Instead of digging into the macro organizational tangles, they enthusiastically wrote of the buzzing motors, fast boats, kids, families, mom & pop business sponsorship, winner's circle, donated prizes, and teamwork making most local races so enjoyable.

The Maine Outboard Racing Association was one of the many happy home-brew groups netting this contagious brand of press. Too busy on the water to agonize over nuance rule revisions, MORA just coalesced its ordinary service runabout membership into something called "family utility 'B' class." Anyone with a typical 12-foot boat that was at least 46 inches wide, and not fitted with a stabilizing fin, was part of the gang. The boats' standard transom length also kept garden-variety 20-cubic-inchers, like the Merc *Lightning KE-7*, or Chris-Craft *Commander*, competitive. (This came in response to for racing-only motors like Mercury's KG-7H, 20H, or Martin "60" Hi-Speed fitted with short tower housings and ultra-sleek gearcases.) Other "Down East" racing with unique categorization occurred on the Bagaduce River in Castine, Maine. The event was the province of a local Lions Club's 4th of July (1954) celebration, and had spots for competitors in Class "1," meaning any boat with a 10-horse motor; Class "2," for craft bearing 7-1/2- hp kickers; as well as Class "3," hulls powered by outboards from 16 to 25 horses. Some midshipmen and a teacher from the Maine Maritime Academy helped the civic organization run the well-received race. There were many such ad hoc stock outboard get togethers throughout the country well into the sixties.

Their class designations might not have translated into APBA vernacular, but according to resulting press, a good time was had by all anyway.

The advent of Kiekhaefer Corporation's "full-size" 7-1/2+ horse motor necessitated a change in the Class "AU" rules. Introduced in 1950, Mercury's *KG-4* (or *KG-4H* with the *Hydro-Short Quicksilver* lower unit) sported a piston displacement (14.89) nearly four cubic inches larger than its 11-cube *KE-4 Rocket Deluxe* 7-1/2-hp sister. The new *Rocket Hurricane KG-4* also bested the original Champion *Hot Rod's* 12.5 cubes, giving credence to the belief that it was created primarily to blow off any "AU" competition a plain Jane *KE-4* might not be able to handle. Whatever the reason for *KG-4*, the strong motor's displacement advantage caused the APBA to recognize that early Champion *Hot Rods*, Martin "60" CHS motors, and even the old *Rocket Deluxe KE-4* Mercury needed protection from KG-4. Officials granted the smaller "AU" engines an option to compete (without *KG-4* or *KG-4H*) in a subcategory dubbed Class "AU-1."

OMC's 1951 release of the Johnson *Sea Horse 25* and Evinrude *Big Twin* quickly poured tens of thousands of the popular motors into the stock runabout stable. When some of these new 35.7-cubic-inch mills showed up to race, however, the regulations dictated them being thrown into Class "DU," the province of far-faster (just under 40-cube) KG-9 Mercs. Understandably the imbalance only discouraged OMC *25* owners. Mercifully, APBA rules added "DU-1" (ranging from 30- to 36-cubes) to accommodate these stockers. Later, the OMC Big Twin types resulted in a class called "36." Additionally, a "CU-1" Class was offered. It reserved 20 to 25 cubic inches in order to allow motors like Sears and Roebuck's mail order *Elgin 16* to enjoy a little stock action. Even so, the "dash 1" classes were activated only as a courtesy to novice or casual competitors. No official Association records or *High Point* credits (typically accumulated throughout a season) could be assigned to their winners.

Here's what a full APBA-sanctioned stock runabout race card looked like around 1953:

Class	Over	Piston Cubic Inches (Up to and including)
JU	0	7.5

(JU originally called for a 10-cube limit, but the popularization of Merc's 7.2 cubic inch, *KF-5* twin prompted the APBA to make the tiny class more Mercury friendly by limiting it to 7.5 cubic inch displacement maximum. Under the original rules, stronger 9.6-cube Chris-Craft *Challenger* 5-1/2 mills possessed too much of an opportunity to rule the "JU" roost.)

Class	Over	Piston Cubic Inches
AU-1	7.5	12.5

(This was a *KE-4* friendly category.)

Class	Over	Piston Cubic Inches
AU-2	12.5	15

(Here, the new almost 15-cubic-inch, *KG-4* and *KG-4H* reigned. When no AU-1 entrants competed, "AU-2" was often just called "AU.")

Class	Over	Piston Cubic Inches
BU	15	20

(Some organizers divided BU into a service lower unit and Quicksilver lower unit classes, typically BU-1 and BU-2, respectively.)

Class	Over	Piston Cubic Inches
CU-1	20	25
CU-2	25	30
DU-1	30	36
DU-2	36	40

Most active among the special sections was "AU-1," 11-cube Mercs were plentiful and seldom the object of envy associated with the *KG-4 Rocket Hurricanes* and most larger Kiekhaefer mills. Consequently, few elevens were hacked up or cannibalized by parts-seeking racers. Dated trophies and oral histories suggest that long after *KG-4/KG-4H* had made obsolete the old 11-cubic-inch "AU" Mercs, these *KE-4* motors and even the newer Mercury *Mark 7* (1953-55) engines were pressed into "AU-1" service. Those ubiquitous fishing kickers saw much of their post-1950 racing action in rural pockets of the U.S. and Canada where the plebian spirit of the old stock utilities lived the longest.

Diversity

During the 1950s, America was very slowly becoming a land of opportunity for more than just young white folks. Mainstream pop music and major league baseball were but two avenues where people in racial minorities helped make American culture envied and emulated around the world. While there were still yacht clubs closed to non-caucasians, *Boat Sport* couldn't make any sense out of barring somebody entrance into stock out-boarding on the basis of skin color. With a generous use of photos, several paragraphs of narrative, but no by-line, the little publication covered fledgling outboard racing pusuits among African-Americans. It was a Missouri marine dealer named Bob Prater, who decided to organize a local racing club in 1938. By 1952, his St. Louis Outboard Drivers Association included "fifty active members" experienced in running everything from stocks in JU through DU, to alky A through F runabout and hydro. During that time, Leon Simmons, Gene Slaughter, Art Kennedy and his son got the outboard bug and applied for S.L.O.D.A. membership. These fellows happened to be most interested in stock utility work. They also happened to be black in a society grappling with a constitu-tional definition of equality. It appears that the St. Louis club was primarily concerned with one color, green. Simmons, Slaughter, and the Kennedys paid their membership dues, and then bought Mercs painted in that particular hue. Of course, motor color has little to do with the engine's real soul. So, after doing well in "AU/BU" action, the senior Kennedy switched to Class "F" with a blue/silver Evinrude. Next, some of the guys were seen campaigning a *KG-7Q* sporting a bare, polished aluminum fuel tank. A few observers might have been shocked that this was no longer a "Kiekhaefer of color," but the mill (which was apparently used "round-robin" by several of the club members) seemed to perform well anyway. Through it all, the unidentified *Boat Sport* reporter stood impressed by the number of white and black spectators that the new drivers' activities were attract-ing at local races and marathons. The 34-year-old Slaughter was identified as "one of the Missouri region's toughest competitors in AU and BU," generating his share of fans. And a prop-riding acceleration shot of Simmons' AU rig, got the famous magazine's nod as "the most exciting photo *Boat Sport* has ever published."

The Martin "*200*" and Mercury's Response

Publicity pictures of Martin's new Class "B" hopeful were bugging the staff at Mercury. Images of the Martin "*200*" had shown up in most boating periodicals by early 1953. Even the likes of the widely circulated *Popular Science* featured information on the black and silver hammer-tone 20-horse twin. Charlie Strang — the *Motor Boating* columnist, erst-while APBA racer, Association official, and by then a top-level Merc executive- read the literature and ordered a "*200*" so that his team could really see what the engine could do. Strang had been recruited to the company by Carl Kiekhaefer in June 1951. Then, his new boss began putting most of his energies into NASCAR pursuits.

Although Mr. Kiekhaefer actively served in stock outboarding's first couple of years, by the summer of 1951 he was not playing much of a role . . . if any in Mercury's stock racing ['Q,' and 'H' motors] program. As long as we kept *winning everything*," Strang recalled, "he kept a hands-off position." That's why the racing organization operating within the Kiekhaefer Corporation wanted to find ways to counter-act any advantages the new Martin might exhibit over a competing Mercury *KG-7H*. Several hundred of the "*200*" engines participated in the 1953 stock racing season (with plans for a shorter, racier Martin "*200*" exhaust snout in the works for 1954). Most of the big Martins got beat by Mercs, but Strang and his crew still kept working on ways to keep Carl from worrying about the competition. Meantime, the Martin factory hoped at least one "*200*" might be showcased in 1953's renowned Albany-to-New York Marathon. Alas, that great race was canceled for lack of a sponsor. (Oil companies usually footed most of the bill, but increasing insurance costs and other liability concerns stalled the cash flow.)

Carl Kiekhaefer's engineers developed a new motor designed to counter the Martin "*200.*" The old man was shown the powerhead, and then took a day off from his cars to do some schmoozing with a Milwaukee design artist named Dick Wiken, who did most of Mercury's styling. There was the matter of properly clothing the replacement for Merc's *KG-7H*. Kiekhaefer, Wiken, and Charlie Strang decided that the new engine should wear green and gold. (Other paint combo options were also planned, but soon rescinded.) Wiken whipped up some sketches showing this colorfully proposed Mercury *Mark 20H* with a short steering handle. He didn't know much about the stripped-down necessity of racing, but thought the truncated tiller protrusion made a nice visual statement. There was talk that it could be used as both spark control and for emergency steering. An advertising artist's rendition was as close as the imaginative steering arm ever got to the production line, but Class "B" buffs embraced the new engines — now with a side-mounted spark lever — as soon they shipped from the plant.

Alcohol-fuel Stockers and Rebirth of the NOA

Jack Leek's assembly area couldn't really be described as a factory. It was just a workbench and motor stand in his small Tacoma, Washington, outboard repair shop. But there, in 1954, the 30-year-old put together a rather amazing Merc, then proceeded to do something long-time alky drivers knew couldn't be done. Leek decided to challenge the old order by attempting to crack the mile-a-minute mark in a little Class "A" hydro. He gathered a bunch of "scrap" and aftermarket parts to fashion into a *KG-4H* that could run on alcohol-based fuel. In the process, exhaust and intake ports were squared, a pair of two-ring Wiseco pistons were installed, a *KG-7* carb was found for the project, and then drilled for alky use. The related carb opening and reed block also got the enlarging treatment. *Speed and Spray* (June 1955) asked alky engine builder Randolph Hubbell to cover the motor in an article titled *Old Iron vs. The New*. He reported that Leek's resulting creation

Why is Ivan Harris, the driver in the foreground smiling? Actually Jon Culver, the owner of boat 516-S should be grinning as he just won top "D" stock hydro honors at the 1953 Syracuse Nationals. Harris is probably still happy that he got to be the "DSH" champ in 1952. The motors are KG-9H Mercs.

yielded some 16.5-hp @ 6000 rpm.

Johnson's KR racing "A" powerhead had been introduced back in 1931, nearly 25 years before the Tacoma Merc was made up. It was over a cubic inch smaller, but could generate 18-hp @ 6500 rpm on alcohol. "A" expert Bill Tenney used one to zip his Fillinger hydro (*Hornet XIII*) to 53.746 mph at the start of 1954's competition season. Within a few months, however, Leek's Merc alky concoction upped the stakes, and completely shocked Tenney when it zipped the young Pacific Northwesterner's finless, high transom Swift (*Gotta Go VI*) through a carefully measured course at an average 61.069 miles per hour. For this achievement, Leek received the APBA One-Mile Championship of North America Trophy. As reported in the June 1955 *Speed and Spray* each year, the award went to "the driver who boosts an existing one-mile world record by the greatest margin." Some said the 12-perecent speed increase and associated prize could be linked to the sleeker — than *KR*'s — *Quicksilver* lower unit. It got several old-timers thinking about mounting their *KR* powerheads on

The NOA was first nationwide organization to sanction those who liked modifying their stock racing outboards — often converting them to alcohol. One of the most overt signs of such tinkering is an open exhaust, something pure stockers feel to be anathema. In fact, there are probably several 21st Century vintage outboard devotees who'd like to clobber these three guys for wrecking a perfectly good Mark 20H and Quincy exhaust stack!

Quickies. Mostly, though, it just got alky outboarders thinking and wondering whether their OMC engines' competitive days were now numbered.

Sometime back in early 1936, the original National Outboard Association's secretary received a letter from several Pacific Northwest outboarders concerned about motors that were revamped in some small way for racing or overtly modified to run on alcohol. According to the *NOA ARK*, that correspondence urged the passage of rules promoting a class of engines that could be raced on runabouts and allowing "absolutely *no* mechanical changes of any type on [these] service motors." Contrary to most mid-1930s outboard speed events, this brand of stock competition seemed to be taking hold in the Puget Sound region, so the Seattle-area racers suggested it might fly on a nationwide basis. During a subsequent (original) NOA executive meeting, "there was considerable discussion as to the advisability" of effecting such statutes, but the proposal got shelved because "it was felt that it would be hardly possible to administer it if it were adopted." Those old-time NOA execs were skeptical of being able to legislate away racers' nearly universal desire to tinker. Perhaps citing the group's biblical *Noah's Ark* logo, some NOA brass might have argued that the Ten Commandments hadn't been very well obeyed before or after the Flood, and that neither Moses nor Noah had to contend with alky racers who owned a drill press, could work a lathe, and had a penchant for doing their own thing. In that spirit, the new NOA was founded by erstwhile APBA official Claude Fox and friends during the fall of 1951.

To be sure, the reborn organization had rules, but they were designed for those not able to resist the temptation to experiment. Fox's long list of alky driver compatriots fit snugly into this psychographic. He envisioned a responsive organization geared toward outboarders with high-speed Evinrude and Johnson gear orphaned by OMC's post–World War II abandonment of racing. There was also the matter of the rival APBA riding high on (and catering to) the early through mid-1950s stock outboarding craze. It was heady, unifying stuff for racers to see the painted image of what looked to be a "BU" runabout (representing outboarding itself) depicted on the cover of *Motor Boating*'s 1954 boat show issue. As noted, though, even the seemingly homogenized stock milieu had its liberals and conservatives.

During the Eisenhower administration, the powerboat racing community entered a period of intense conflict. The APBA wanted its breakaway alky members back, while the NOA touted its independence. Hank Bowman's son, Craig, grew up hearing both sides of the issue. At the family's home office, his father wrote about all outboard racing endeavors for *Boat Sport*, thus the inside scoop from both camps flowed freely. "The APBA spent most of the fifties," he recalled, "battling Claude Fox and NOA. Their policy ranged from extending an olive branch to *Let's get rid of that renegade outfit!*" It wasn't unusual to find some retaliatory barbed salvos in the NOA's *Rooster Tail* publication. The October 1955 edition is a case in point. "True enough," the smaller outfit's newsletter admitted, "NOA

Had organized stock outboard racing cultivated its stars, the sport may well have been able to continue attracting the vital fan base that seemed to plateau around 1957. Certainly, personalities like young Dean Chenoweth (seen here in a Mercury catalog testimonial – though Merc misspelled his name) were capable of rivaling NASCAR notables who propelled auto racing to spectacular family entertainment heights. But, after Mercury drifted from the genre around 1960, good publicity became harder to tap. And, when outboard racing found itself to be a relatively dwindling community, further withdrawal from staging races to please the public had a negative effect. In fact, during the early 1960s, one boat racing magazine editor lamented that many races and participants weren't particularly friendly nor looked very presentable — an exact opposite of the NASCAR success formula.

does have competition in the administration of this nation's outboard racing, but we always shudder at the thoughts of the sport being mishandled even by <u>them</u>. We wish that even our [APBA] competition would have rules that would govern their races in a manner so as not to reflect unfavorably on our sport."

At issue was a newspaper article reporting that one of APBA's regional championship event victors got his crown in a coin toss. According to the story, two drivers earned equal points and elapsed time in their endeavors, sending a "puzzled referee to the [APBA] rule book." The matter was then given over to the chance of a coin toss during which "a driver called 'heads,' and 'heads' it was . . . and he [became] the Regional Champion." *Rooster Tail's* writer promised he meant no ill will against the "fine drivers or officials involved in this incident," but did "not hesitate to take a punch at the [APBA] persons responsible in being so careless all these years in the rules revisions of that sanctioning organization." Shame on that Eastern establishment organization, the NOA correspondent (probably Fox) concluded. "To those of us who are fighting so hard to get more publicity for our sport," he scolded, "we regret very much that such [APBA] incidents happen which makes it much more difficult to get our newspaper reporters to take an interest in our sport."

A master at publicity, Fox well understood that flipping a quarter to determine a racing winner was likely the very angle that drew the journalist to prominently chronicle that outboard event. But, in that case, the Yankee-headquartered association had handed his Tennessee-based group ammunition for a skirmish, and so a volley the bigger organization did receive. A variation on this "us vs. them" theme was an NOA favorite, The North-

South Race. Initially staged in 1951 and 1952 at Lake Cumberland in Somerset, Kentucky, this entertaining event featured drivers, pit crew, and fans in civil war garb (typically an inexpensive Gettysburg souvenir hat) divided into tongue-in-cheek fighting factions according to their north or south hometown locales. Fox went all out with the motif, provided appropriate flags and even placed some tangled barbed wire between rival pit areas. This seemingly goofy style of "team" racing, with a General Grant and General Lee leadership, provided an added dimension to organized competition. At stake was a huge "Captain Waide Hughes" trophy going to the high point winner and his soldiers. To be sure, participants took their roles seriously. In the middle of 1952's North-South shindig, "B" Hydro notable Bill Tenney had to be taken to the hospital after his efforts as that year's Grant ended in an aggressive flip at the starting gun, and a "badly cut leg." *Boat Sport* featured a stunt photo of him "wounded and defeated with torn [Union Army] uniform and [truly] bandaged leg" as he relinquished the trophy to a "Southern" alky outboard conqueror.

NOA Classes

The NOA boasted four categories by 1955. At the top of the list was the *professional Division I*. Here, the most latitude for motor concocting reigned supreme. Fox wanted honest play among the engine-wizard class, so his rules mandated that even though "replacement parts for Division I mills could come from any individual or company in good NOA membership standing." According to the group's *Official Rulebook*, these aftermarket gizmos "must be available to everyone at a fair price." No record of "gouging" is evident, so the term "fair," must have been intrinsically under-

The hot Mercury KG-4H that Jack Leek built from parts looked a lot like this Rocket Hurricane. His had a bigger fuel line and carburetor throat, however, as it was converted to run on alcohol-based fuel. Boat Sport contributor and master boat builder Hal Kelly took this shot to illustrate the (improved) deeper reach of Merc transom clamp brackets that allowed Kelly to shim the motor 1 3/8" above the transom and still have a good grip on the boat. Sometimes just jacking up an outboard the width of a broken piece of yardstick would raise the lower unit enough to dramatically improve propeller performance.

stood. Most any other improvement was OK in Division I, with the exception of a tractor lower unit.

Division II or *Utility Class* (later referred to as *Pleasure Craft Class*) called for the use of outboards "run strictly as manufactured." The only leeway came in spark plug, prop, steering bar, automatic shutoff hand throttles and related slow-speed carb needle options. This category was an early attempt at Outboard Pleasure Craft or "OPC" racing.

Division III was the *Stock* zone. Semantics were at play in this one, as, unlike APBA Stock, these rules allowed for things such as open exhaust.

Modified Stock was the descriptive name of Division IV. Racers with a sense of Division I mechanical adventure, but a desire to run postwar motors, became most comfortable competing here. They were supposed to use "manufacturers' original or manufacturers' replacement parts," except for pistons, rings, wrist pins, carbs, sparkplugs, props, motor bracket, fuel tank, gaskets, intake valves, and various adapters. Mixing and matching different makers components was acceptable. Machining and adding metal also passed muster with inspectors assigned to Division IV.

Interestingly, the smaller NOA classes' piston displacements (listed below) were different in Division I from the other divisions. That's because the Evinrude *Midget*, alky favorite in "M," came in just under 7 1/2-cubic inches. It was not raced on gas/oil, and so never went stock. In Divisions II through IV, the diminutive motors utilized were Martin's *"60" Hi-Speed*, KE-4 Merc, and early Champion *Hot Rod*. The latter mill just kissed 12.5 cubes, and so became a motor of choice. None of this trio, however, could legally compete in APBA "JU," though, because its ceiling was 7.5 cubic inches [although it spent a couple years at 10] to make Kiekhaefer's 7.2 cube KF-5 feel right at home. The little Merc never had much connection to NOA.

The accompanying graphic from a 1955 National Outboard Association *Official Rule Book* shows the categorical roster.

Roster Categories (1955)

Division I		Divisions II through IV	
Class	*Cu. In. Disp.*	*Class*	*Cu. In. Disp.*
M	less than 7.5	J	through 12.5
A	7.5 to 15	A	12.5 to 15
B	15 to 20	B	15 to 20
C	20 to 30	D-1	30 to 37
(There were no D or E alky motors)		D-2	37 to 40
F	50 to 60	F*	50 to 60
X	Unlimited		

(*Div. IV only. Utility designated by "U" as in "JU," etc.)

One obvious hole in Divisions II through IV centers upon a Class "C/CU" absence. In the case of our mid-1950s sampling, "C/CU," the "great compromise class" was missing because its related 30-cubic-inch Mercury *Mark 30H* hadn't yet been formally introduced and approved. Getting a sanctioning body's blessing on a particular model's use was key to being able to sell the motor as an accepted stock racing engine. Claude Fox smiles when recounting a National Outboard Association rule barring newly debuted motors from gaining approval in the middle of a racing year, and especially not at the *National Championships*. That way, members' existing gear stayed competitive at least through the end of any given racing season. For example, Merc would release something new in early summer but the NOA wouldn't allow it until the next spring. Drivers could more easily handle the financial burden of having to buy the latest mill if they had several months breathing room.

Hollywood Meets Outboard Racing

There were Monday phone calls to a number in Wisconsin from a star in California that sure did something positive for the Kiekhaefer Corporation's switchboard girls. They got to the point where they'd almost know his ring, then bubble, "Good afternoon, Roy."

"Well purty Miss, dontcha mean 'good morning'?" the caller might twinkle. "Remember, it's a few hours earlier out here in Hollywood." Movie and TV western good guy Roy Rogers was dialing the factory for some advice. He'd gotten especially interested in Mercury motors right after the company introduced its four-cylinder engines in 1949. The "King of the Cowboys" even visited Kiekhaefer's test facilities to get an inside look at one. Of course, Carl Kiekhaefer wanted to meet him and offered Rogers a chance to try a *KG-9* quad on a fast utility hull. Talk about a great photo opportunity! With the star's wholesome weekly television show spreading through America's airwaves, Roy Rogers represented the ultimate stamp of consumer approval. Plus, here was a man who practiced what he preached. Kiekhaefer understood Rogers' genuine even-keeled likability generated the kind of publicity made in heaven. "Evinrude should be so lucky," some Merc dealers beamed.

By the mid-1950s, a brand of offshore outboard racing was becoming especially popular on the coast, and Roy Rogers was one of its prime movers. Salty stints from the Los Angeles area out to Catalina Island typically comprised the course. In 1954, the western hero drove a garden-variety 16-foot open sport runabout the 23 miles and back in record time, 110 minutes and 28 seconds. It had been a "predicted log" race, timed by the US Coast Guard, with Rogers promising them that he, his two passengers (just along for the ride), and sleek new, four-cylinder Mercury *Mark 50* could make the trek in about 110. Not only did his prescient estimate make the grade, but he beat 121 other boats to the finish line, too.

The next year, Rogers bought a Glasspar family runabout hefty enough to hold a pair

of just-released Mercury *Mark 55E* powerplants. His phone calls to Kiekhaefer got direct-
ed to the small group of Merc men assigned to stock racing. Mercury's Messenger reported that they made some suggestions about performance boosters for the 40-horse motors
that helped Rogers establish a "new [1955] record of 39 minutes and 10 seconds for the
22-plus mile open sea route." He had a chance to win the whole enchilada, but true to his
western hero TV persona, stopped on the return leg to help a fellow racer who was in
trouble. Mercury distributor Elgin Gates (of Seaboard Equipment) often accompanied
Rogers in competition. Gates remembered the musical cowboy "singing all the way
across" the vast racecourse. He continued crooning the praises of outboarding — and racing off-the-rack, family-style motors/hulls — by buying stock in the Yellow Jacket boat
company and running Mercs on them in pleasure craft events whenever breaks in his TV
show filming schedule would allow.

Etched into the ground not far from the movie studios was a little body of water
sometimes dubbed "the puddle." With a bit of Hollywood transformation and euphe-
mism, it became the Venice (California) Marine Stadium, and served as home to many
outboard-oriented events. For a little while, this tiny lake also doubled as a studio for a

*Los Angeles' KTLA(TV) did a live broadcast weekly of the Speedboat Rodeo show. Had the station's crew been
able to use today's digital recording/editing, and/or satellite syndication distribution, the program might have
survived and even gone national.*

weekly television broadcast devoted to stock boat racing. Video cameras in TV's golden age were heavy, cable-laden monsters demanding a relatively stationary vantage point. In 1955, scouts from Newman-Priest Productions recognized that small boats traveling in a well-defined route could work within the restrictions of fledgling telecasting technology. Thus, the show business people began brainstorming with members of the local *Valley Speedboat Association* on a plan. Sanctions for TV/spectator races were secured by the club, a nice 5/8th mile course was buoyed, and a major L.A. station — KTLA(TV) Channel 5 — came in on the deal.

During the resulting program's late 1955-early 1956 run, two or three [depending on time] stock classes made it to the airwaves. The two-hour *Speedboat Rodeo* also featured trick water-skiing as well as interviews with drivers and boat-related celebrities like Roy Rogers. The ratings especially shocked the TV station, which was notified that *Speedboat Rodeo* amassed over half-a-million viewers, making it the most watched Sunday afternoon program in the Southern California media marketplace. Merc distributor Seaboard Equipment Company and Sta-Lube Oil sponsors were certainly happy. And, N-P Productions was planning to take the broadcast national. They even solicited offers from other clubs wanting to institute similar weekly television shows. Those are some of the reasons viewers were so surprised that the show was cancelled after fewer than six months on the air. The live television format required more than 190 people to produce and promote *Speedboat Rodeo*, a number that, according to one of N-P's principals interviewed in the March 1956 *Speed and Spray*, "caused problems . . . that ha[d] been, at times, almost insurmountable."

Unfortunately, good ratings weren't enough. *Boat Sport* (September/October 1956) lamented that personnel issues and "reported financial difficulties encountered by the TV producers" prevented this black & white "shot in the arm" for stock racing from surviving. Broadcast historians would point out that *Speedboat Rodeo* came and went just a few months before to the introduction of video tape. Had this cost-effective technology been there for N-P Productions, their show might have been able to thrive. And, one can only speculate how the mid-1950s stock outboard racing heyday would have mushroomed had *Speedboat Rodeo* been syndicated from coast to coast. After all, it was a time when it seemed the whole country was going bonkers for boats.

Bonkers for Boats

People going bonkers for boats is what exasperated the owner/operator of Doc's Airpark. After years of success catering to airplane buffs, his establishment was suddenly drained of clientele. "We have battled to keep the airport open," he told the July 1956 *Boat Sport*, "but it has been a losing game. There is little interest in civil aviation in this section [of the country anymore]. Those who formerly flew for recreation have turned their attention to boating." Some of the boaters inadvertently responsible for the summer 1955 closure of that Quincy, Illinois, flight service and airfield probably knew O. F. Christner. Not too far from the defunct landing strip, he ran a busy shop where racers could get Mercury outboards modified to run on alcohol fuel. Many of his Quincy Welding Works' conversions made the scene wherever "stock mod" rules permitted. While interest in this genre was growing, the era's biggest chunk of racing still focused on ready-to-race engines pretty much right out of the box.

Everyday-use outboards — never designed for racing — helped ordinary folks star in a Lake Winnebago marathon designed just for them and ten thousand onlookers. A 45-mile course — beginning at Mercury's hometown, Fond du Lac, Wisconsin — was planned for *strictly-stock* motors without racing lower units. Standard service or non-racing boats were also mandated for use by entrants of this Fisherman's Outboard Marathon. During the running, and just a year before that airfield folded, the field of 44 included outboard cruisers, family runabouts, and even an Aluma-Craft rowboat with two guys and a *Mark 20* Merc. The "dead start"-style watery adventure was slathered all over the local press as "*just a bunch of amateurs having fun racing their fishing boats.*" Technically true, but the event managed to be won, overall, by a Mercury dealership mechanic helming a nicely tuned *Mark 40.* It nevertheless made for some excitement and old fashioned schlock, as spectators crowded to see winners being presented their trophies by Lake Winnebago's *Sturgeon Spearing Queen.* She appeared in all her midwestern innocence, brightly smiling and decked with an Uncle Sam top hat. The whole shebang really fit the bill, because in those pre-video game, DVD, or Internet days, people were always looking for something "outdoorsy" and wholesome like that to do.

Perhaps that's a major reason why (through the mid-1950s) stock outboard events kept springing up almost everywhere possessing even the most modest pond. An obscure upstate New York magazine can be used to illustrate this point. The tiny Eisenhower-era *North Country Life* appeared only four times a year, was kind of a self-published affair, albeit neat and professional, and primarily concentrated on topics of Adirondack nature, history and folklore. Next to its article about Fort Ticonderoga, several bucolic book reviews, as well and an interview with a local collector of antiquities rests a listing of the summer of 1955's outboard races. They were showcased in the booklet's calendar as if most readers expected such information to be there, alongside some poem about fresh mountain air. Also telling, are several of the stock outboard racing venues that year. Even a longtime Adirondack "summer native" like me had to consult the Rand McNally to pinpoint a few of them. More than one of those beautiful, but rather remote race locales had fewer than 500 inhabitants. An interstate highway system we now take for granted was then largely the province of project engineers and lines on their planning maps. So, the most direct routes typically slowly funneled motorists through villages, towns, and cities. Travel was not the 65-mph cruise control and relatively carefree process we enjoy today. Nor were cars and trailers, with old-style ignition and tube tires, completely dependable or protected by extended warranties.

Imagine dragging a double boat trailer/motor box (filled with a couple of *KG-7H* Mercs, tools, props, parts, miscellaneous gear and gas) behind some 1952 Chevy bumping over half a day's worth of back roads. Such transport challenges generated enthusiasm for lots of local races. During the early years of stock utility competition, some of the less formal hometown contests were swelled by vacationers able to enter the likes of their 12-foot fishing boat and 1951 Goodyear *Sea Bee* 12-horse twin. It might be said that crummy roads, accepted isolation, "run-what-ya-brung" rules, and $40 worth of trophies provided stock racing with the most variety and greatest number of folks trying their throttle hand at the sport. Like a proverbial community talent show, the easier it is to qualify, the more people there'll be on the stage and in the audience.

People from all over Central New York packed the State Armory in Utica on May 6, 1956, to wander through their area's *All Racing Speedboat Show*. APBA- sanctioned clubs in the region got together to stage the shindig to raise public interest in boating competition. Costs helped raise some dough for the purchase of their upcoming season's awards. Outboard drivers — and even a few inboarders — trailered their rigs to the huge building so as to assemble what the May 1956 *Speed and Spray* labeled "the largest indoor pit area in the history of racing in the East." A hot meal was offered to racers who volunteered to help with the setup. Everyone in attendance got treated to a Referee and Inspector Clinic, plus boat and motor displays featuring showroom quality products from makers like Sid-Craft, Speed-Liner, Swift, Mercury, and Champion. On display were Champ's new model 6N-HR Class "B" *Hot Rod*, or Merc's just debuted *Mark 55H* "D" motor, and Class "C" *Mark 30H*. The 30-cubic-inch mill was especially perused since it might prompt long-anticipated "CU" runabout and "C" stock hydro activity. Several hundred *30H* motors were sold nationwide right off the bat. That represented a sizable sale in racing terms, so Kiekhaefer minted more. There was another sales surge, but by 1958 and the slowing of the stock outboard racing bubble, racks of them went gathering dust in the warehouse, eventually to be turned into standard service outboards. Curiously, though, sudden orders for these 30-cubic-inch racers — and for Merc's other four-cylinder competition motor — popped up at the close of the decade. As a result, a few white, square-top versions of *Mark 30H* and *Mark 55H* dribbled from the factory between 1959-61.

After World War II, neither Evinrude nor Johnson ever expected to spend time issuing stock racing engines from their already overbooked plants. In May 1959, *Time* reported that the Outboard Marine Corporation had — during the previous boating season — cranked out $131 million worth of what were intended to be strictly "family service" motors. Even without the factory's blessings, though, some of these OMC pleasure outboards were drafted into formal competition by a waterspout of owner support. "Quite a few of the members of the outboard boat clubs in our area," a Sacramento, California, man told the editor of *Speed and Spray*, "have Johnson 25s and good fast runabouts." He

The alky-burning "C-Service" Class had a respectable following during the 1950s. Aficionados usually possessed sufficient machine shop skills to make their mills out of Evinrude Speeditwin, Elto Super C parts, and other sundry components. Battery ignition, a solid-steel flywheel, a drip oilier, hogged-out Vacturi carburetion, and fuel tank clamp straps were often mainstays in the mix.

indicated in his spring 1955 letter that many of them have gotten together with their big "Johnnys" for some informal racing, and found that the 25-horse machines and related utility craft were "well matched." The correspondence came with the hope that someone might put the large, dependable, and increasingly ubiquitous twins to work on a nationally sanctioned racecourse. There had been some competitive usage of the Evinrude *Big Twin* and Johnson *Sea Horse 25* clamp-ons (in 1951), as soon as a respectable number of them hit showrooms, in an ad hoc sub-D or "D-1" Class. And, from 1951 through 1954, some races were well represented with these mills. More than a few stock purists considered the OMC 25 as a real way to revisit the dream of racing with such an "everyman's" motor. For 1955, grass roots support and lobbying caused the APBA to put its new "36" (because of the engines' 35.7 cubic-inch displacement) Class into probationary effect. Proponents beamed that the average family's OMC 25 water ski outboard could be made race-ready with a $16 speed prop (Oakland-Johnson had a suitable one, and Michigan Wheel's bronze AJC-461 worked well), some steel for a steering bar, and a safety throttle attachment retailing for about five bucks.

Original rules pretty much barred any tampering with the powerhead, except some timing change and .020" oversized cylinders in 1951-53 motors. Furthermore, the 25's bulbous shift-type gear foot couldn't be touched. Cowling could be left intact, but along with the recoil starter, typically got removed. Much to the chagrin of the aforementioned purists, little of the official racing in "36" Class occurred with a family-style boat. Instead, most every "DU" stock utility runabout of the day became a popular partner for the drafted OMC "racing" mills. Riggs Smith, who set one of the last "36" Class's speed records (before it was phased out in the 1970s) helmed a Chrysler-powered Sid-Craft, but others drove everything from Van Pelts and Speedliners to Switzers and home-brew hulls from *Science & Mechanix* magazine plans. The "36"ers usually built up their boats transom to about 17 3/8-inches in order to get the "fishing" lower unit near the water's surface (thus eliminating drag). With such a big gearfoot, however, the changed elevation could cause porpoising and twisting, making "36" drivers very aware of the value of a nice soft set of knee pads.

The OMC's reliability made for a good marathon motor, as long as models with the old two-hose pressurized fuel tank system were well maintained and didn't get persnickety because of a punctured line, leaky gasket, dirty valving, or wimpy spring. Evinrude and Johnson viewed the number of their 35.7-cubic-inch motors solely purchased by racing buffs as a drop in the bucket and so didn't worry about planned changes for 1956, the year when the "36" Class was officially adopted by the APBA. First, the parent corporation came out with a 35.7 cube Buccaneer brand 25-horse motor, and then bumped up its big Johnson and Evinrude models to 30 hp. Actually, they'd increased the lower unit's exterior dimension for extra strength in 1955. Admittedly, the enlargement was slight, but *Boat Sport* admitted this represented potentially greater underwater drag. Plus the magazine noted, the '56s wore differently domed pistons among other power head nuances. "Registered [APBA] members of the class were polled [on one of the issues] and wisely voted that the [microscopically more slender] 1951-54 lower unit should not be allowed in combination with a 1955-and later powerhead." OMC's engines were prominent in the "36" Class into the 1960s when West Bend (later Chrysler) motors began beating the Johnsons and Evinrudes. Even with a more gentle evolution than other stock classes, though, "36" was never the kind of "fish with it on Saturday/race on Sunday," one-design class that the early *Big Twin* and *Sea Horse 25* sport racers envisioned.

Flyin' Flivvers

Stock purists tried again in 1957. They watched Sailfish sailboat racing catch on, and figured a similarly affordable hull and outboard would draw lots of new blood into the sport. Labeled "FF-class," this one-design boat/motor combo offered an equilibrium that truly left victory up to chance. The "FF" stood for Flyin' Flivver, brand name of an eight foot, unsinkable fiberglass hull that looked a bit like a big old-fashioned bathtub wilted from too much direct sunlight. Fitted with a 1957 Mercury (approximately 6-hp) *Mark 6*, "Flivvers" could scoot right along "demonstrating," as a *Boat Sport* editor witnessed, "the most praiseworthy reluctance to capsize under the most extraordinary handling imaginable." The Kiekhaefer Corporation purchased a bunch of the boats for an outdoor writer's convention it staged at Cypress Gardens, Florida. By the 1957 model year, sales of stock-racing engines had begun to slow. The decade's entire run of Quicksilver-style racers, however, looked paltry compared to the numbers of ordinary little kickers — like *Mark 6*- Merc — was selling. And, figured Fond du Lac, if the writers successfully planted seeds for an "anybody can race one" craze, this "FF-class" sure could generate some remarkable *Mark 6* sales volume. Pictures of the funny little boats (often Mercury-powered) appeared in dozens of late 1950s magazines, and, in fact, a few informal "FF-class" events sprung up among owners. Then, just as suddenly, the movement lost steam. Perhaps its premise had simply been too simple? Alas, an unalterably standardized boat, and a common motor didn't leave any leeway for tinkering.

Choice Parts and Propellers

"Fatootzaling." That's what I overheard one outboard racer say he was doing in the pits. "Let's see if some fatootzaling with the carb will give us an extra RPM," the guy thought out loud while searching for a small wrench. When I commented about the dime soldered to a slot in the stem of his high-speed needle valve, he noted that it had replaced a "much slower" washer that the *KG-4H's* previous owner had "stupidly thought would work." Another stocker whose theories made lots more sense prepared for competition using the "Hundred Percent by Quarters Rule." That is to say, victory comes in four parts: boat 25 percent, motor 25 percent, propeller 25 percent, and driver 25 percent. Equal attention to these elements adds up to a 100% chance of winning.

Because original stock rules forbade the addition or removal of metal from stock motor parts, serious racers would buy every piston and connecting rod they could amass for their particular engine until coming up with a balanced set of the lightest components. Those would go into *the* motor, and it'd go a tenth of a mile-per-hour faster. Soon thereafter, the "heavier" parts would be sold to the competition. Over-the-counter pieces were never completely identical, so obtaining a "magic" stock part was a possibility for those who knew how to look. Outboard expert Lou Eppel knew this to be true of both motors and boats. For January 1953 *Yachting*, he stated: "It is no secret that there are variations in every motor coming off the production line. Usually one motor will measure up a little better than others, and it is the little differences which can mean better speeds. Yet these motors are strictly stock and out of the box. The same holds true in getting the right hull. Any boat builder will admit that within reason all hulls of a given model are identical but that occasionally one will, because of slight differences in materials, temperatures while building, and many other factors, come out with a bottom that is a little straighter or somewhat better than the regular run."

Aside from expertly concocting a "legal" motor from rare "lucky" parts, or finding some serendipitous hydro, stock outboarding's major variables included driving skills and the *right* propeller. Just the right "wheel" often made the difference between winning and losing. A Connecticut stock racer once told me his tale of placing almost last in every "ASH" heat. After observing this consistently disappointing status, a more experienced competitor approached him with a question. "Ya wanna go racin'?" the guy taunted, "I mean really racin'?" The novice's nod prompted the old sharpie to hand over something wrapped in a shop rag. "Here," he cautiously announced after looking both ways, "Gimme seventy-five bucks quick and try this." In the very next event, the newcomer placed second. Nothing had changed but his prop. And to the average observer both looked identical.

Quincy's O. F. Christner often compared changing a propeller on an outboard to the quick-change rear-end gearing on old race cars. The correct wheel best handles the motor's revving capabilities, the weight of the driver, boat, boat type, water conditions, and particular race course. Its related outboard's transom height and motor angle proves critical, too. Novices were taught to buy at least two props. One was for a reference, while incremental pitch changes were made to the other. Some drivers were reported to have repitched their blades on any available trailer hitch ball, but a leather mallet often served as the pros' choice. In-water testing came next, with upwards of 50 trial and error runs commonplace before gaining that elusive extra 1/2 mile an hour. The Michigan Wheel Company gets credit for making some of the postwar stock era's first high-speed propellers. Engineers there had been surprised to see Carl Kiekhaefer equip his 1947 *Lightning KE7* 10-hp with a slow three-blade item when an aggressively pitched two-blade would better help the new motor blaze a faster reputation. Michigan then embarked upon its *Aqua-Jet* project in which racing-style props were developed for the Mercs, as well as a host of other circa 1950 motors with potential for stock or cottage competition. Mercury noticed Michigan's success and soon countered with a line of KAMINC (<u>K</u>iekhaefer <u>A</u>ero <u>M</u>arine, <u>Inc</u>orporated) propellers. They figured it was only right that Mercury customers should buy Merc wheels. Craig DeWald, experienced with both brands, and subsequently a leading maker of racing propellers, felt "Kaminc props were good early on, but that Michigan caught up and surpassed them. Eventually, Merc propellers — under the *Quicksilver* banner — became popular again with the advent of the 'cleaver' prop in the 1970s."

At the 1957 APBA Stock Outboard Nationals, *Boat Sport* said that DeWald was one of the first to try Michigan's newly perfected "cupped" high tensile-bronze speed wheels. He and a few other notable competitors were given the props and established seven new world's records there. DeWald upped existing "AU" and "ASH" by three miles per hour. Even the manufacturer was surprised. Michigan quickly issued a press release identifying the two-blade wonders as "standard factory models used exactly as furnished - a departure from the previous practice of altering or reworking."

Racer Les Stevenson noted that inventor and professional alky driver Bill Tenney was surprised, too, and rather annoyed. It was Tenney who actually discovered the prop-cupping process and had been fitting one of his new "cupped" propeller prototypes to an alky outboard's prop shaft when a "factory man from Michigan Wheel" [happened to be] in the pits. Minutes later, Tenney's hydro just ripped past the competition. The Michigan guy figured the startling speed augmentation must have come from the unusual propeller, which he copied and had "quickly patented."

Oscar Johnson contributed greatly to outboard racing through his line of Super O-J (stock classes) and standard O-J wheels [C-Service and alky]. He began practicing the propeller trade during the mid-1920s, when inboarders were the only one's with engines fast enough to require his talents. At 76, Johnson was still active during the 1955 racing season. From his small Oakland, California, cinder block headquarters, he spent days shaping and polishing props and testing props in an effort to, according to *Boat Sport*, "develop faster and more efficient propellers." Johnson Propeller Company literature indicated each prop was "custom-built," cast in the firm's own foundry of special bronze from patterns exact in every detail, that is, blade area, contour, pitch and spacing, as well as boring for perfect alignment of bore with the blades. Racers often recall Oscar Johnson as being well liked for helping outboarders select the best wheel for their motor and boat combo. This service took place free of charge, even if it meant recommending somebody else's prop. Whenever stock outboard racing was at its best, the field of competing motors ran on a theoretical even match. Props represented a stocker's biggest edge, given equal horsepower. (Humid, hot weather with low barometric pressure decreased the engine power of every motor on a given course. According to *Speed and Spray*, that's why manufacturers standardized hp ratings based upon a dry, 60-degree day with a 29.92 barometer reading.)

The Racing Culture Spreads

Stereotypically, visions of a "regular" stock race might center on a US lake surrounded by folks with "American accents." During the 1950s, however, the sport spread well beyond state borders. American servicemen were instrumental in this promotion, as dozens of racers in uniform around the globe staged competitions in their free time. During the immediate post-World War II period, their "iron" consisted of surplus OMC outboards originally built for fighting the enemy. *Boat Sport* got a letter from a reader in Sweden noting, "here we have a lot of ex-U.S. War Department 50 hp *Stormboat Motors* obtainable quite inexpensively. I would like concrete advice on how to get one to go as fast as possible." Johnson *POs* and Evinrude *Speeditwins* also passed from military to recreational hands for fledgling races in far-off places. Nor was it uncommon for the Kiekhaefer Corporation to ship motors to Americans who were even casually interested in promoting some stock racing while living abroad. Army guys helping to rebuild Japan, for example, were cut some pricing slack on a KE-7 Lightning if several were ordered and sportily paraded around Nipponese waters. By 1952, outboard racing began mushrooming as a spectator sport in the Land of the Rising Sun. Around 1953, Japan boasted 1,040 registered stock outboarders (including 30 women) who raced in nine cities, and drew four million paid attendance. To ensure predictable water, 10 Japanese outboard racing "stadium" courses were built in 1953. While Mercs were used early on, the island nation's domestic manufacturers (like Fuji and Yamato) eventually took over. Originally, copycat motors (the Yamato 60 was sort of a combined *Mark 20H/6N-HR Champion Hot Rod* knock-off), the Japanese competition outboards eventually established their own designs that led some to prominence in contemporary stock action.

Mercury products imported for some local boating enthusiasts in Singapore scored

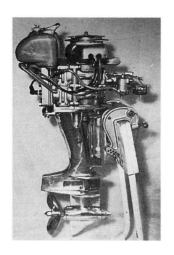

Before the 1980s when Yamato became one of the major players in American and Canadian stock outboard racing, the Japanese firm amalgamated ideas from US makers like Champion and Mercury, as evidenced in this 1960 Yamato "60" Class "B" machine.

big in that Far Eastern island republic's first stock outboard regatta. Kiekhaefer Corporation's September 1953 *Mercury Messenger* boasted photos of smiling Singaporeans with their Merc-won trophies. Some of the long, thin, high-sided native craft used in the fishing boat class looked interestingly anachronistic with a *KG-7 Hurricane* rigged to the stern. The sight was probably nothing compared to the expression exhibited by a Merc sales official who tore open a letter with an unusual return address. The aforementioned factory publication included a copy of that envelope's contents. Kiekhaefer publicity people thought their US-Canadian dealer network might get a kick out of seeing a brief typewritten note requesting the shipment of: "1 fast racing boat, 2 square propellers, 2 remote control equipment, and 2 motors called *KG-9H*." They were to be delivered to His Majesty Boa-Dai, Emperor of Vietnam.

Mexico actively participated in out-of-the-box outboarding during the 1950s. Its Federation de Mexicana de Lanchas y Motores (Federation of Mexican Racing Boats and Motors) started sponsoring a yearly Pan-America Regatta in about 1952, often inviting an American team to participate. While some racing was held on a cocoa palm-lined saltwater shoreline at Acapulco, much of the 1956 contest ran in Lake Tequesquitengo, a water-filled volcano. *Boat Sport* called the permanent one-mile course there, "as near perfect a layout as possible." The era's "increasingly popular Mexican outboard racing schedule call[ed] for a minimum of one major regatta each month [for men and women stock 'pilotos']," Typically, their names were emblazoned on both sides of their hull. Mexico's alluring tropical weather allowed for lots of races, and drew a number of Southern Californian competitors, as well as other "northern" drivers and their spouses looking for interesting cultural contrasts.

Canada and the United States have long shared many similarities, including a colorful history of outboard competition. Although some "clamp-on" events held in provincial waters were sanctioned by the American Power Boat Association, numerous races have taken place under the Canadian Boating Federation banner.

For example, the 1955 CBF regatta schedule (for the Ontario and Quebec zones) included some 34 outboarding contests run between May 23rd and September 10th. Winchester, Ontario, alky racer Harry Keyes, recalled that prior to the CBF's 1950 founding, though a Canadian Power Boating Association was known to have sanctioned 1930s

Here's the six-boat and motor box trailer of O. F. Christner. He operated Quincy Welding Works, makers of numerous racing accessories (like the Visu-Matic safety throttle), and modified outboards. The firm's most famous mills were dubbed "Quincy Loopers," because of their loop-charging fuel induction. (NOA photo)

events, "there were races held by towns along the rivers, and by hotels on lakes in Ontario and Quebec for profit — or in [connection with] some towns' holiday celebrations. Back then, the classes were [arranged] mostly to suit [and attract] the local boating heroes who went out with their Johnson *PO-15* against some [stranger's] "C" alcohol-burner, and were completely embarrassed [by the alky rig] in front of their friends, and understandably not in the best of humor. [Of course, this often added an exciting measure of drama to press coverage in the event community's paper, and served to generate great publicity for future races.] Prizes were usually trophies or a small amount of money, or all the beer [the winner] could drink. [Just like in the US] origins of the various racing organizations started with a 'club' of enthusiasts who all went to the same regattas." Once established in the 1950s, Canada's stock outboard program was initially built on an OMC/Mercury divide. With a venerable factory presence in Ontario, OMC (Evinrude/Johnson) had many loyalists there who were suspicious of Mercury. So, a strict utility "U" section developed, designed with garden-variety OMC motors in mind. For the interloping Mercs (especially ones) with *Quicksilver* racing lower units, a performance class, dubbed "Z," went into effect. Eventually, as was the case in America, Mercury dominated the stock scene, and the OMC stock categories faded. Around summer 1954, though, the CBF line-up looked something like this:

Class	Typical Motors (believed to have been used)
MZ	Mercury *KF-5*
JU	Johnson *Sea Horse 5*
AU	Evinrude *Fleetwin*, Johnson *KD-15*
AZ	Mercury *KG-4H*
BU	Evinrude *Super Fastwin 15*, Post War *Elto Speedster*, Johnson *QD*
BZ	Mercury *Mark 20H*
BZ-1	Mercury *KG-7H*
BZ-2	Mercury *KE-7, KF-7*, or *KG-7* (standard lower unit)
CU	Evinrude *Speeditwin*, Johnson *PO*
DZ	Mercury *KG-9H, Mark 40H, Mark 55H*
DU	Evinrude *Big Twin*, Johnson *Sea Horse 25*
DU-1	OMC engines as above, but w/ after-market racing foot
EU	Evinrude *Speedifour*
FU	Evinrude *Big Four*

Later, the CBF introduced Class "T" for motors up to 10 cubic inches; "36-U" to handle OMC "Big Twin" outboards; "C-1" for German König engines of about 30 cubes; and a "C-2" Class in which Merc 30H motors were run. Related hydroplane (as opposed to utility or runabout) classes were subsequently added, too. Nicely representative of Canadian stock skills were the 1950s endeavors of racers like John Webster and Keith Cavanaugh. Each exhibited a specific style through frequent participation on both sides of the border. From the Toronto area, Webster began throttle-squeezing during the early fifties. His ties with the Merc distributor there prepared him with the latest gear. Still winning races at the time of this writing, he's long been dedicated to the sport, as well as a fan favorite.

Recognized as one of the most consistent Canadian stock outboard racers, Keith Cavanaugh's secret might be described as "quiet perfection." He always went to a race specifically to race ... not to socialize or party. The machinist from Peth, Ontario, was one of the only men in Eastern Canada who studied every detail of the (motor specifications) rule book, and then went to the max with the lathe and drill press. Outboard collector Ron Tackaberry, who in the 1990s re-built Cavanaugh's best "AZ" motor (from parts found in basements and swap meets) said when the no-nonsense competitor got finished machining his *KG-4H* crankshaft to the absolute end of the letter of APBA/CBF law, "it looked [and performed] differently than everyone else's ... but it was legal." Using mail order sets of Hal Kelly plans, Cavanaugh constructed runabouts and hydros in the "A"

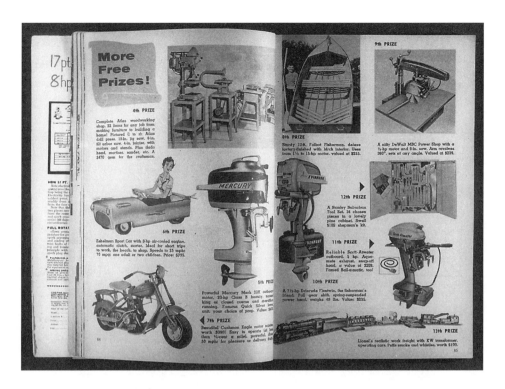

To illustrate that family boating and stock outboarding were hot commodities in the 1950s, here's a 1955 Popular Mechanics- type publication. Some 40 percent of the prizes — for a home workshop craftsmanship contest — in this magazine spread are outboard boat related. Up for grabs was a new Mercury Mark 20H racer.

class realm. They helped him attain the rank of Canadian High Point Champion in both "AZ" [runabout] and "A" Stock Hydro from 1956 through 1959, as well as become the Canadian National Champ in those major categories during 1959. Then, just as quietly as he started, Cavanaugh left the sport the following year, and delved into private aircraft.

Newspaper Support

"Can we really safely say that, or shall I change the figure?" asked a *Boston Globe* staffer assigned to compile the press book for the1957 Nationals. "Six hundred boats should be an accurate estimate," replied the contact from the South Shore Outboard Association, a local group with an APBA sanction to stage the big races. By the time August 22-24 rolled around, 702 entries were on Lake Quinsigamond, in Massachusetts for the spectacular. The *Boston Globe* spent much of the summer plugging its sponsorship of the competition, and planned for 250,000 spectators. Much of preparation for the public went unused, though, because rain kept away all but a few folks. Adding to the snafus, employee disputes at the newspaper prevented it from being printed during the four-day event. Consequently, coverage was at a minimum. The idea behind holding National

Germany's König brought competition outboards to North America in the mid-1950s. Its stock equipment never caught on here, but the alky (racing) models were adopted by NOA drivers, and then APBA racers.

Germany's König brought competition outboards to North America in the mid-1950s. Its stock equipment never caught on here, but the alky (racing) models were adopted by NOA drivers, and then APBA racers.

Championships before September was in response to the large number of student stockers having to be back in classrooms right after Labor Day. Such scheduling worked and made the 702 entrants part of the biggest stock outboard championships on record up to that time. Some went home feeling there were too many boats competing in certain heats.

Flips and spills were not uncommon in these get-togethers, but at Quinsigamond they seemed to be happening with alarming regularity, especially on the turns. In a run of the "D" stock hydros, some racers got ahead of the starting clock, requiring a restart. On the next try, 10 screaming Mercury *Mark 55H* hydros jockeyed for the best position around the first corner. One of the pack, a sleek boat driven by Bill "Buck" McClung, got hit by another craft. The impact ejected him into the swarm of hydroplanes and propellers. He died a few hours later. A year earlier, McClung had been at the 1956 Stock Nationals where a Champion Hot Rod driver hit a wave that lifted that fellow's hydro on its stern, then slammed him "face down against the automatic throttle." Fortunately, that racer survived. Another outboarder did lose his life in 1957, though, while testing an alky Johnson PR-65 on a three-point hydro. The flywheel disintegrated, shooting shrapnel through his life jacket. Rain and cold, windy conditions at the Nationals eerily accentuated McClung's accident. Some speculate that if not for the tragedy and bad weather, The Worcester Nationals might have kept stock outboarding's bull market charging. The assembled multitude of U.S. and Canadian racers was legendary. And it represented the first time the giant stock event was run in New England, where the respectable population base with numerous waterways at its disposal could have been enticed into the sport. Its organizer, the South Shore Outboard Association, was all ready to spread stock's message. The press book for the big race said South Shore's "well over a hundred racing members" made South Shore the "second largest outboard racing club in the nation." Also willing to promote stockers, the *Globe* was a well-heeled partner. The publication was famous for respecting marine endeavors, causing the National Association of Engine and Boat Manufacturers to grant it the 1956 "Golden Award" trophy for being America's top boating newspaper. From 1945-1956, it led the nation in the amount of boat advertising and information it offered readers. The fatality and poor spectator turnout at Lake

A gentle pathway for young-sters to enter outboard com-petition was through the lit-tle "JU" runabouts and 7.2-cubic inch Merc fishing engines. Billy Schumacher won the 1955 Nationals in this diminutive rig. Note that metal braces facilitated a dramatically high transom board. The added height allowed the motor's lower unit to be closer to the water surface (for better prop action).

Quinsigamond, however, permanently cooled the daily's interest in throttle-squeezing.

The *New York Herald* and the *Milwaukee Sentinel* were among other papers once friendly to outboard racing. While the *Herald* concentrated on promoting many of the Albany-to-New York events, the *Sentinel* was known for its connection with the Winnebagoland Marathon. Hassles on the Hudson eventually caused the Big Apple daily to cut ties with the race. Mercury's desire to shift Winnebagoland's focus from small stockers to bigger boats boasting six-cylinder powerplants soured the *Sentinel*. It liked covering the human-interest angle of youngsters, like Craig DeWald, having a chance to best older, better-financed rivals in the 92-mile event. When Kiekhaefer officials contin-ued pressuring the paper to include larger, more expensive craft (even calling for a course featuring the six-poppers and just a consolation jaunt for little plywood stockers), the *Sentinel* said no, and then dropped its association with the Midwestern classic. Merc went ahead with its brand of the run for a few years, but without the status conferral of the press, widely distributed, exciting publicity for the race was hard to come by. And at least as a partial result, so were the youthful spectators and future participants who might have been reached for the sport through that influential paper.

The editor of the APBA's *Propeller,* enthusiastically rolled the presses for important information in its August 1957 issue. FLASH, its front page boasted, arrangements have been completed with the *New York Mirror* newspaper "for a [June 1958] rebirth of the largest stock outboard marathon ever to be staged by American Power Boat Association." The Albany-to-New York race was to be revived! People started talking about the classic contest again, and how it'd capture worldwide sporting attention. They were mostly the seasoned pros, anxious to make the riparian trek no matter what. Challenges like weath-er, infamous water conditions, and getting one's rig and crew to Albany hadn't changed significantly since the event's first date in 1928, or its initial pure stock run nineteen years later. Unlike many of the renowned race's cadre of optimistic late-1940s stock competitors, though, few novices who read of the race's proposed 1958 revitalization harbored any thought of attempting such a test in their family boat. That's partially because even "stock" outboarding had become quite specialized and required boats and motors that in 1958 were not as prominent in the average marine dealership, as had been the case just a few seasons earlier.

By the late 1950s, safety worries, costlier insurance policies, and intricate legal questions also started to loom larger than the plain old common sense modus operandi accepted by organizers and racers a half-decade or so before. "What if?" concerns first took their toll on low-budget meets. "Before the advent of massive litigation," long-time APBA official Craig Bowman noted, "there was lots of organized local racing for weekend fun or just plain play." Some participants only got involved in the sport during, say, their town's annual 4th of July regatta. Typically, folks like these couldn't really afford the latest *Mark 20H*, and so whizzed around their informal course with obsolete gear. Somebody still won the race, plus everyone got to give it a go. But then, village officials reviewing the community's basic insurance policy invariably got read the riot act by their attorney who warned them they'd be risking a potentially huge liability. That paradigm shift often resulted in more than a few boating buffs to wonder, "Hey, what happened to the outboard race that was supposed to be run this year?" And so it went with the big guys in the Empire State, too. Only days from the June 1st race date, word surfaced of these kinds of liability problems, and even a seemingly arcane worry regarding the copyright use of the *Albany-to-New York Marathon* name. Negotiators suggested a name change might solve the technicality. Then a couple of those involved in the bargaining proposed shifting the race (and the stock outboard racing sport in general) toward pleasure craft, and used the last-minute sessions to try squeezing in a few classes of family-style outboard boats.

In the end, neither issue mattered. "Due to circumstances beyond the control of the *New York Mirror* and the American Power Boat Association," *Propeller*'s front page copy stated, "It is necessary to cancel plans this year [1958] to run the Hudson River Marathon from New York to Albany. . . . Drivers in Stock Runabout Classes AU-BU-CU-DU-36 . . . please remove this date from your calendar of places to race." Seeing those words in bold, capital lettering caused more than a few stockers to muse about how such a cancellation killed off some needed evangelism for their family sport. Some speculated that it served as a sign that stock outboarding's populist heyday was ending.

Alky Endeavors

There was a rumor going around that Hugh Entrop picked up. Sometime in the mid-1950s, he'd detected scuttlebutt about Mercury toying with producing a six-popper that'd fit perfectly into Evinrude's old Class "F" niche. The Boeing-based craftsman had raced four-cylinder Mercs, and so knew a bigger version would hold true promise for record-breaking speed . . . on the right hull. He got right to work building a boat perfect for the

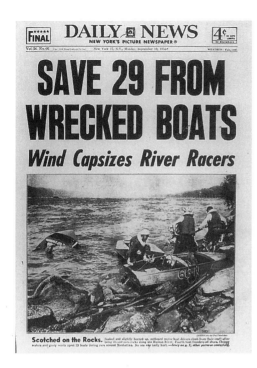

Scotched on the Rocks. Soaked and slightly burned up, outboard motor boat drivers climb from their craft after being shoved onto rocks along the Hudson River. Fourth boat founders off shore. Choppy waters and gusty winds upset 29 boats during race around Manhattan. No one was badly hurt. —*Story on p. 3; other picture centerfold.*

During the Eisenhower era, Outboard racing's Super Bowl — the Albany-to-New York Marathon — was an on again/off again, and sometimes truncated affair. Fearing accident liability, even the event's most ardent original sponsors backed away. They feared negative publicity from the likes of this front page New York Daily News story that began, "Soaked and slightly burned up, outboard motor drivers climb from their craft after being shoved onto [Hudson River] rocks." Small print went on to say that "no one was badly hurt," but such coverage took its toll on what had been outboarding's major crowd pleaser — stock marathons.

ethereal Kiekhaefer mill. Two years later, though, there still wasn't any such Mercury, so the unusual hydro sat in Entrop's basement for want of a particular motor someone had mentioned might be ready in 1956 or maybe 1957. That was about the time a few other racing outboards showed up in the U.S. rather unexpectedly. Dieter König brought some of his German engines to America during 1956, and then Bill Tenney began importing British Anzani competition motors not long thereafter. As alcohol-fired machines, neither brand wasted much time while shoving most of the old-line OMC alky mills into retirement. They even gave Merc-based Quincy "modified" (alcohol-fired) engines stiff competition.

König's original intent was to sweep his products into stock, as well as "pro" action. The "J" class through "C" line included a König for each genre. NOA officials began accepting the German alky motor for the 1956 season. Here and there some König stock (which used regular gas/oil fuel mixture) activity occurred in NOA circles, too. APBA "out-of-the-box" enthusiasts wanted nothing of it, though, so enthusiastically responded "NO!" to a Stock Outboard Racing Commission poll regarding the use of foreign motors. So loud was the rejection of König stock racing models that regulation wording even warned of using Canadian loopholes to get around the spirit of the rules. APBA approved "stock" outboards, reported *Boat Sport* in June 1956, would be "only engines built in the United States or by bona fide Canadian subsidiaries of" those U.S. makers. Tenney took note of that armed camp, and aimed his Anzani artillery solely at NOA/APBA alky targets. By the early 1960s, his imported iron dominated that arena in Racing Outboard Classes "A" and "B." Tiny ads the seasoned racer/inventor/businessman bought during that era stated that British Anzani motors "hold more APBA World Records in their [alcohol-fuel] classes than all other motors combined!"

Stock outboard racing proved popular wherever there was water. Here in 9150 is speed buff Weston Hook in Hawaii. The "Flyin' Hawaiian" concentrates on keeping his Mercury KG-7H powered hull skimming towards the checkered flag.

It's strange how a man rather solidly convinced that all other outboard makers were trying to psych him out didn't care about König and Anzani successes against altered versions of his Mercs. Charlie Strang clearly recalled, though, that his boss Carl Kiekhaefer "had zero interest in alky" endeavors (with one exception mentioned later.) Staffers crafting the 1955 and 1956 Mercury catalogs were allotted only a few words to note Mercury's *Mark 40H* "with *alcohol fuel*, [had been] officially timed at better than 77 mph." That was faster than any contemporary Evinrude or Johnson claimed, but for some reason the Old Man gave nary a hoot about exploiting such public relations weaponry.

Stock Racing's Decline and the Rise of OPC

By mid-1958, Mercury was the only remaining American company producing stock racing outboards. Actually, this survival didn't provide Carl Kiekhaefer with much to savor in the stock avenue. While his *Mark 30H* and *Mark 55H* were listed as current models in the Mercury 1958 brochure, any of those engines sent to dealers came from an earlier, unsold inventory. Charlie Strang recalled that by this time, "the stock category had simply run its course, demand had dropped and the [company's] stock racing effort was reduced." The sale of each four- and six-cylinder outboard made it evident that they created a remarkable profit center. Merc's plans for 1958 included helping to grow the Outboard Pleasure Classes (OPC), using standard, family-use engines of mostly 50 hp and up. For Mercury, phasing out traditional stockers to cultivate OPC business, is analogous to the record industry of the late 1980s, which gladly gave up pushing vinyl records in favor of compact discs. Even though a record album and a CD cost about the same to produce, the public perceives that compact discs are worth more, and is therefore willing to pay the extra retail price.

There were those in the National Outboard Association who felt the wording in their rule book about *outboard pleasure craft* was just so much surplus baggage. Around 1954, regulations had been penned outlining ways to include truly stock "average Joe" boats and motors into the competitive picture. Not much actual OPC activity materialized, though, until 1957. Scott-Atwater decided to come on board that year with a brand of "factory-fostered" OPC racing designed to give its motors' image some needed pizzazz. Bob McCulloch, known for his speed penchant on land and water, had recently bought the second-string outboard maker. He spotted OPC as a virgin territory in which to make Scott's mark. NOA's *Rooster Tail* newsletter indicated that 1957 provided an opportunity for such a sortie because of its "many marathons and some closed course racing for the Pleasure Craft Division." At season's end, the Association debuted its Division II National Championships for "pleasure type boats and motors." The Gallatin, Tennessee, event represented one of the first pleasure boat racing, national title opportunities. The 1957 inaugural version turned out to be primarily for NOA's fledgling Class "EP," which was won by a Mr. J. C. Leatherwood and his Scott-Atwater 40. In fact the chance to win a sanctioned race with generic gear earned companies like Scott some useful publicity among boaters who fancied some informal competition. NOA's class delineation for its OPC Division II looked like this in the late 1950s:

Class	Cubic Inch Piston Displacement
JP	0 to 12.5
AP	Over 12.5 to 15
BP	Over 15 to 20
CP	Over 20 to 30
DP-1	Over 30 to 37
DP-2	Over 37 to 40
EP	Over 40 to 50
FP	Over 50 to 60

As in all other racing classes, the OPC had rules dictating allowable boat size and types. Here, a no-exceptions, family/fishing boat and motor situation reigned as both letter and spirit of OPC law. In the "JP" class, for example, competitive standard equipment could mean a 12-foot Lone Star aluminum Little Fisherman rowboat powered by an 11-cubic-inch Scott-Atwater ("Bail-A-Matic") 7 1/2- horse kicker. Organizers felt Class "DP-1" had some of the greatest potential in that it encouraged the use of garden variety 13- to 16-foot family runabouts (often with windshield and up-front steering wheel) and common outboards the likes of a 1956 Montgomery Ward Sea King 25. To really catch the public's imagination, however, OPC advocates dreamed of a standard-issue but sexy motor that had a reputation for everyday reliability, and ideally one that had the power to hit 100 miles per hour.

100 mph!

Ten days before Christmas in 1954, three Italian brothers, Carlo, Dore, and Massimo Leto di Priolo, sent a Western Union telegram to Charlie Strang saying that Massimo had piloted a 12-1/2-foot Italian-built interpretation of a Swift Big Dee (normally an 11-footer) hydro and Lesco brand (dubbed "X-4") outboard to 100.382 mph. Power producing this remarkable ride came from a 162 hp @ 7,000 rpm, four-cylinder, four-cycle one-of-a-kind motor with a supercharger and dual overhead cams. Its push helped make Massimo Leto di Priolo the first person to ever achieve 100 hundred miles per hour with outboard power. This got Strang thinking about coming up with a Mercury that could get on speaking terms with the century mark. That's where Hugh Entrop's aforementioned rumor started.

Whispers were also seeping out of the Scott-Atwater factory in Minnesota. Throughout the fall of 1957 and into the first few days of 1958, the Scott people had been hoping their hybrid *Square-Six* outboard and unique Flying Scott hydro (by Bill Tenney and boat builder Shorty Fillinger) would give their outboard company an NOA United States Class "X" (up to 61 cubic inches or 1,000 cubic centimeters piston displacement) record and steal some of Mercury's "fast motors" reputation. With no company backing, Hoosier racing great Paul Wearly had done just that in late 1955. He built-up a bored-out Evinrude *4-60* (mixing in some Johnson *PR* parts) which shot his Neal hydroplane through a one-mile Mississippi River course at 85.106 miles per hour. Scott would hope to best the Wearly record, and then surpass the European's triple digits mark. During testing in January 1958, and only minutes before a sanctioned NOA measurement, Scott-Atwater's unusual powerplant ate up its lower unit overdrive gears at 90+ mph. Spectators on the Fort Loudon Lake (Tennessee) beach shook their heads in disappointment, as this was, technically, but not "officially," faster than Wearly's Old Man River run.

Jack Leek, who'd broken speed records with his little 15-cube alky-Merc, knew that the century mark wasn't long for this world. And, he figured that a boat stacked away in a friend's cellar could do the trick, *if* the right outboard were made available for the venture. Leek wrote to Charlie Strang asking whether Mercury might provide Leek's buddy Hugh Entrop with a *Mark 75H* as depicted in the Kiekhaefer Corporation's December 1956 four-page *Boat Sport* advertising spread. Standard-service versions of the 59.4-cubic-inch, six-in-line (*Mark 75*) giant had finally hit dealer showrooms for 1957-58, but an artist's rendition was about all the public saw of the "H" racing edition until Strang decided to oblige Leek and Entrop.

Actually, the Merc exec was in a mood to give world record breaking a try. Legendary outboarder and then-Mercury distributor, "Doc" Jones (no relation to Seattle boat builder Ted Jones) had gotten wind of the early 1958 Scott-Atwater attempt, and notified Strang. With proof that some other manufacturer was out to steal Kiekhaefer's potential speed thunder, Merc readied for the goal. No more than several dozen *Mark 75H* motors were slated to come out of the Fond du Lac factory, and one of the first was shipped to Mercury's Lake X Florida proving grounds. Staffers were notified the motor would be put under Leek's mechanical jurisdiction and converted to run on alcohol fuel. Tests indicated that the tall, alky-modified powerhead on a shorty "H" length Quicksilver racing lower unit, registered in the 80+ horsepower range, as compared to a stock (gas/oil-fired) *Mark*

With bigger motors emerging as Mercury's (and other brands') real profit centers, manufacturers were very willing to support the kind of racing that gave their high-end mills positive publicity. Twin Merc 800 engines (80-hp apiece) helped Stan Groff and Chuck Mersereau win the 1960 Alaska to Seattle outboard marathon. Seven of the eleven starting boats finished. Unlike participation in smaller class ("A" through "D") marathons, this high profile, big horsepower racing typically required aggressive financing/sponsorship, as well as professional planning, crew support and driving.

75H's 60 hp. Hugh Entrop remembered that:

> When Kiekhaefer decided to go for the 100-mph record, Charlie [responded to] Jack
> Leek, and Jack drove up to Seattle from Tacoma to inform me that Carl Kiekheafer
> wanted me and the [basement-stored] boat to go to Lake X in Florida immediately. So
> Jack and I contacted my supervisor at Boeing and he gave me a month leave of
> absence. We [maneuvered the hydro out of the cellar and put it] on top of my old 1950
> DeSoto, and headed for Lake X. [This water body] was not really long enough for a
> 100-mph record [run], and we needed more prop work, but we did get to 96 mph.
> Plus, my month away from Boeing was running out. As it was, Kiekhaefer was
> acquainted with Ted Jones, who lived on the shores of the east channel of Lake
> Washington. So arrangements were made to take the zand 75H] to Ted's place. With
> the help of Ted's son, Ron Jones, [who tweaked the two-blade propeller] we were able
> to go 107.8 mph through a measured kilometer [on Lake Washington] on June 7, 1958.

Thus, Entrop's skillful driving, his home-brew hydro, Strang's *Mark 75H* project, and
Leek's fine-tuning clobbered the 1954 Italian outboard speed record, doing so with only
half the horsepower used by Leto di Priolo. Strang proudly pointed out to the boating
press that, while the *75H*'s strength was notable, the run actually made stars out of the
motor's sleek gearcase, skilled propeller engineering, and an aerodynamic hull design.

As soon as the 107.821 mph fly-by occurred, Merc public relations people were ready
with a press conference. News of the 1958 record run was irresistible. Even in the minds
of the most ardent landlubber, it came at a time when America needed a technological
success. Soviet Sputnik satellites and Communist state-controlled military might propa-
ganda was sapping confidence in the long-held American belief that real power rested in
rugged individualism. Word of a lone hobbyist zipping well over 100 miles per hour in
his little homemade plywood speedboat while using a Midwestern-built outboard that,
hypothetically, any average citizen could get from the local Merc dealer sure sounded
patriotic. Anyway, it earned an American a true world's record . . . meaning those pesky
Soviets in the USSR certainly hadn't been able to pull off such an accomplishment.

Entrop's record helped set the stage for a profound change in outboard racing. The
watershed performance reinvigorated Carl Kiekhaefer's interest in marine competition.
Over the remainder of the 1950s, news stories, photo essays, and single-captioned pictures
of the *Mark 75H* feat appeared in literally hundreds of publications from niche U.S. boating magazines to major European newspapers. Few of the period's boat buffs could claim
they'd never seen at least one publicity still of the *75H* and *RX-3* with Entrop crouched at
the helm. More than a few outboard-minded grade schoolers pontificating on the play-
ground started highlighting six-cylinder Mercs in their "dream-team" bull sessions.
Compared to one of these tall powerhouses, even that old favorite, the *20H*, seemed mundane.

Bigger Becomes Better

Throughout the summer of 1958 and beyond, Mercury's crescendo of publicity preached that big motors on fast family runabouts were hot. The company's discontinuance of Class "A" and "B" stock racer models implied that small motors — as far as impressive records went — were passé. Already in this informational mix were many other articles about the Kiekhaefer Corporation's legendary (late 1957) 50,000-mile endurance run with "stock" *Mark 75* motors. The year-in-review front page feature on the January, 1959, *Mercury Messenger* boasted "Mercury Makes Outboard History in '58," first noting Entrop, then touting the 50,000 mile enduro, a Mississippi River Marathon win, and some world's record water ski jumps . . . all thanks to *Mark 75* "performance and dependability."

Big "modern" outboard motors like the six-cylinder Mercury made speeds previously associated with lightweight, spartan, competition nautical punkin' seeds possible for average family runabouts. Forty miles per hour and exciting acceleration was now a reality to be enjoyed in comfort. No need to be kneeling down, wedged into a one-person hull, when *tower-of-power* Mercs now allowed casual speedsters the luxury of sitting down on a cushy, upholstered seat with a loved one at your side and, for extra fun, a couple of water-skiing kin in tow. For most folks who enjoyed water sports, traditional stock outboard racing had lost the core of its novelty and excitement. Going fast in a bigger (14-18 foot) pleasure craft felt safer, too. This made more people want to do it. Life jackets didn't even seem necessary, anymore. Of course, personal flotation and crash helmet requirements were for anyone wanting to race their family boat in a sanctioned Outboard Pleasure Craft event.

Strang and Jim Jost crafted an APBA version of the rules for this quickly emerging brand of "stock." With the *Mark 75* publicity, and through Roy Rogers's earlier *Mark 55E* pleasure boat racing endeavors, OPC took over the Kiekhaefer Corporation's competition program interest (of the late 1950s and 1960s). Strang's Oshkosh, Wisconsin, home served as summit headquarters during his and Jost's Outboard Pleasure Craft rulemaking. Somewhat more encompassing than previously mentioned NOA Division II regs, these "Oshkosh Papers" brought the genre into wider acceptance by the larger racing body — APBA — and then on to dozens upon dozens of sanctioned regattas and marathons.

Coverage of this late 1950s-early 1960s paradigm shift from single-passenger racing boats to OPC runabouts never reached the pages of *Boat Sport*. In a fiscal downsizing effort to save stock outboarding's best-known chronicle, its publishers merged it into a similarly ailing sister publication. After a single consolidated June-July 1958 *Aqua Sport* issue, however, even this periodical vanished. A few copies lingered on newsstands while Entrop broke the world's outboard speed record (and then grabbed an APBA Class "F" competition title at 103 mph). But Hank Bowman had written most of the copy months before the cover date, so word of that milestone never appeared there. Neither would *Boat*

Sport (nor its long-gone former rival, *Speed and Spray*) be around to note the Champion Outboard Company's demise, Swift hydro's and Sid-Craft's closure, or editorialize about Mercury, dropping from its 1959 catalog, all remaining "H"-model stockers. In one of *Boat Sport*'s last issues (June 1957), Bowman did express continued concern about the shrinking availability of new stock racing motors. With fewer "store-bought" stockers on the open market, outboards utilised to continue the sport were more and more of the "re-vamped in the home machine shop" variety. This would drain racing from the average family's purview.

A Final Decline

"Only if stock outboard racing is placed [back] on a firm foundation of competition, with equipment that is essentially identical in any given class, with motors so constructed that those isolated few who may seek unfair advantage over honest fellow competitors can readily be detected," Bowman warned, "will the fast-growing game of stock outboard racing continue to flourish." Regarding the state of the once seemingly universally available Mercury "A" and "B" Class motors, his editorial's last three words had been written more in the spirit of a hopeful cheerleader than about what he knew loomed on the horizon. With Kiekhaefer's *KG-4H* and *Mark 20H* production halt (1953 and circa 1956 respectively, though leftovers of the latter were offered in 1957), by 1960, the winning power-heads in these smaller categories were becoming somewhat of a treasure hunt, mix-and-match affair, and largely the province of significant home shop mechanical acumen.

Each time a marine dealer stopped speaking the stockers' language, it served to drive the increasingly tight-knit racing community a bit further underground. Though veteran participants often made hand-me-down rigs available to newcomers, the days of a novice claiming the checkered flag with a brand new, just-out-of-the-box stocker had already begun to wane by the time of Bowman's June 1957 article. Some 1958 Mercury pamphlets showed green *55H* motors and sunset orange *30H* mills and noted prices. For the next year, *30H, 55H* (as square-top models in the artist's rendering) and "F" Class *75H* were depicted near the words — "These motors' [records] prove the stamina, built-in reserve power and reliability found in every Mercury" — but none was listed in the actual spec sheet. (Because today's few remaining *75H* engines are tagged Mark *75HA*, it may be that they were 1959 models, as the company used an *A* suffix that year. Some surmise that *A* meant alcohol motor, but the *75HA* owner's manual refers to gas-fired and alky versions.)

To be sure, the brand of outboard motor racing (Classes "A" through "F") most-loved by *Vintage Culture* readers survived the equipment shortages Bowman prophesied. In fact, Kiekhaefer production included some tiny, uncataloged runs of *Mark 55H* and *Mark 30H* motors during 1959-61. And McCulloch offered an *F* racer (model *590* triple) in the early 1960s. Additionally, the "Corn Popper" tuned-exhaust conversion sets for 1954-57 *Mark 20H* Class "B" models could be ordered from the factory up until the mid-1970s.

Even so, those who stayed with the sport, while others switched to OPC, tunnel boats, or went into Honda motorcycles, sports cars, *GTO* convertibles, *Corvettes*, etc., saw their ranks and spare parts supply shrink.

The alcohol-burning crowd was also thinning out by about 1959. Senior demographic attrition and the introduction of foreign motors (even the APBA eventually let them into its alky club) pretty much signaled old blood to get out, leaving the few newcomers, along with their German König and British Anzani mills, lots of empty beach in the pits. Screaming noise from alky exhausts, as well as the unique howl of a stock *Mark 20H* with "corn popper" (or "toilet bowl," due to their bulbous appearance) tuned pipes tower housing, irritated residents whose waterfront homes sprung up all over North America. Event insurance costs jumped, and increasing numbers of local officials gave thumbs-down to outboarders hoping to stage a closed course race. Finally, with some "B" and "C" boats capable of exceeding the mile-a-minute mark, many parents now considered the sport far too dangerous. Out of the way, bucolic areas once home to 1950s-style family camping along with stock outboarding seemed to fall off the event schedule first. The aforementioned Adirondack New York region dropped from several dozen annual races in the early 1950s, down to pretty much zero a decade later.

Around 1965, I found a tattered *Boat Sport* filled with grainy black and white pictures of old *Quicksilver* Mercs, and begged my dad to take me to the Plattsburgh, New York, Mercury dealer for such an engine. The proprietor of that first-rate franchise hadn't opened up for business until 1957, and so was bypassed by the stock zenith, but he had heard of a Vermont dealership where a *30H* reportedly went unwanted at one end of the used motor rack. After asking what size the engine was, my father instantly determined that a four-cylinder racer was not suitable for our eight-foot plywood hydro. The Merc guy also suggested a visit to the converted garage shop of an erstwhile Kiekhaefer outlet in Saranac Lake where races had once been regularly run.

It wasn't until the following summer that we ventured to the purported gold mine. The little outboard repair shop appeared to have sustained occasional visits from others looking for engine parts. High-pitched two-blade bronze props and safety throttles were among the leftovers. The elderly fellow who owned the place said he thought a club in Quebec still raced *KE-4 Rockets* and even *KE-7 Lightnings* on scrounged racing lower units. They'd been to his place "four or five years before," the old gent noted, "and just might come to buy again." That made me rummage faster. This quest and 25 bucks netted me some Michigan *Aqua-Jet* racing props and a "Q"-length (long) *Quicksilver* lower unit to hook to a lawn sale *KF-7 Super Ten* powerhead. I must have spent 15 minutes trying to decide which "Quickie" to pick from the waist-high pile of cast-off stock racing stuff. Many are the times today when I try remembering his inventory and wish I had known then what to look for. Mostly, though, I just recall trying to keep the *Super Ten* going, sustaining incredibly sore knees while taking a pounding on the waves, and wishing mine was the fastest boat on the lake. That honor went to a family down the beach. They'd bought their smooth riding, 16-foot fiberglass runabout with comfortable seats and electric-starting Johnson *Sea Horse 75* at the boat show.

Chapter Three

Race Day!

"Local drivers have no advantage [in this 90-mile, St. Lawrence River outboard race. Last year] 85 percent of starting drivers finished; only five percent were local entries. The marathon weekend schedule includes driver's dinner, marathon ball, and marathon queen contest. Six chambers of commerce are joining forces to present this event and are making a combined effort to make this the largest [outboarding] event in the East."
— *promotion for the 1956 1000 Islands International Stock Outboard Marathon*

"While powerful inboards [at big regattas] compete for the coveted trophy, the bouncing outboards supply the fans with the most thrills."
— Speed Age *(September 1954)*

THERE WAS A QUARTER-MIDGET car racetrack at Seekonk, Massachusetts, that wasn't doing so well. One of the owners of this 1/2-mile banked "bowl" shook his head with disappointment, and then remembered hearing about a new way to boost attendance. An associate had reported seeing some pretty exciting outboard racing action, and suggested such motorized marine thrills 'n chills would translate perfectly to a flooded midget bowl. "After all," the compatriot likely gestured, "this place already has parking, seating, a loudspeaker system, and johns, plus a snack bar!"

While winter 1952 blew through the Seekonk Speedway (not far from Providence, Rhode Island) management called in water trucks bearing fifteen million gallons. The results made for a neat little oval lake. Later that day, an eager Mercury *KG-7Q* hydro driver got free use of the new facility. The preseason test was caught on camera by the nascent aqua speedway's optimistic owners who sent the shot to the equally fledgling *Boat Sport*. A subsequent magazine picture prompted youthful racer Dick O'Dea to head to Seekonk for a look see. Weathered bleacher seats only a few feet away from the water allowed patrons to feel the action, sometimes quite literally. "They had cyclone fencing all around the [aqua] track's perimeter," O'Dea recalled. "Boats would be whipping through the

It appears that this old black and white photo — found in Hank Bowman's file cabinet — came from the 1953 Winnebagoland Marathon winners circle. Actually, it was shot to show the Class "B" stock victor Dennis Grenia (right) with a big smile and handfuls of stuff he'd been awarded a few minutes earlier at the prize ceremony. The young man received a nautical desk lamp, racing steering wheel, safety throttle, trophy plaque, assorted gift certificates from local merchants, and a beautiful new Mercury Mark 20 and six-gallon gas tank that he enlisted a buddy to tote.

turns [and] then get way too close to the barrier. There'd be crashes, spray, splinters, and ripped deck fabric as the hulls broke up [like grated cheese] on that fence."

Such a tight course no doubt added to spectator appeal and probably some stiff necks, but Seekonk Speedway's early 1950s setup of what ostensibly amounted to boats racing in a big swimming pool was relatively unique. Typically, a lake, ocean bay, or river provided runway space for galloping shingles. Routes were either an oval (circular if space was at a premium) *closed course*, the mapped-out "here-there-and-back again" style for a marathon, or an interesting amalgamation of the two, dubbed a "predicted log" event. In the latter, competitors would guess the exact time it would take to complete a course. The person with the most accurate estimate won. Another variation, called "bang-and-go-back," also pitted all classes of boats heading for a single buoy. As soon as the first boat rounded it, a gun was fired, signaling everyone to turn around towards the finish line (which had been the starting point, too). Like predicted log, drivers were not allowed to alter their original throttle setting. Theoretically, that gave all motor sizes and boat types an equal chance at victory. Of course there were additional racing games, especially in local "outlaw" clubs. These events ranged from relay racing to a funny procedure called the "spark plug race" (where drivers, with their motor's sparkplugs in hand, responded to the starting gun by running to the boat, installing the plugs, and getting underway) to "bath tub" or decorated rowboat racing; and even outboard speed competitions with a water skier in tow. While nationally sanctioned closed- course, and marathon programs were most prevalent, each genre attracted particular drivers, sponsors, and spectators. The aforementioned offbeat practices seemed to gain the most favor at events where family fun and chambers of commerce sponsorships were active.

An enthusiastic group of Southern knee-padders hit upon a plan it hoped would equip boat racing with the kind of fan following enjoyed by baseball, wrestling, or stock car action. Members of the Memphis, Tennessee-based Rebel Outboard Club, dreamed of "a spacious artificial lake built just for boat racing — plenty of pit area, beautiful country surroundings, with a huge natural grandstand sloping up from the water's edge, rest rooms, ice cold drinks, sandwiches, an NOA sanctioned race with cash prizes every Sunday afternoon — plus FREE GAS AND OIL." That's the way *Speed and Spray* described the utopia shaping up in the fall of 1952. There, some of the visionaries formed a corporation, found a site, and "built" their Tomco Lake alongside a mile-long levee. It was all ready by the following April 26th, generating a decent crowd to watch the rooster tails. The Pure Oil Company donated free gasoline and quart cans of oil to all Tomco race drivers for the entire1953 season. Coca-Cola fitted the judges' platform with a powerful public address system. Newspaper reporters, and TV and radio coverage also helped kick off Tomco's. Outboarding officials they interviewed predicted the site could give Mid-South throttle-squeezing a "place with other American sports events which have a regular following of spectators." While most of the racers came to Tomco to see whether they could net a little green (in NOA's professional Division IV), folks gnawing on a chilli dog in the grandstand admitted that they liked the "Fishing Boat Races" staged with ordinary craft and garden variety motors of ten horses or less. "Free-for-All" events also netted fan attention, especially when the guy on the new P.A. system added a bit of ad-libbed humor while describing what was happening out there on the lake. Purists sometimes wondered how John Q Public could assign higher ratings to those antics than to the actual sanctioned competition Tomco was built for.

As quintessential as today, a vintage outboard (alky or stock) race got underway by way of a *flying start*. For up to five minutes, participating craft buzzed around the judges stand area with a goal of going full throttle over the starting line just as a huge (six feet or greater in diameter) timer clock hit zero, a white flag waved, and a shot fired. Any driver "jump-

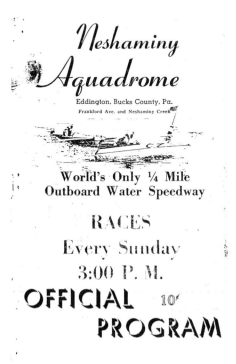

Neshaminy Aquadrome

Eddington, Bucks County, Pa.
Frankford Ave. and Neshaminy Creek

World's Only ¼ Mile Outboard Water Speedway

RACES

Every Sunday

3:00 P. M.

OFFICIAL 10'

PROGRAM

While to an ordinary person it might just look like a cheaply printed and faded document, this long ago race day program cover holds significance for outboard speed buffs. It came from the tiny Neshaminy Aquadrome, a short-lived, seat-of-the-pants, outboard raceway operated by Hank Bowman in late 1940s Bucks County, Pennsylvania.

ing the gun" was out of the race. That anxious outboarder's only hope is that he was not alone. If over half of the contestants were also over the line prematurely, a restart may be ordered using the red signal flag. Even so, the driver who led the early birds was unequivocally disqualified. And, it was generally true that only a single restart was allowed in an American Power Boat Association bout, while a pair of them could be legal during National Outboard Association action. Sometimes racers would happily cross the finish line in the lead, only to soon learn their boat had jumped the gun (perhaps by just several inches).

On the closed course, racers have a love/hate relationship with buoys anchored in strategic locales to mark the circuitous route. Many were constructed of upside-down peach baskets affixed to automotive tire inner tubes. Often a small flagstaff marker protruded from the overturned container. Like the starting line, these boundaries were to be approached "just right." Ideally, one's hull would barely kiss the buoy's outside surface while tightly negotiating a right-hand turn. Instant dismissal was the fate of any driver cutting corners. Champion stocker Dean Chenoweth was noted for his ability to keep his rig closer to the legal side of a buoy than most of his contemporaries. Once though when a sizable truck wheel's innards were serving as boundary, his twin-cylinder Mercury-powered boat speared it. Chenoweth's runabout continued on with the big black tube (and related dragging anchor) captive on the bow. Hopefully safe around the markers, boats race the course for five miles. Upon the leader's entrance into the final lap, officials display a green flag. A checkered one gets waved at the first [in most cases] three craft crossing the finish line. These 1st, 2nd, and 3rd place "winners" can smile, but never breathe a complete sigh of relief until after sweating out a successful officially sanctioned inspection of their equipment. The rest of the race isn't over until all the other boats report past the finish line, then turn left (out of the incoming traffic) toward shore. In some cases, even a 5th place driver is eligible for a small prize and some of his or her Association's ranking points (to be added up at the end of the season). These points were also doled-out to marathon winners. At season's end, a high-point winner was announced, and then showered with a trophy and various kudos. Like a Mr. or Ms. America of Stock Outboard (or "alky" Outboard) Racing, the high-pointer is apt to be invited to make the speaking rounds at boating trade shows and civic club luncheons. There, the honored guest would share a few tales of the recent racing year, then probably answer questions from neophytes about what it's actually like to be in a race. That would bring a description of the practice of running two, five-mile events, called heats, per class. Optimally, each featured 12 entrants. Results from this pair of heats (with a brief pit-stop in between) added up to the actual race score. Inspection of the "unofficial" 1st, 2nd, and 3rd victors' gear occurred after this second heat or completed race set. They also had to report immediately to the inspectors' tent. Momentarily detouring back to one's station wagon for a waiting sandwich, or some dry digs was strictly forbidden.

Spectators knew that anything was possible when several boats vied for the closest position to the marker buoys during closed course racing's hairpin turns. No doubt some who witnessed this event long-recalled driver Dean Chenoweth cutting a corner a little to tightly and his Speed Liner runabout wearing a marker (truck tire inner tube) buoy to prove it!

Closed course racing's claustrophobically close quarters — with a possible dozen swarming boats — could make a driver long for the comparatively wide open spaces of marathoning. But such freedom often came with a price, like rough water, uncertain routes, floating debris or other obstacles, and just plain fatigue from pounding through tens of miles of chop on one's knees. Most marathons, like the Mennen aftershave lotion company's 1957 *Grand National* at Worcester, Massachusetts, ran for about one hundred miles. The Thousand Islands event measured 90; Winnebagoland, in Wisconsin consisted of 92; and the Albany-to-New York grind spanned 130 taxing, unseen mileposts. Seattle's rugged *Sammamish Slough* (pronounced "slew") pitted contestant against winding, shallow water for just 14 miles, but even that short distance was brutal enough to disable many competing craft. "The modern guys think going around buoys is racing," Pacific Northwest-area Evinrude distributor Jerry Bryant was fond of saying, "but real racing happened at Sammamish Slough! He'd stress the route's dangerous hairpin turns, like one that'd throw its sharp angle at you directly under a very low bridge. "If you didn't duck at just the right second while also paying attention to your throttle, water depth, and dozens of other boats trying to squeeze by," the veteran outboarder warned, "you'd get your head knocked off! Oh yeah," he'd conclude, "there'd be farmers' barbed wire waiting to snag anyone who got even a little bit too close to the creek bank."

Moviemakers at 20th Century-Fox heard about the

In the first heat of "BU" action at the 8th Annual Tri-State Outboard Regatta (Lake Chautauqua, NY), this accident occurred. While, in a tightly packed fleet of screaming outboard boats, it's easy to collide with a recently overturned craft — as was the case here — this brand of mishap was rare.

After the starting gun and its crowded field of contestants, the marathoner's trek may actually seem lonely. This is especially true for those way out front, or lagging behind. The big water feel of most marathons even caused some novice drivers to get lost. Of course, if conditions weren't terribly rough, the marathoner might almost be able to relax and wave to the thousands of spectators typically lining the shore. Here, a "DU" racer heads down the New York side of the Saint Lawrence River before passing historic Boldt Castle.

Slough outboard challenge, and sent a camera crew to Seattle. Setting up various shots, they loved the way livestock grazed so near the waterway. Only several feet from the race-course, one waterside farm even featured a chicken coop that the show biz people just couldn't resist. In a staged scene, Fox film caught alky racer, Al Benson, whip down the Slough, then veer off smack into the rickety barnyard building. Theatergoers laughed at the goofy sight of splintering wood, a chagrinned throttle-squeezer, and shocked chickens flying all over the place. Benson didn't make the Seattle trek look easy. Even without poultry trouble, it wasn't. Anyone skilled enough even to finish long after the winner had achieved something valid for the racing resume.

During stock's heyday, Craig DeWald earned a lasting reputation as a championship marathon man. Actually, though, upon entering the marathoning game, he was well under voting age. Perhaps his naiveté provided him motive to practice without getting overly discouraged. For one of DeWald's early long-range races, he and his family traveled to the James River at Norfolk, Virginia. He'd nonchalantly pulled his Mercury motor out of the cellar the night before, and tossed it in the car for the ride. On race day, trouble showed up in the on-board fuel pumping system, resulting in his 10-minute late start. That meant the teen was the last one to get into the middle of the river. That meant there wasn't a lead rooster tail — to follow — in sight. Within a few minutes, the youngster and related Hal Kelly plans runabout were hopelessly lost. "It's tough to know where you're going in one of those races when there's no one else to follow!" he admitted.

Before his next marathon, he watched in horror the Hudson River's huge tanker wakes. "I've got to remember to find someone to follow," the high schooler pledged. Noticing an easy-going veteran racer preparing to tackle the treacherous swells, DeWald wondered, "Gosh, how do you survive those waves?!" The old-timer smiled, wrapped the starter rope around his motor's flywheel, and boasted, "Just do what I do, kid and you'll be all right." On the first wave, DeWald stared in disbelief as the vet got thrown completely out of his boat!

The Seattle Slough race was particularly challenging because of erratic water levels and various obstructions — under, on top of, and/or sticking out into the water. This event's most outdoorsy spectators could literally pull up a tree and seat themselves for a close look-see. Here, a couple of spectators watch Kenny Feroe anxiously pilot his homebrew "AU" runabout through the tenuous course. Had they been on the other side they'd have noticed a long gash in the youngster's boat where it came in contact with something mighty sharp. He's skillfully balancing the bow up high enough to keep out the water.

By an early Top 'O Michigan Marathon, he'd just began picking up needed confidence to handle most anything. Rather than high seas, this time part of the course included a crooked, narrow river. All around, there were ducks and otters. He swerved to avoid a critter, hit a log, and got spun to the adjacent shore. His "A" Merc stopped after its prop gunked up in the sand. The 14-year-old checked for oncoming boats, stepped in the ankle-deep water, pushed the boat out into the middle, started the KG-4Q, and then proceeded to finish 5th. Fortunately the water pump kept working. DeWald also credited his respectable showing to about a week's worth of practice on the course prior to the race.

Finishing well on the big day took lots of stamina, and then placed the racer on the next rung of Association ladder of success. For American Power Boat Association people, the pinnacle was always the Nationals. The organization handed reporters a Press Booklet

Right before leaving for a race, boat builder/racer Hal Kelly snapped a photo out of an upstairs window of his New Jersey home. No doubt he was taken with the sight of his ready-to-go boat and motor trailer rig. It could hold a runabout, hydro, tools, motors, and — as the "on sale here" notes — the latest copies of Boat Sport. *Kelly served as the magazine's art director and often advertised his boat plans therein.*

prior to its 1957 National Stock Outboard Championships. It outlined the pathway from regular seasonal to regional, then divisional, and finally on to national competition:

> The Nationals move from one area of the nation to another, as much as possible, to spread the main event of the sport across the entire nation. The APBA has divided the U.S. into 19 boating REGIONS [and then further divided these regions into] five major DIVISIONS. Each region has during the course of its season a series of closed-course races, paid for by local sponsors, and sanctioned by APBA. This season is followed by a REGIONAL championship event, in which the first three drivers in each event automatically qualify to run in the later DIVISIONAL championship. Frequently, a regional winner cannot compete [in the divisional event] because of personal [typically, travel affordability] reasons. Elimination heats decide the eligible starter. All drivers who place first, second or third in the Divisional championships are eligible to start in the NATIONAL championship event. As before, some eligible drivers, unable to give time for a cross-country trip to attend the Nationals will leave "vacancies" that are again filled by eliminations. In seasonal, regional, or divisional racing, each heat is limited to 12 starting boats. In the Nationals, there [is room for] 16 competitors.

There was also opportunity for MILE TRIALS at the Nationals. Usually run early in the morning, mile trials gave racers (many of whom hailed from tiny towns) a chance to set a "world's record" over a ruler-straight course of exactly 5,280 feet. "This event," noted the aforementioned handout, "is open to any racing driver that has finished first, second or third in any APBA-sanctioned event during the current year. The driver must be driving the boat and motor [or equipment of the same model and manufacture] in which he qualified during the season. APBA's rival National Outboard Association offered its membership similar opportunities. Its main event, however, was self-branded with *worldwide* (as opposed to national) status. Successful local NOA-affiliated club racers progressed to District, and then National Zone contests before admission into NOA's nationals or

World Championships.

No matter which organization sanctioned a particular race, spectators there noticed different numbers on the boats. During outboarding's early days, the boat/motor's class was included in the ID emblazoned on the hull. "A-22," for example would indicate the twenty-second Class "A" registrant. Later, a state-by-state, single-letter code (for example: N = New York, P = Pennsylvania, D = Connecticut, E = Washington) replaced what had been a class distinction symbol. This letter preceded its related numbers on alcohol-powered boats, and came after the digits on stock outboard hulls. Also meaningful were odd numbers, assigned to amateur drivers, while even figures belonged to the pros. Winners of national events won the right to display the "1" designation (along with their associated class's letter) for a year after the victory.

Through much of the 1950s, outboard racing appeared to be North America's number one motorized spectator sport. That's because, unlike auto racing, it was typically free to the spectator. Marathons, covering dozens of miles of shoreline, also yielded extensive, no-charge exposure to the action. For some reason, though, outboarding never quite capitalized on a "driver as star" approach. The guys on wheels did. NASCAR shared outboard competition's humble beginnings, but had fully eclipsed APBA and NOA's popularity nationwide by the 1960s. Access to the drivers, if only through a brief track-side public appearance and publicity picture, seemed to provide the glue needed for new fans to stick with the zooming oval lap sport. Significant numbers of NASCAR enthusiasts came from the female ranks.

Filtering outboard racing through women's intuition, Blake Gilpin predicted in a 1952 *Boat Sport* article that unless race day was aesthetically pleasing, understandable, and accessible to spectators, the crowd would quickly disappear. She was one of the sport's all-around veterans with savvy insights about competition, event organization, and follow-up promotional reporting. Gilpin had often witnessed race locales void of adequate public parking and/or directions for where the event might best be seen. Printed programs, sold to attendees, were typically informationally deficient, too, she noted. They were usually more filled with generic "Good Luck To The Racers" ads from bars and gas stations, than with details fans could use to better understand what was going on around the buoys. The proverbial shorted-out, intermittent, over-modulated, or undersized public address system also received her thumbs down. Almost quintessentially, these electronic marvels made an art form out of either distortion or announcer pantomime. The P.A. "system that might do good service for a square dance caller in a moderate sized room," Gilpin wrote, " is no competitor for a dozen or two unmuffled outboard motors."

Drivers who complained that the general public served as a nuisance at a race really baffled the boating magazine writer. After all, curious spectators were the hometown people whose presence made sponsors want to support a boat club. She'd been to numerous events where casual attendee and active participant didn't mix well, especially in the intriguing pits. Gilpin closed one of her prescient admonitions to outboarders by stating, "if the spectators had a reasonably interesting place to be and a spot to call their own, then they could be more readily controlled and kept out of the pits." Pointedly, she wondered, "Is it too much for the spectator to ask for a place to park, a place to sit, boats and drivers he can identify, a race he can see, and results he can hear?" Annual races without organizers who were sensitive to these needs usually shrunk — year by year — in attendance, sponsorships, and municipal cooperation. Eventually, all that was left were a handful of outboarders having to look for a new venue.

To be sure, there were many well-presented outboard races during the sport's golden age. These yielded definite positive ripple effects that brought countless families into general boating and some new blood into racing. One such noted regatta was the enviable province of the Kingston, Tennessee, Lions Club. Deep in National Outboard Association country, the civic organization sponsored its first race in 1948, some three years before the postwar NOA's formation. By 1955, the local Lions annually attracted 10,000 spectators to the Fourth of July competition. This in a town of (then) less than 1,700 residents! Food concessions, and 50-cent "lucky donation admission/raffle tickets" (for a new boat, Evinrude motor, and trailer) generated thousands of dollars for subsequent distribution to worthwhile community projects. It was done with a bit of NOA help, lots of volunteer planning, and significant promotion. Such public relations included press releases and racers' photos to every newspaper within 50 miles of Kingston, a guest spot on the area's TV sports show, and most importantly, radio coverage before, during (via a live, on-the-scene remote broadcast), and for a few days after the race. Wisely, the "radio relations" Lion arranged for some of the local drivers to be interviewed on the air. Spectators who'd heard those programs admitted they came rooting for the racers they got to know over the radio. Many also reported seeing a picture of the contestants in their local weekly. Participating drivers were pleased with the Kingston Lions's various work committees that provided great pits, parking, potties, and prizes. An officials' barge, accurately measured and marked course, workable inspection area, and various facilities for the public added to the overall cooperative mood. Additionally, all the effort primed the pump for the next year's outboard regatta. The June 1956 *Boat Sport* suggested this Tennessee event was a model all other stock outboarding functions would do well to copy.

To keep even the most casual outboard racing spectators happy, some organizers concentrated on "in-between" outboarding events. The object was to prevent boredom resulting from lulls in the hydro/runabout action. One club enlisted the services of a college jazz quartet, senior citizen banjo player, barbershop singing club, and teenage rock band. These aspiring musicians, doing a song or two between races, were often happy to go "public." Typically, they could be persuaded to hang around doing their tune weaving for several hours without charge. Another civic group sponsor whipped up a "swim suit beauty contest" for added flavor to the race day program. Before to the final judging, par-

Enthusiastic competitors often emblazoned the exteriors of their boat trailer's motor box with their name, hometown, and main class endeavor. The inside walls of the motor box might have penciled-in performance notes or names and phone numbers of people with spare parts for sale. This rig was seen at a 1967 Antique Outboard Motor Club meet during which time the owner put on a racing demonstration.

ticipants would be chaperoned around the regatta site signing autographs or just waving at the crowds. Talent shows, modest water ski demonstrations, and water "thrill extravaganzas" also ranked high with spectators. In a 1955 *Boat Sport* article, Hank Bowman suggested filling race day down time with a plywood ramp, de-finned "B" runabout, and — most important — volunteer daredevil. "How difficult would it be," he proposed, "to set up a shortened version of a Cypress Gardens show, or present a 10- or 15-minute interlude of spectacular stunt driving?" Lots of folks came to the race primarily to see such a performance. With imagination, these kinds of extras made for a full racing package. Ancillary events (even the most corny localized ones] also gave the racers and their families something else to see besides an assigned patch of muddy shoreline.

Smart organizers knew the importance of transforming the water's edge into a serviceable pit area. A general rule of thumb called for at least five feet of firm waterfront per boat. Ideally, deluxe pits included docks and nearby electric/water hook-up for participants' campers, cars, or trucks. Realistically, though, more than a few consisted of about a half-dozen running feet of muck. Every footprint created suction, and thus exposed some sharp underwater object or maybe gnarled roots of the pulpy trees that bordered the beach. It was no place to drop a sparkplug. Pit Stooges, defined as those who crew for a racer, quickly got to know every busted beer bottle that lurked a few inches under water in their jurisdiction. For them, race day meant back and forth between their driver's parked vehicle and trailer/motor box/boat. Every detail needed attending before any member of outboard racing's "pack mule" crew could roam the race venue for some food, or sightseeing.

"The Pit Stooge," *Boat Sport* wanted readers to better appreciate, "is simply the guy [or gal] who lugs boats, holds engines, keeps his fingers crossed while his driver is out on the course, gets cussed out when the engine won't start, gets cussed again when the engine starts and his driver doesn't win, and then carries [again] boats and engines at the end of the [race] day." Those experienced in this line of servitude could be easily distinguished from novices by their rubber hip-waders. The alternative flip-flops and cutoffs in cold,

A National Outboard Association inspector scrutinizes a rack of 1st, 2nd, and 3rd place Johnson-based alky "C" motors at the NOA's 1954 Outboard Championships. If the 1st place engine is disqualified, motor number 2 becomes the victor — unless it, too, displeases the official. By the way, no inspector was expected to reassemble the perused outboards. Sometimes the winning driver in a "small" race would take an automatic disqualification so that his motor wouldn't have to be stripped down and rebuilt prior to a major contest like the Nationals.

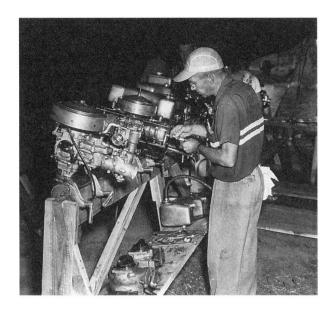

murky water could make teeth chatter. And, such footwear had a habit of popping apart whenever the heavy end of an outboard and submerged broken glass were in the picture. People who pit stooged outnumbered the race driver contingent by more than 2 to 1. The most successful worked with a checklist so that long before heading to the race, all needed components were loaded up for the big event. Tales of hopefuls arriving without a starter cord, propellers, Association membership card, tool kit, or driveshaft are legendary. About 200 miles from home, one first-time helper of a Class "A" alky race driver, remembered that "uh-oh," the boat trailer's motor box was *sort of empty.* He'd meant to put those two KR Johnsons in there, "but . . . well . . . with all the other stuff to do. . . . " Not all pit crew possessed above-average mechanical ability. They often made up for it on race day, however, by knowing the names of all available tools, then almost instantaneously producing them when requested by their leader. A pit stooge who kept track of equipment made himself or herself mighty valuable.

Occasionally curious spectators would wander into the pits. Most just wanted to get a closer look at the action. Some hoped for free advice on how to get their own "regular" motors to go faster. And there were always kids wanting to touch a real live hydro and *Mark 55H*, like the ones they saw in a boat magazine at the corner variety store. Maybe there'd be the vital question: "Mister, if you was gonna sell a boat and Mercury like that, how much would it be?" A quick pit stooge might just smile, "Fifty million bucks, kiddo. Now get your nose outta the motor box before I get suspicious." During the innocent 1940s and '50s, theft in the pits was relatively uncommon. More often than not, when an adjustable wrench, prop nut, or something went missing, it had been hastily utilized, then forgotten someplace like on top of the curved trailer fender. That's not to say pre-Kennedy days were completely void of crooks, but most racers, their families, and crew were a rather close-knit community. They kept a pretty close eye on what was going on around their gear. If something got clipped, word spread fast, making it tough for the robber to fence any high-performance motor or parts without raising suspicion.

Because even in honest Harry Truman's day, the world wasn't completely perfect, racing clubs and associations called for inspection to be part of the race day schedule. This race element served to ensure that each rig was "legal" or acceptably comparable to all others in its class. Good facilities for this brand of once-over typically included motor racks, and workbench, all under a conspicuous tent. A dockside scale was also standard equipment. "In stock outboarding, the measuring and weighing of boats, the inspection of the motors for illegalities, must be carried out," Hank Bowman indicated, "in order to maintain as closely as possible a level of competition in each class; to give every driver an opportunity to compete on as even terms as possible with his fellow participants."

Every race day, the fastest boats in each class (typically the top three) were guilty until proven innocent. That trio of happy drivers and their pit crew would head to the inspection area immediately after seeing a checkered flag. Their lucky outboard received an official inspection tag as soon as it got shut off, and then was subject to complete disassembly. Some inspectors, many of whom had ties with Kiekhaefer Mercury, might ask a racer to show him one particular internal component of the motor as sort of a random spot check. Others, like Mercury VP Charles Strang (originator of many "*H*" Mercs) was most confident of compliance after seeing the whole motor reduced to parts lined up on the workbench. The racer and his assistants provided all the tools and wrench turning for the teardown. An inspector's job was simply to look at and measure the resulting pieces.

There's a story about a family that thought it'd be fun to buy a new boat and motor it could race. This took place during the 1960s when Outboard Pleasure Craft racing was gaining attention, and caused the folks to select a nice fiberglass runabout and pricey 100-horse Merc. What a thrill it was to win a big race! Dad, mom, and kids — minus a teenaged son who volunteered to help the inspector check their winning Mercury — were all so excited, that they went over to a nearby restaurant to celebrate. Their oldest found them an hour or so later, and told of a technicality that caused officials to disqualify their expensive mill. Seems the "factory-sealed" powerhead suffered from a reed stop that was just this much too high (a production error). An even greater state of shock awaited mother and father, however, upon seeing their fleeting prizewinner reduced to a lower unit and several boxes of parts. The sight immediately weighed down their enthusiasm for any future OPC competition.

Drivers, as well as boats — minus accumulated water and all nonpermanent attachments — hit the scales to make sure both were in tolerance. There were cases when the combo was fine before the race, but slightly underweight upon return. This was true especially in marathons where a racer could lose a few pounds on the grueling course. Yes, such a suddenly skinny driver could get disqualified! If everything matched the official factory specifications as "stock," the competitor's status shifted from "unofficial" to "official" winner. The victor went home with a trophy, prizes, and a box of parts that composed the winning engine. It was a good idea to have a generous supply of new gaskets for the inevitable rebuild. More than once, a driver superstitious about having to take apart his "magic" winner power head only a week away from some bigger regatta, would skip the inspection, thus forfeiting his win. The idea was to keep from messing with a great-running motor he'd slated to save for the Nationals.

There were some tricks unscrupulous racers tried to get past inspectors. One of the most legendary involved a certain Class "A" stocker from below the Mason-Dixon Line. Reportedly, he noticed in a Western Auto catalog the 12-horse Merc-built Wizard boasted an 18.34-cubic-inch piston displacement, but had a block that sure looked like the "A" legal 14.89-cube *KG-4H*. The switcheroo was not externally obvious, and certainly gave him the winning edge. After a few trophies, his *Southern-A* cylinders were scrutinized by inspectors who beached the guy for dishonesty. The use of an ultra thin gasket between the block and crankcase for added compression was also a known scam. So were shady practices like cutting tips off water pump impellers to reduce friction, using hot fuel additives in a gas/oil stocker, or polishing lower units and other parts that weren't that way from the factory. Even slightly enlarging a motor's prop shaft shear pin hole, *Boat Sport* noted in a list of no-nos, could cause inspection trouble. In so doing, one is removing metal, and that changed the dimensions from "stock" specs. It might also allow the use of a heftier prop than those who didn't drill out the hole could use. Officials looked for any physical thing that gave a driver an advantage over the competition. Sometimes the inspectors were a bit overzealous. So, APBA rules permitted a written appeal and $25 application fee (in the late 1950s) to be filed with the official Referee no later than an hour after the day's last race. Should the disqualification be overturned by the ref, the money got returned along with a reinstatement. Otherwise, the dough went to the Association

A rich schedule of marathons crowned stock outboard racing's heyday. The Midwest's most popular long-haul event was the Winnebagoland Outboard Marathon. Officially, it was sponsored by the Milwaukee Sentinel newspaper and the Fond du Lac Association of Commerce, with help from the Fond du Lac Park Board, but one might speculate that a particular Fond du Lac-based outboard maker probably had something to do with the race, too.

and the original ruling stuck.

Every so often, inspectors, referees, and drivers all felt trapped by extenuating circumstances. While "removed metal" resulting from one's skeg getting chewed up by an underwater obstacle might have been graciously overlooked, other deviations from stock could not. After the 1953 Winnebagoland Marathon, the inspection tent turned somber when the overall winner had to be disqualified. The inspection team noticed higher-than-permissible reed valves on Bob Switzer's just-out-of-the-box Mark 40. They knew he'd never altered the engine. Like the case of the aforementioned, new 100-horse motor, it resulted from a factory mistake that would have delighted the average owner. Even so, the components were technically not within factory specs. The officials had no choice but to take Switzer's 1st place win away. Another Merc boo-boo was more obvious. It surrounded incorrect porting accidentally cast into some Class "A" *Mark 15* blocks. Kiekhaefer people caught the error in time to stamp the offending parts "Not For Racing." Anybody who tried to run one of those through the inspection tent clearly deserved anything he got!

No race day would be officially over until the victors received their prizes. Alcohol-burning outboard racers competed for cash, while stockers were relatively happy with a trophy and possibly some assorted merchandise. And this bounty was often a grab-bag jumble of gizmos rounded up from civic-minded, Main Street sponsors. Flyers for the 1956 90-mile International 1000 Islands Stock Outboard Marathon promised a huge "perpetual" (turned over to the next winner the following year) trophy. Plus, there was loot for the winners to keep, like radios, hardware, gas, oil, small trophies, jewelry, auto accessories, water skis, boat trailers, outboard motors, and magazine subscriptions. There were instances where stock racers won money, but it was supposed to be turned over to his national sanctioning organization for "credit." The winner was then instructed to give headquarters a shopping list so that the check could be laundered into goods. That way, with no actual currency going to the winner, a stock competitor's amateur status wasn't legally compromised. Stock outboard marathoner Craig DeWald got into the 1000 Islands winner's circle. He recalled that Mercury always provided a motor prize, typically a *Rocket KE-4,* of which the company had an excess. Not relating to much of the stash, DeWald, then a junior high school student, was awarded items like a paint sprayer, electric coffee percolator, gift certificates from sundry local clothing shops, and at the end of his list of winnings being announced above applause on the public address system, *two cases of beer.* "Hey wait" the APBA master of ceremonies whispered urgently to an associate slightly off mike, "We can't give alcoholic beverages to a 14-year-old kid!"

"That's true," DeWald's dad suggested as he stepped toward the podium at the conclusion of that long ago race day, "but you sure can give them to me."

Part Two

Governance and Structure

At every race, outboard clubs ostensibly staked their reputations on their inspectors — the people who had the power to disqualify and demand that a victorious motor be dismantled bolt by bolt. That's why these crucial officials were well identified, with the most equitable and professional in high demand. Here a serious looking inspector feels whether or not everything is kosher in this winning OMC "36" Class motor's lower unit and prop. Though we can't see what the two men in the background are thinking, no doubt they'll breathe easier when and if the official smiles.

Chapter Four

Clubs and Organizations

"The purpose of the Oklahoma Boat Racing Association is to promote outboard racing in general. The rules concerning conduct, inspection procedure, scoring, course layout, flag signals and starts, rules of the racecourse, protests, disqualifications, boat numbers, and prizes will be enforced in accordance with the National Outboard Association official rule book."
— *from a 1952 OBRA booklet*

SOME OF THESE OUTBOARD BOYS WORE real crash helmets, a couple of them co-opted headgear originally designed for football, and one kid could only manage to scrounge up an old construction hard hat. Their boats and motors were an ad hoc mishmash, too. During one official race, an odd runabout tagged along in a field of "A," "A/B," and "C" hydroplanes. Power ranged from a leftover 1958 stock Champion *Hot Rod,* garage sale KF-7 on a skegless (it broke off on some rocks) long *Quickie,* to a modified 20H with exhaust megaphones. But they were organized; all members in good standing of the *Hydros* Boy Scout racing club.

While not up to top national competition standards, the *Hydros* division of Saint Paul, Minnesota's Explorer Post 248, held races twice a month all summer, and always managed to have fun. Their second-hand plywood passports had been willingly forfeited by APBA and NOA racers dedicated to a belief that winning is everything. Most of the motors were likewise castoffs from people phobic of finishing last. In the meantime, the *Hydros* were affected by a more attractive contagion. They simply loved firing up their rigs for some spins around the lake. Victory was happily relative, since the variety of craft meant comparing apples to oranges anyway. Universal to outboard racing, there was also family adding to the enjoyment. It's likely that this outfit had more moms in tow than did counterpart organizations. And the coveted victory merit badge was probably exclusive to this brand of boat racing group.

Boys' Life magazine heard about the modest outboard club, got caught up in the group's enthusiasm, and made the *Hydros* a 1961 cover story. The periodical sent a reporter with the "caravan of cars towing boats and a repair trailer, clearly marked

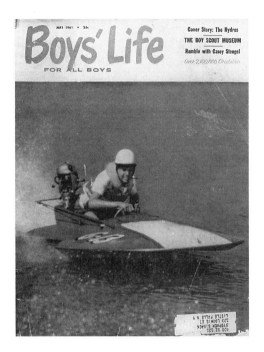

With well over two million young, enthusiastic readers (plus their encouraging parents), Boys Life *might have breathed longer life into stock outboard racing's heyday had the magazine run this cover story several years earlier than 1961. By then, few marine stores carried racing boats, motors, and related accessories. (Boy Scouts of America established a Motorboating Merit Badge in the summer of 1961, and even though Mercury helped produce the program's Outboard Scouting training film, racing wasn't emphasized.) Mitigating the supply problem was the hand-me-down/donated status of many of the racing troop's gear, which also made the endeavor especially affordable. The Scout shown is running a Mercury Mark 20H that never received the tuned exhaust tower housing and carburetor upgrade that the fastest Class "B" racers used after 1958. No matter, the kid looks like he's having the time of his life!*

Hydros," as the group made its way through the streets of Saint Paul and onto nearby School Lake. "Also trailing along with the fifteen young racers [were] friends and relatives. Especially relatives, for this trip [was] really a family affair. . . . Mothers act[ed] as cooks as well as rooters, Dads work[ed] as pit men for their sons. They also supervise[d] the starting and timing of the race . . . and abide[d] by [safety] rules of the Midwest Power Boat Association." Just ahead of a picnic lunch, the scouts got their motors humming. Everybody had a chance to shoot rooster tails around the buoys. Then somebody at the grill shouted out that the hot dogs and burgers were ready. There'd be more time for high-speed water adventures after chow. "A small crowd ashore cheered the boats as they slowed and circled. Moms and girlfriends waved handkerchiefs. Dads whooped and clapped their hands. The *Hydros* had just finished another race." Parents who led these scouts knew the importance of having rules designed for fair play. That's why, between the launch ramp and the cookout, they made sure the Boy Scouts Of America preparedness and kindness protocols were followed on the water. Rules were outlined to participants before racing would begin. Such sanctioning conferred status on the kids' endeavors.

Traditionally in boat racing, there have been two branches of organization . . . national bodies and local clubs. Best described with a television broadcast analogy, the national associations are like the major broadcast networks a la CBS or NBC, while the individual hometown racing organizations might be considered local TV stations. Like coast-to-coast networks, the national groups provide a schedule of programming (specific boat and motor categories, boat numbering, the promise of a season's finale *Nationals* race) and rules for their successful implementation. Most notable are the "points" which may be accrued during any race, throughout the country, sanctioned by a national body. Racers most concerned with these digits are shooting to become "High Point Champion" within their given umbrella association and class. The nationwide organization is also needed to approve and grant recognition to any speed accomplishment that is to be considered a truly national record. Meanwhile, back to our aforementioned comparison, individual broadcasters, in this case, hometown clubs know best how to use some of the network fare (and customized home-grown event offerings) to reach their "audience" or local racer/spectator/sponsor community. Each is vital, but works best in connection with the other. Over the years, national associations have provided regulation universality, referee/facilitation, insurance, franchise assistance, and universal clout. Local clubs specialized in race course particulars (site selection, starting clock, buoys, and prizes). Sharp ones also printed membership development literature, held banquets, swap meets, youth boating education, and might even commission a 15-minute film of a hometown race. During some snowy February evening, gung-ho members showed the movie to their community's VFW or Lions civic clubs perhaps in hopes of securing a 4th of July race sponsorship. While the projector was being readied, a gregarious officer of the racers' publicity committee might warm up the audience with some chronological background. . . .

Historically, outboard competition started when a few local rowboat motor owners wanted to see whose newfangled engine was the fastest. As noted in Chapter One, only a shred of pre-1910 "clamp-on" racing documentation exists. Even so, it's safe to assume that sometime during the twentieth century's first decade, somewhere on the same stretch of shoreline, at least two people showed up for vacation with a Submerged Electric (a circa 1900 battery-powered motor) or maybe a 1907 vertical cylinder Waterman kicker. It would be a stretch to postulate that these outboarders simply ignored one another. And if even these motor owners initially showed no interest in their rival's rig, kids on the beach were in a position to egg them on.

"Hey Mister, my friend says that other fellow's engine is best, but I bet your motor is faster."

"See that tree sticking out over the water way down there where the shore juts out?" one outboarder then likely asked the other. "Whatdaya say we give those boys a show?"

"On your mark, get set . . . GO!" got shouted by the kids on the dock. With a sudden air of determination, flywheels were spun, engines popped to life, and a duel was underway. Every time this happened it added to the universe of people talking about outboard racing. One may hypothesize that such characters represented outboard racing's pioneer organizers.

While there were plenty of informal outboard racing clubs — some with only a single race to their credit — from outboarding's earliest days through the very early 1920s, serious enthusiasts groups began gelling here and there. Of course, Judge Cohn's Ohio gang is among the first (and noted in Chapter 1). A nascent arm of what became the

Seattle Outboard Association (officially formed in 1929) staged speed events on Washington's Green Lake around 1924. This was about the same time as the Oshkosh, Wisconsin-based Mississippi Valley Power Boat Association added outboard competition to its traditional inboard regatta schedule. But it took a larger club, the American Power Boat Association, to move a truly national brand of outboard racing throughout the U.S. and parts of Canada. Although established in 1903 as a swanky Long Island Sound inboard racing group, the APBA noticed the successful clamp-on doings of its Mississippi Valley counterpart. "In 1924," its rulebook long noted, "the emergence of outboard motors efficient enough to stimulate racing interest prompted APBA to put into print a set of rules for boats propelled by outboard detachable motors." Within a few years of such seminal, nationally recognized competition, books addressing the topic emerged. One, the 1930 *Outboard Motor Boats and Engines* by Bradford Burnham, stated: "The sport of outboard racing has become well organized under the sponsorship of the Outboard Division of the American Powerboat Association and the Outboard Division of the Mississippi Valley Power Boat Association and all races must be sanctioned by one of these two associations if records made thereat are to become official."

Others got into the act of declaring rules around 1930. There was the National Outboard Racing Commission, which made sure an unbiased referee surveyed the race course, timed the boats, and arranged for winning motor inspections. This serious ref didn't actually perform such mechanical scrutinization; instead he called in an authorized inspector of the Outboard Motor Manufacturers' Trade Association to do the job. "Furthermore, the [owner of any winning engine was required to show documentation that he/she is] a member of some local club belonging to the APBA or MVPBA." In less than a decade, outboard racing went from loosely organized putt-putting to a paperwork beauracracy.

During the late 1920s, local, outboard-only organizations affiliated with the afore-mentioned national groups began dotting sundry shorelines. There were dozens, with the likes of Outboard Boating Club of Chicago, and the New Jersey Outboard Association being among the earliest. These two have since disbanded, but the 1928-born Connecticut Outboard Association still sanctions races, making it one of the oldest such bodies in the world. Also noted for longevity is the Oklahoma Boat Racing Association. It was formed in 1923 by pioneer Oakie outboarders,

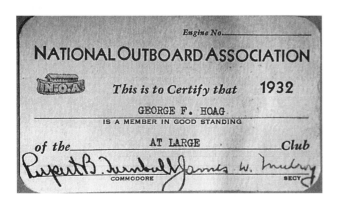

and even survived the Dust Bowl 1930s. Over the years (1935, 1959, and 1960), the OBRA hosted several nationally attended outboard events. The Association's members have often exhibited their creativity through a rich tradition of motor modification. In 1966, when OBRA had lost lots of old timers, dwindled to five people and zero races, the remaining membership elected Dudley Malone to spark a

renaissance. Within a year, a hundred boats were filling the determined core's event schedule. Once again during "the late sixties," noted Malone, "this club was one of the largest outlaw organizations in the country." Adhering primarily to their own customized rules (hence the label "outlaw" or outside of APBA mandates) gave Oklahoma and Texas racers reason to get involved with the resilient group. As a legal backstop, OBRA officials had made some connections with another alphabet agency called the National Outboard Association (NOA). In time, however, the southwestern knee padders wanted complete independence. The larger outfit from which OBRA broke away around 1971 was the second incarnation of the National Outboard Association. Of all such entities, the NOA has a most colorful history.

A short-lived concoction called American Outboard Association inadvertently set the NOA in motion back in the twenties. When the AOA failed soon after starting, major motor makers wanting a united public relations voice got a hold of AOA files, and parlayed them into the Chicago-based National Outboard Association. That was in late 1928. At the New York Boat Show the following winter, Caille, Elto, Evinrude, Johnson, and Lockwood hosted a small contingent of outboard enthusiasts who were aiming to form a sort-of nationwide small boating version of the American Automobile Club (AAA) with everything from insurance to racing rules and score sheets. By late March, the resulting NOA had hired George O. Hoehn to serve as executive secretary. Association officers like Commander Eugene F. McDonald, founder of Zenith radio electronics soon refilled the executive secretary position with Jim Mulroy. He would come to embody the prewar outboard organization. Management chose Noah's Ark (with its phonetic pronunciation mnemonic with "NOA") as a logo. Their publication, or official bulletin, mailed to NOA membership was named *The Ark*. Noting the outboard industry's disparate system of horsepower rating, Mulroy quickly pushed for a universality that would better allow buyers to compare makes and models. He won the support of the Pittsburgh (Pennsylvania) Testing Laboratories, an unbiased organization proficient in measuring and certifying rated horsepower, and then got his bosses to sign on to the plan. Thus the NOA's first success was a new honesty in the actual horsepower versus revolutions per minute labeling. Within a single boating season (1930), the term *"Certified NOA Horsepower"* accrued a value in the minds of outboard consumers. The organization authorized the production of little oval-shaped NOA decals a manufacturer or dealer could affix to the fuel tank. They were akin to the "UL" Underwriters Laboratories stickers for approved electrical goods.

Because it was not uncommon for the purchaser of a racing outboard to revamp the new motor to run on alcohol fuel, normal gas/oil-fuelled NOA horsepower ratings were not assigned to factory-built competition models. That didn't mean the Association was uninterested in speed. Upon its founding, Burnham reported, "this orizonization ha[d] charge of all rules and regulations pertaining to outboard racing." The NOA also promoted "the development of inland waterways [like the then-proposed Tennessee Valley Authority lakes], and other interests pertaining to the sport."

Here is the logo of the venerable Connecticut Outboard Racing Association.

When Mulroy needed someone to help officiate races in Tennessee, he remembered a young throttle squeezer around Knoxville who displayed a willingness and capability for the post. W. Claude Fox had been a part of that region's outboard circuit since the mid-1930s and loved racing, but was ready to try a related but less punishing role. Fox vividly recalled that his knees hurt so much after each outboard race that it was painful to have the under-dash car vents open during the drive home. Just the wind blowing on his raw joints stung like crazy. When he began doing NOA refereeing plus racing, things got pretty hectic, begging the question of which one to exclusively pursue. A call from Mulroy in Chicago provided perspective. "Claude, face it," the NOA chief intoned avuncularly, "you're a much better official than you are a racer. We need your help in our organization." Shortly thereafter, Fox sold his racing rig so there'd be time to work more closely with NOA. That relationship as well as his love for boating prompted him, in 1938, to open a marine dealer-

The Philadelphia Outboard Racing Association hosted many notable outboard motor regattas on the Delaware River, and never courted anyone from the schooner set. Enigmatically, its logo featured a traditional sailing ship's wheel.

ship in Knoxville. Well- attended local races seemed to generate traffic for the store. And, his welcoming, knowledgeable demeanor often turned his visitors into friends and customers.

America's entry into the World War II cut off the supply of new pleasure boats and motors. Knowing his background with small craft and organization, the Army offered Fox a commission in the Amphibious Engineers. He sold the shop and shipped out to the Pacific. With its sponsoring outboard makers refocused on defense work, and racing deemed "nonessential," the original NOA closed. Its important racing documents were then merged into APBA files. That left the American Power Boat Association as the sole nationwide sanctioning body at war's end. Other organizations, like the Mid-West Power Boat Association, reactivated racing around 1946, but their influence was regional. Fox noticed the void upon returning to Knoxville. He started another boat and motor store and volunteered for service in the APBA. Still, something was missing. Many of the racers recognized Fox from his prewar NOA days, admitting to him they "sure wished the old Ark was back in business." It was worth considering. "When a motor manufacturing APBA sponsor got wind of the [fact that he was thinking about restarting the NOA]," Fox told a biographer, "the sponsor offered [him what sounded like Plan "A"] the presidency of the APBA." But he recalled

soon finding out that the job offer was designed to keep him from starting a rival body. "That was the wrong thing to say to me," he noted. "I don't believe in any manufacturer controlling the associations." It weakened his confidence in the august organization. An incident at the 1951 APBA Nationals (discussed

It didn't take long for NOA to come up with a logo. By 1952 it had settled on a red, high-speed outboard prop on a field of blue and bordered with five white stars.

An APBA map showing its numerical regions. The "new" NOA followed similar cartography. Generally, both groups used similar lettering systems to identify the boat owner's home state, and with some nuances and exceptions, it's as follows: A= Maine, New Hampshire, Vermont; B= Massachusetts; C= California, Arizona, Nevada, Hawaii; D= Connecticut, Rhode Island; E= Virginia, W. Virginia, Maryland, Delaware, DC; F= Florida, Georgia, Alabama; G= Minnesota, S. Dakota; H= Indiana; I=(none); J= New Jersey; K= Kentucky, Tennessee; L= Louisiana, Mississippi, Arkansas; M= Michigan; N= New York; O= Oklahoma; P= Pennsylvania; R= Oregon, Washington, Idaho, Western Canada; S= Ohio; T= Texas, New Mexico; U= N. Dakota, Wyoming, Montana, Colorado, Utah; V= Illinois; W= Wisconsin; X= Iowa, Nebraska; Z= N. Carolina, S. Carolina, Eastern Canada. Some listings say CE= Eastern Canada, CW= Western Canada.

in a subsequent chapter) activated Claude Fox's "plan B." Establishing its headquarters in Knoxville, he chartered a new National Outboard Association and then founded a related publication called *The Rooster Tail*. For many oldtimers, used to Fox's Southern hospitality, the NOA revamp certainly felt like home.

Speaking as one who observed boat racing primarily through magazines, and other vicarious connections, the group's congenial aura was apparent. While never organizationally sloppy, the postwar National Outboard Association did have an "old shoe" quality that seemed to make room for just about anybody who wanted to race an outboard. If the APBA were a Republican caucus, the NOA would be a Mayberry town hall meeting. It was first to embrace folks with foreign motors, made room for outboard drag racing, and encouraged competition between pleasure craft owners. There were even some events on the NOA roster for those wanting to race a boat while pulling water skiers! Almost any motor would fit into at least one of the group's classes. Whenever my compatriots and I would spot a fuzzy *Boat Builder's Handbook* photo of an 11-cubic-inch "J" mod alky-burning Martin "60" Hi-Speed, imported König "B" stocker, or some cartoon-

Incorporated during the spring of 1950, The Canadian Boating Federation and its Racing Commission drew membership from its nation's many water speed buffs. Most Canadian boat racing enthusiasts living near the U.S. also signed up with the APBA. And, in 1962 the APBA and CBF arrived at an operating agreement that "has for its object and purpose the mutual benefit of both organizations… and a sound understanding and cooperative international relationship between the [the CBF and APBA]." Each organization, though, retained a few uniquely arcane (regulatory, class designations, racing number assignments) protocols.

ish amalgamation of Merc/Hubbell/Quincy/Johnson PR-65/homebrew parts on a backyard hydro, we'd happily speculate in unison . . . "Gotta be N-O-A!" The organization's unpaid leadership post was supposed to be the province of various volunteers. Fox figured on being NOA Executive Director only temporarily, but was kept at the helm from 1951 through the mid-1980s. About that time, an accident occurred during a Philadelphia race not sanctioned by NOA. One of the boats careened onto the beach, killing some spectators, and "everyone sued," Fox remembered. He got a call about the tragedy and couldn't help but think what would have happened had it been his group. Shortly thereafter, sizable insurance cost increases caused the second National Outboard Association to close its doors. The 1980s shutdown also resulted from the effects of a meeting in Memphis. There, a misunderstanding and tired leadership inadvertently allowed for a sea change like the one that produced the postwar NOA from that APBA split in 1951.

During the early seventies, veteran Oklahoma racer Dudley Malone and his associates got together to talk about ways the NOA might be made better for its southwestern membership. Overall, they liked the organization, but had some issues and possible changes they wanted to discuss with officials. It was decided Malone would lead a small Oklahoma-area delegation formed to attend the NOA's national get-together and bring their concerns to the leadership's attention. During the long drive to Memphis, they rehearsed ways to best express their views. Hopes were dashed, however, when the contingent couldn't even get on the meeting's agenda. Silence on the way home was eventually broken with the resolve . . . "The heck with this! We should just start our own association." A new outfit, dubbed American Outboard Federation was born of those frustrations in 1971. Dudley Malone was chosen executive director. Arthur McMeans (cocreator of the C-Service *GO-MAC* lower unit discussed in a subsequent chapter) became its first president. They well realized the political nature of racing often made it necessary, as Malone put it, to "win on the shore as well as on the lake." That is to say, knowing how to properly argue about rules and disqualifications can be as vital as understanding hydro handling in rough water. Especially responsive to drivers' interests (like the NOA in its 1950s heyday) the AOF saw appreciable membership growth. Of course club rosters are really just a mirror of an era's people and the intensity level of their pursuits. Sociologists might qualify that statement with words like "demographic" (gender, age, income) and "psychographic" (personality traits, likes and dislikes), but outboard racing organizations have been a reflection of their era's socioeconomic trends.

Fishers Landing Racing Club is a case in point. The Thousand Islands, New York-based organization came to life in the summer of 1946, hardly a year after the war was over, and just as vacationers began seeking all kinds of ways to enjoy the fruits of peace and emerging prosperity. But the FLRC didn't begin with big budgets in mind, rather the fledgling club focused on fun. It was something wholesome for the kids to do. Parental founders made sure participants were not required to invest heavily in gear. There was the "5 HP Class," where ubiquitous Johnson *TD* and Evinrude *Zephyr* kickers reigned; as well as a "10 HP Class," filled with Model *KD* Johnsons and Evinrude 9.7 horse *Lightfours*. Of course, this garden variety started changing when the faster 10-horse+ Mercury *Lightning* made its 1947 debut. No matter, many members still showed up with the family fishing engine and did Okay. The adults saw to it that modest craft had a place to compete. Most FLRC faithful were under16 years of age. Twelve-foot utilities by Wagemaker, Barbour, and Thompson represented the state of the art. In a pinch, though, any floating hull would do.

Pioneer member Riggs Smith ran his first race in an old de-masted sailboat powered by one of those little green Johnson fives. The other grade schooler who beat him that day drove a regular wooden rowboat. Her motor, however, was a "bigger" 5.4 hp Evinrude. Though victorious, the girl dropped out of the club. Alas, all was not lost, as during the late 1940s and early 1950s, there were plenty of other kids (and some good sport grownups) to take her place. Many of the young people weren't yet old enough for a driver's license. So, when a race was being held a dozen miles up river, rather than trailer their rig, they went by water. It was strictly local racing through 1948. Ever serious about club activities, Smith began upgrading his boat and motor combos. Along the way, there were home-brew, then commercial racing craft. Once the old Johnson fishing kicker was retired, power upgrades included a 1949 Elto *Speedster,* and a 30H Merc. Most of his fellow FLRC friends improved their equipment inventory, too.

The group's technical assistance with the well-publicized 1000 Islands Marathon sparked additional local interest, often generating new membership. Naturally, the Fishers Landing Racing Club flowed with the 1950 stock racing salad days and ebbed when the supply of competition outboards, specialized speed parts, and those with a desire to work on them dwindled by the late 60s. Neither did generalized complaints about boat noise, pollution, and fear of racing accidents help marshal new recruits each succeeding summer. Universally, insurance costs jumped and sponsors disappeared, as did the running of the region's famed marathon. There weren't many eager spectators left, anyway. During the early 1970s, they were encouraged by the media to get busy pursuing more environmentally friendly pastimes, like waiting in line to buy gas. Meanwhile, the Fishers Landing Racing Club ran out of people and was abandoned. But, there's a twist. Some twenty years after the club folded, a few young boating enthusiasts — including Smith's son Scott — got to thinking about all the neat Thousand Island racing stories they'd heard from the oldtimers. The next thing you know, novice and veteran knee padders staged a few informal events on a course . . . "say from here to that buoy and back." At first their gear was only a rather ad hoc jumble of stuff long dormant in local boathouses, but when they resolved to reorganize under the APBA banner, strictly contemporary competitive boats and motors became the standard. Then this second Fishers Landing Racing Club was off and running again, generating interest, new members and a body of memories. The same thing has been happening elsewhere, too.

Ideally, this case study narrative can cause us to remember that the history of any organization is really about individuals and how they relate their interest to others. Every great race was set in motion by a club. And, each successful club was empowered by those members happy to work toward its goals. In 1954, *Boat Sport* noted stock and alky outboard racing's steady rise. It used word of the healthy popularity increases to remind readers that "much of the credit for this growth can be placed where it is deserved but so often overlooked . . . the officers of the various [outboard] clubs. Almost without exception, the various key jobs of an outboarding club are non-paying, thankless and rewarding only from a standpoint of the success of the individual club."

Don Guerin was a notable local boating club worker, in addition to being an APBA president. Also the Association's 1954-55 stock outboard vice president, he owned a Mercury distributorship in Rochester, New York, and, like some other Merc sales-related people, became a part of racing for two main reasons: He believed racing was a great way to promote selling motors, and had a son who was interested in the sport. Through much of the 1950s, Guerin worked tirelessly on both the national APBA level, and as for his area's local club. One of the many young upstate New York competitors who admired Guerin was Gerald Mosier of Phoenix, New York. At the 1953 APBA Stock Nationals (in nearby Syracuse), Moshier won "BU" class, and then left racing. When interviewed in the late 1990s, he admitted forgetting details about his throttle-squeezing career, but retained vivid recollections of Guerin's knack for promotion and ability to make even the club's novice racers feel important. "The real reason Syracuse got selected as a site for that nationwide event," Moshier noted, "was due to Mr. Guerin's persistence and influence with APBA. He also treated the racers right."

In the 1960s, Mercury bought his distributorship, and then turned the Rochester facility into a Kiekhaefer Corporation branch. Guerin went on to help with Merc distribution in Canada, and then became a pioneer MercCruiser stern-drive sales manager. He passed away in the 1990s. Merc's Charlie Strang recalled a story representative of the gentleman's devotion to organizing an enjoyable race. Seconds before leaving this world, perhaps envisioning a sunny day on the lake and a final outboard event to orchestrate, Guerin is said to have suddenly smiled. "OK," he whispered from his bed, "let's get those D stock hydros in the water."

Chapter Five

Outboard Racing's Civil War

"The fact that there are two major sanctioning bodies for outboard racing complicates the picture somewhat in that two sets of records must be kept and two sets of champions must be crowned. Yet the very existence of two major Associations has provided for a greater number of regattas . . . which is good."
—*Tracy Ogden,* Outboard *magazine (February 1955)*

---

*T*HINGS HAD BEEN GOING so well. The old alky-burner racing circuits, drained during the war years, were notably refilled by 1951. And, newcomer stock outboarding was then growing so fast that almost every community situated near water saw at least a race or two each summer. Enthusiasts living within larger population centers had the

pleasurable dilemma of having to pick and choose which event they'd attend on most any given warm weather weekend. The folks at the American Power Boat Association happily watched the sport's explosion. They'd outlasted their biggest pre-World War II rival, the Chicago-based National

Claude Fox had a knack for mixing just the right amount of goofy fun into serious outboard racing. Here a "Yankee" team racer nets a trophy while a rival "Johnny Reb" leader looks on. One couldn't help but speculate that the popular NOA North-South championship event was predicated on APBA (Eastern establishment) vs. NOA (Good 'ol southern boys) feuding. (C. Fox/NOA photo)

Here is Claude Fox, arguably outboard racing's greatest organizer and promoter. Seen here in this late 1940s APBA publicity still, he's wearing an official APBA lapel pin. A few years later, he'd be helming a competing organization, the "new" NOA.

Outboard Association, effectively gaining controlling interest of boat racing's largest market — outboarders.

A benevolent monopoly, the APBA appeared secure in its supremacy. That's why no one at the Detroit headquarters worried about anything going wrong with the upcoming outboarding world series . . . the Association's capstone '51 Nationals at Knoxville, Tennessee. There was enough preregistration activity to schedule two full weekends of top-level competition. National championship hopefuls from eight outboard alky classes, a half-dozen stock utility categories, and a trio of stock hydro departments were readied on the card. Enthusiasts began rolling into Knoxville for September 8-10, and 15-17 events. In those pre-interstate highway system days, even late summer travel didn't come easy. The added responsibility of suitcases, provisions, boats, trailers, and full motor boxes represented a true commitment on the part of attendees from even a state away. But having the chance to set a world's record was the wild card making lengthy travel on two lane roads bearable.

Utility stockers quickly forgot travel woes as soon as their turn at the mile trials came on September tenth. Speeds were remarkable! When those runabouts ripped through the finish line, more than a few observers stared at their stopwatches in total amazement. They were incredulous, but waved off by officials who heard their suspicions that something was wacky in the measuring department. APBA's newsletter, *Propeller* commented: "Because of the rapid progress which has been made during the last two years in Utility racing — and because of local reassurance [that the mile course equaled 5,280 feet] the records which were established by Utility drivers going through the 'mile' were not too severely questioned." The next weekend, the alky hydros zipped over that same distance. When they bettered existing records by more than five miles per hour, someone decided to measure the course. Sure enough, it was short. That meant none of the reported speeds were accurate. Most stock participants had already left for home by the time the discrepancy was uncovered.

Grade schooler Allyn Guerin had driven to Tennessee with his father and their "JU" rig. He set a pretty impressive competition record, headed back to Webster, New York for a hometown welcome, and then learned his victory had been unfortunately won on a "funny" mile. The APBA called with bad news, causing the youngster to "very graciously agree to waive any claims to a new record established on this doubtful competitive course." Having to disappoint a kid who'd gone all the way to Tennessee with his little runabout and five-horse motor in tow made APBA officials rather steamed. They were especially mad at their race committee chairman of the Stock Utility Championship, referee of the alky races, and ranking local APBA official at the 1951 Nationals. All of those jobs had been taken on by Claude Fox.

Outboard racing was second nature to the Knoxville boat-and-motor-dealer turned-APBA volunteer. Fox started serious throttle squeezing in the 1930s, all the while helping the original National Outboard Association run its Southern contests. Following the war years, the old NOA's closure prompted the APBA to seek his promotional and organizational talents in parts of Dixie. He'd been instrumental in swinging the 1951 nationals to his hometown. There was even talk about him becoming the American Power Boat Association's chief executive officer, but when that offer came from a motor maker, he declined on account of manufacturer control and influence issues. Now he was being reprimanded by the APBA president, Jack Horsley, whose apology "to the entire membership of the stock utility and outboard racing classes for the manner in which the National Championships were conducted at Knoxville, Tennessee," made front page news in the Association's *Propeller* publication.

Horsley then admitted "it was obvious to everyone who attended these races that they did not meet the standards set by previous National Championship events." The CEO also noted that participating racers were innocent of causing the problems. There was also an all-clear for Dr. Harter, the APBA referee sent as a troubleshooter to Knoxville. "It is unfortunate," said the president, "that the championship performance [of the racers and HQ's ref] was not matched by the local race officials." Then the charges were suggested; short mile, inadequate boat/motor inspection areas, and questionable inspection procedures. "Dr. B. P. Harter as referee," set forth an official Association explanation, "refused to endorse the lower unit inspection procedure followed by [local club] Measurers A. Sel Preston and Robert Flagg." There was also a revelation that APBA headquarters had not received an approved race course chart from Mr. Fox even though he "definitely promised that an approved chart would be furnished immediately." Finally, Horsley suspended APBA's top Region 14 official "as of Monday the 17th of September 1951, and set November the 2nd, at the Biscayne Terrace Hotel in Miami, Florida, as the date for his hearing. If Mr. Fox is not to blame," the APBA exec stated, [also reported in *Propeller*] "then he will be exonerated by [the] Council on November second."

As with any controversy, there were at least two sides. Knee padders who had sundry gripes with the APBA rallied around Fox. Some filed Association accusations against referee Harter and Horsley for overriding findings of inspectors at the 1951 Nationals. Fortunately, a conference session was convened with Horsley, Fox, and other concerned parties. Enough of a spirit of cooperation prevailed to allow all the charges in the matter to be dropped. But the seeds of secession had been planted. Rumors of a new, outboard/stock-only racing organization were filtering through the throttle-squeezing community. The APBA began nipping such scuttlebutt in the bud with a couched warning. Readers of the December 1951 *Propeller* noticed in the "This and That" column.

"Outboard and Stock Utility drivers who are being urged to minimize their heritage in APBA on the grounds that its elected officials and hired help are obstructing their desire for high-grade racing, should STOP, LOOK, and LISTEN! Does the sun really rise in [Claude Fox's hometown] Knoxville?"

That's where all the 1951 Nationals trophies were anyway. And no one from Detroit wanted to venture down there to recapture them. "Convinced of the futility of reaching final agreement with W. Claude Fox and his fellow members of the local race committee" officials preached, the APBA instituted "an independent course of action in order that drivers who participated may receive credit for National titles and High Point awards" Victors were offered "printed certificates, suitable for framing, as a token of recognition from APBA." They were also given coded advice to forget about ever getting their trophy from "the Knoxville Boating Club, in whose name [the 1951 Nationals] sanction was issued." From the rhetorical tone, it seemed that cannon-equipped Confederates were holding the original prizes hostage.

Shortly after the big races, members of APBA's Knoxville Region 14 chapter got together for their annual meeting. Parts of the session sounded like a local union hall after some factory lockout. Detroit was anxious to see what went on in what it perceived to be the unfriendly territory. The main APBA Council had a session of its own [on January 12-13, 1952], and wanted to know why minutes of the Southern get-together hadn't been sent to APBA's home office. Fox was at the New York Council meeting to remind his fellow council people that suspensions from the 1951 Nationals incident had left Region 14 without any elected officers. Nonetheless, he pledged to mail a copy of the October proceedings to APBA officials, but predicted they wouldn't like what the text revealed. "I didn't instigate it, and I didn't start it," Fox mentioned, then announced most of the Region 14 membership had just decided to quit the APBA. But he offered to continue serving in his APBA Council volunteer position "barring objections from his fellow members." Those colleagues immediately began firing loyalty questions his way, however, causing Fox to write up a quick resignation letter and make a departing speech, it began with an indication that the split wasn't his idea. Lots of drivers wanted him to help them get a real outboard racing group. "I have this new deal now," he said as if having just made up his mind, "and I intend to regard *your* organization just as I would regard any other competition. Personally, I don't think competition can hurt boat racing — and you are going to get some too."

With that, Claude Fox went back to Knoxville and spearheaded the formation of a new National Outboard Association. For several years (around 1949-51), it had been an ethereal "secret weapon" to be exposed only as a potential bargaining chip. Until the 1951 Nationals incident, no more than a handful of racers on the APBA roster ever truly figured on jumping ship. Before the mid-September event was over, however, it was obvious there was enough of an irreconcilable rift to create dark boundary lines. And for the cause of the oppressed, Fox represented an able general. His promotional power to find race sponsors in even the smallest lakeside burg had already become legendary. For drivers, sponsorship translated into attractive prize purses. Although it was not his ideal first choice, the flamboyant Fox possessed all the ingredients needed to pull off a split.

Like any fledgling outfit, this version of the NOA had pockets of membership here and there, mostly in the south. Many early joiners who sent their dues to Knoxville were alky burners, with "NOA Stock" being somewhat of an oxymoron. Even so, the APBA did not like the thought of a sliced outboard pie. Speaking in a Cincinnati hotel at the bigger Association's (November 16) 1952 annual meeting, one council official said the NOA was "a one-man rump group. We should find out how much they are hurting us," he pleaded on the PA mike. Then wondered "how many members do they have, how many sanctions [for races] did they grant and what geographic spread have they been able to achieve?"

The labeling was scribbled for editorial comment by some racing buff after this cartoon originally appeared in Speed and Spray, but the resultant zinger is consistent with the epoch's tensions. Before eventually bowing to frequent rule change requests, most APBA stock outboard officials eschewed the idea of allowing stock motors to be modified. Meanwhile, the NOA quickly made a home for tinkering racers who favored making "mods" on their mills. Perhaps our scribbler sided with the latter group?

Hydro maker and APBA treasurer Joe Swift knew Fox's promotional skills had already made for some pretty-well attended NOA contests in Swift's Florida region. He took to the floor and frowned, "We are not too cheerful over the NOA situation, and we are all agreed that we should work out a plan to combat the inroads of the NOA." Veteran alky driver and marine dealer Jack Maypole raised his hand to speak about the threatening new group. "We all know," he confirmed, "that the sport has suffered for the simple reason that it is too small to support two organizations." Then Maypole proposed appointing a committee aimed at acquiring the infant National Outboard Association. Another councilman echoed that saying he "didn't want to give one inch to the NOA," and pushed for an investigation of the fledgling group so "that APBA does not lose face." Bill Tenney, a world-class outboard racer, supported the committee idea, but felt it should include people willing to "reach an amicable settlement with [NOA]. We don't want to fight them in a effort to beat them down," the gentleman competitor said at the council meeting, "because if the wounds cannot be healed, and everybody cannot get together it will be the welfare of the sport that suffers."

Tenney's colleague Paul Wearly testified that his name had been placed in nomination for NOA vice president. He declined the offer, but told APBA associates that he "did not feel the NOA is a menace," and that "they have put on some good races." That fact really upset some in attendance. For a moment, pensive silence engulfed the Netherland Plaza Hotel conference room. Then, Joe Swift admitted what most of the others had known all along. "The only answer," the hydroplane pioneer noted, "is to beat the bushes and show the [renegade] members that APBA can give them more than NOA . . . *give* it to them rather than *promise* it to them." Heads nodded vigorously in agreement. "They will come back to us," someone in the back loudly announced with enthusiastic resolve. The big organization's (November 1952) *Propeller* quoted the fellow as saying: "We're going out and selling APBA to drivers and race sponsors harder than ever before. Although they broke away from us, we are leaving the door open and we will be prepared to take them back when everybody feels that APBA is the best deal and for that reason they will want to come back!" Not long after that pep talk, "aye" echoed around the room authorizing the American Power Boat Association's Outboard and Stock Outboard Racing commissions "to appoint a study committee to look into all aspects of the [NOA] situation." Of course, that would have required a team of social scientists as the whole scenario simply demonstrated the presence of human nature within boat racers and their chosen groups.

Alas, there wasn't much else APBA could do about its erstwhile compatriots. For years, some of the committee kept sputtering about outboarding's civil war, and repeated accounts of who caused it. There was even a longstanding NOA Negotiating Committee within the APBA. But neither faction sustained mortal wounds from the conflict. By the end of the next September, however, most accepted the fact that NOA was probably not going to fizzle. "Doubts and skepticism about the Tennessee-born, national in scope, National Outboard Association were erased" commented *Boat Sport,* "in Lake Village, Arkansas [September 18-23, 1952], and Dallas, Texas [September 27th-29th]" during the new NOA Nationals. Hundreds of drivers showed up for the traditional alky, as well as modified stock action. The boat-racing magazine happily concluded that "taken overall, both the Lake Village and Dallas events were every bit as successful as NOA's spark plug and executive director, W. Claude Fox might have wished."

American Power Boat Association loyalists took no comfort in those words printed for all *Boat Sport* readership to see. Resentment simmered through the fall of 1954, and then flared. That's when some APBA member stockers [pursuing a racing style generally thought of as an APBA province] showed up to race at NOA's World Stock

Championships in Indianapolis. Upon returning home from NOA competition, the twenty received APBA notification that they were being "beached from further APBA racing because of their participation" in Fox's gang. Appropriately, as the 1954 holiday season approached, a spirit of good will prevailed. Representative committees from both groups got together to air their frustrations and begin fence mending. The February 1955 *Outboard* magazine reported "an APBA spokesperson [stood up to say that there would] be no further ban placed on any of its drivers for competing at NOA events." Fox was especially happy with the truce, albeit an occasionally shaky ceasefire. It let him concentrate on doing what he enjoyed most, promoting races. He stayed at the organization's helm through the lucrative fifties, shifting sixties, and slim seventies, and then finally brought it into dry-dock for disbanding during 1987. All along the way, the world of outboard racing kept changing. Parts of his NOA splintered into another group, the American Outboard Federation. Every club, Fox smiled, has its people, has its time.

In retrospect, even the most loyal American Power Boat Association person came to realize that the NOA had actually been good for the APBA. It had given the bigger organization contrast. The choice tended to make the sport seem customized and more inviting. The truth is, even some of the old committee felt comfortable about giving the NOA a try. For starters, Bill Tenney, Paul Wearly, and Jack Maypole joined in time for NOA's premier Nationals, branded World Championships in later years. It wasn't long before hundreds of racers were part of both associations. About four decades after the APBA/NOA rift, a number of these stalwarts joined another Claude Fox-sparked outfit dubbed the Pioneer Outboard Drivers Association. At most every PODA meeting, somebody there got overcome with a wistful look and started reminiscing about the infamous 1951 APBA Nationals. That always resulted in a spirited conversation about just what happened at that long-ago September event and the day it sparked outboarding's civil war. At that point, not even a free trip to Gettysburg in a hydroplane could have pulled the old friends away.

Part Three

The Culture of a Sport

A teenaged Hank Bowman (left) and friend (believed to be "Doc" Williams) proudly display their newly acquired step hydroplane (on car roof) and Johnson Big Twin. The rig was already well used by the time this 1930s photo was snapped, but represented some real Depression-era summer fun. Note the tachometer drive fitting atop flywheel.

Chapter Six

Hank Bowman: Outboard Racing's Personal Writing Syndicate

"For example . . . "Bowman's *Encyclopedia of Outboard Motorboating* is the most complete and readable volume on outboard motors, boats, and boating I have [ever] seen."
— *Dick Borden.* Field & Stream *boating editor*

*I*T WAS A BIG FANCY CHICAGO press breakfast for America's most noted outdoor writers. But when Hank Bowman saw those nicely embossed name cards on the elaborately set table, he knew he'd be dining alone. That's because trade show organizers had assumed power boating's well-known scribe would enjoy being seated next to associates like Tracy Ogden, Shanon Place, Craig Mallery, Crane Whittaker, Shannon Kelly, and Henry Hotchkiss. Needless to say, the hosts were rather miffed when these guest's places remained empty. And to think no one in the group had the courtesy to RSVP. Bowman volunteered to reprimand his thoughtless colleges upon returning East. Of course, that would have required talking to himself, as the no-shows were all nom de plumes!

The name Hank Wieand Bowman first appeared as a boat racing byline in a tiny column within *Speed Age* magazine. Around 1948, "Galloping Shingles" kept readers of the modest, Hyattsville, Maryland, based pulp publication abreast of waterborne motorized competition. Actually, there wasn't much to report. The war had taken lots of outboard racers out of the action for the duration. Then, OMC made it clear after the war that Johnson and Evinrude did not intend to build any more racing motors. Parts were getting scarce, causing lots of former throttle squeezers to move on to other pursuits. Through his "Galloping Shingles" column and a flooded gravel pit, rechristened the "Aquadrome," Bowman tried to get the old racers back into the alky-burning action. Both were laudable ventures, but neither yielded enough sparks to reignite professional outboarding's glory days. However, a new brand of clamp-on racing would soon provide him with a venue to match his mechanical knowledge and literary talents.

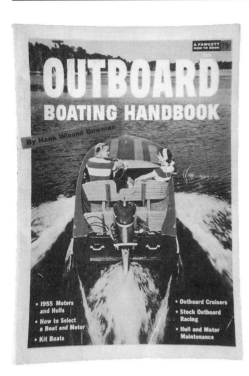

Arguably, Bowman's most widely circulated boating pieces were the Outboard Boating Handbook annuals he did for publishers like Fawcett. Often with a Mercury product featured on the cover, these typically 75-cent booklets served as a portable boat show depicting the latest hulls, motors, and marine accessories. Almost without exception, Bowman managed to convince the editors to make room for a chapter on stock outboard racing (with highlights from the previous season). It was not uncommon for Fawcett to produce some hard-cover versions of these magazines for the library trade. Such a format added years to the literature's life span. In 1986, the author found one from 1954 in circulation at a Missouri community library. The librarian noted that it was still being taken out rather regularly, but let me swap a contemporary small boating book for that well-worn volume.

Riparian, Pennsylvania, in lower Bucks County, where Bowman was born in 1914 provided a great place to develop an interest in water sports. At 12, he acquired his first motor and scratch-built a boat. Unfortunately, its transom fell off, but the river kept calling. Along with fellow teenage compatriot, "Doc" Williams, Bowman souped up a late-model K-35 Johnson for a used hydroplane the duo managed to purchase. The rig had enough life left in it to give a good ride, all the while pulling the pair into a lifelong interest in outboard racing. Later, while studying at the University of Pennsylvania, he helped organize the school's outboard competition team. That small ad hoc squad lasted until his graduation. Right out of college, Bowman followed romantics like Hemingway to Spain to see if he might be of use to rebels fighting in the (1936 – 1939) Spanish Civil War. No one there needed an outboarder, nor gave him an official welcome. He was stopped on a Madrid street and told to get out of the country. Back home, Bowman was pulled into the OSS (a predecessor to the CIA), and given a micro-camera to photograph suspected secret Nazi documents on a German freighter docked at New York harbor. While sneaking into the captain's quarters, however, Bowman caught sight of a Luger pistol appearing around a corner. It was a close call that sent him racing out the door and into the river. His next assignment for the cause of freedom was happily Naval. America's entrance into World War II provided the speedboat enthusiast with lieutenant commander's stripes and a mile-a-minute PT boat. These fast hulls weren't a bad place to spend a war. PT crews were somewhat independent of typical military regulation. Perhaps not exactly like the 1960s TV comedy McHale's Navy PT crews enjoyed loopholes such as growing a beard, wearing rather informal uniforms, and island-hopping shore leave, not available to many other service men.

When the enemy surrendered, Bowman was reclassified as a reservist. Five years later, the Navy "invited" him to serve as a full commander in Korea. He'd had enough fighting, though, so scribbled something equivalent to "GET LOST!" on the official correspondence, and then sent it back. Military police arrived at the Bowman home shortly thereafter to "escort" him to some top brass's office. There it was ascertained the erstwhile PT boatman wasn't at all interested in leaving the Delaware River Valley, resulting in an assignment to a nearby naval airbase public relations department. In the meantime, Bowman's voice was heard track announcing at Philadelphia's Yellow Jacket Speedway, and over the jury-rigged loudspeaker system at his Aqua-Drome 1/4-mile circular hydro course. There was also a bit of early NASCAR racing, and the public address system operation at the old Wall Stadium in Hatfield, Pennsylvania. Once, while he was completely focused on mike work in the track office, the race promoter scooted out with the entire night's receipts, leaving Hank at the mercy of the rough-and-tumble drivers who would not be getting any of their prize money. To make ends meet, he could always whip up some sports fiction, a staple of several small pulp magazines of the day. Usually, though, he simply talked, and his wife, Blake Gilpin, punched out the words on their Smith-Corona. She had the ability to type as fast as Hank could dictate. She could also write expressively. They made a great team.

Bowman had married Gilpin in 1940. The war years kept them apart for a while. So, by summer 1946, with the Aqua-Drome part of the reunited family's life, he wanted her to get more involved in his outboard racing endeavors. That's probably why an "A" hydro was found under the Christmas tree. It was tagged: "To Blake," and she vowed to race it as soon as the warm weather arrived. The couple's oldest son, Craig, remembers watching his mother ripping around the buoys so often that, as a kindergartner, he figured outboard competition was "a women's sport." When the *Philadelphia Bulletin* sponsored a race in which his mother participated, he watched from the pit area. A reporter looking for the story's human interest angle asked Craig when he was going to race, making the youngster feel horribly insulted. "It was like calling me a girl," Craig later laughed.

In the early 1950s, equipped with a portfolio of writing samples, Hank made the rounds to all the Manhattan-based magazines that might buy an article on boats, cars, motorcycles, guns, or even vintage trains. Four of the most notable connections from those forays were *Boat Sport, Popular Boating,* ARCO Books, and Fawcett Publications. Through Fawcett, he gained his widest audience with titles ranging from *Boat Show,* and *Outboard Boating Handbook,* to *Sports Cars in Competition,* and *Antique Guns.* Many of these magazines were actually annuals, or went into additional printings, thus making for a lengthy shelf life. Some were even hardbound for the school and public library market, giving them added influence upon generations of various enthusiasts. Bowman's seminal work in *Boat Sport* is discussed in a later chapter. For fans of this body of literature, it's understandably surprising to learn that, although essentially producing the critical mass of each issue's content, he and his co-contributor/wife Gilpin earned very little from the legendary racing periodical. That's why the publishers were not in a strong position to squawk when the couple concurrently worked with *Outboard,* and *Popular Boating* magazines.

Perhaps like me, other avid consumers of Bowman boat literature pictured him in a luxurious New York City office, gazing through a spectacular window on the 55th floor toward the shipping on the Hudson River. Between leisurely puffs on a pipe, he'd dictate a little copy into a tape recorder for transcription by the secretarial pool, take an early lunch, maybe receive a call from a Mercury big shot, then knock off for the day at, say, quarter past two. Truth is, he worked on an 8 a.m. to 8 p.m. schedule at home. Son Craig can close his eyes and see him sitting at the kitchen table (in the family house in Solebury, Pennsylvania) with a blue editing pencil going over some manuscript. And always battling deadlines from three or four different publications.

In 1953, Bowman began burning extra midnight oil during an 18-month project culminating in *The Encyclopedia of Outboard Motorboating* (A.S. Barnes Co., 1955). Even today, clamp-on aficionados agree that this book is still largely relevant. It included a chapter on outboard/stock racing. Although many consider the *Encyclopedia* to be his finest contribution to outboarding, Bowman was most proud of something related to a more traditional form of journalism. His real writing passion was *Waterline,* the weekly column syndicated to about 200 newspapers like the *Miami Herald, Boston Globe,* and dozens of tiny weeklies. Via *Waterline,* he had a pipeline to every nook and cranny of North America. Because of the need to meet a readership with "mass appeal" boat information, racing wasn't a major focus, but received an occasional mention that sent word

of the sport to millions more than would ever see a copy of *Boat Sport.* Much of the material for *Waterline* came from "adventures" dreamed up by his Boat and Motor Writers organization. The firm's stationery advertised: "Complete photo and text coverage of all types of boating and automotive events." It also boasted a half-dozen "member writers," the likes of those who skipped that aforementioned Chicago

Deep in thought about a test tachometer reading, Bowman (left) gathers data for an outboard/propeller performance article while his wife Blake Gilpin and a manufacturer's rep look on.

breakfast. That left just Bowman and his wife, but they were never short on ideas. In the kitchen he might suggest: "How 'bout I do an article on what it's like to run the Miami-to-Nassau race?" If Blake agreed, Hank would take the concept to the standard roster of publishers until one gave him a go-ahead. Then, he'd call boat and motor makers in an effort to get a loaner rig for the event. Symbiotically, the makers stood to receive positive publicity. He'd get paid for the story, plus augment an already strong readership reputation for having personally been in the race. Because the boating public considered him to be a one-man marine *Consumer Reports*, Bowman did not take his responsibility lightly. There were times when, after borrowing a manufacturer's product for a test run, he was unable to recommend it. He felt the value of his name, and his public would be harmed if he overlooked even a minor production flaw in the resulting "test report."

Mercury factory owner Carl Kiekhaefer knew of Bowman's trusted image, and read everything he wrote about outboard motors. The colorful industrialist didn't take well to even a touch of deserved "bad publicity." Nor did he like to see Hank write anything good about Evinrude or other competitors. More than once, a few lines in *Boat Sport* would cause the Bowman telephone to ring. Primary school-aged Craig might answer, only to hear a hopping-mad voice scream, "Where's that @%&$#! Hank Bowman. . . !@$%*+#!" "Daddy," the then youngster would exclaim, "there's a bad man on the phone saying lots of swear words." Hank would quietly shoo his son into the next room, then yell back, "Carl . . . How many times do I have to tell you not to expose my kids to profanity?!"

Like clockwork, about a week later, a Railway Express truck would pull into the Bowman driveway to drop off a new Merc *KF-5* or something. From about 1953 through the early sixties, Hank would get "shipments" from Kiekhaefer, as an apology for yelling at him or the kids. Once there was a nice *Mark 20H.* Not wanting to be compromised, Bowman typically gave the motors away.

Outboard and stock racing's influence began fading by 1960. Martin, and it's competition line-up, was long gone; Champion had been a recent casualty of closure and Mercury pulled the era's last Quicksilver lower unit-equipped engine from the 1959 catalog. Almost concurrently, the associated publications, most notably *Boat Sport,* had folded. Through several early sixties *Outboard Boating Handbook* editions, Hank kept open a nationwide channel of racing coverage with a few back pages of photos and captioning in tiny chapters typically titled, for example, *The Racing Year, 1962.* To fill a subject void caused by the shrinking closed-course marketplace, he concentrated his evaluative writing efforts on pleasure craft. When *Popular Boating* failed, the publishers of *Rudder* magazine asked Bowman to transfer his "contributing editorship" to their periodical in 1964. Material often came from a boat testing service he headquartered in his home. Through the fifties and early 1960s, hundreds of honestly accurate articles bearing a Hank Bowman byline gave his name a *Good Housekeeping*-like trademark. Marine manufacturers were quite willing to pay (and loan a rig) for a chance to pass muster, thus netting his public seal of approval.

Hank Bowman never raced in a traditional (Class "A" - "F") stock outboard event, like the ones he made famous with his words and pictures. Once OPC took hold in the beginning sixties, however, Bowman "competed in most major powerboat races involving the craft [of] the type used in pleasure boating." According to the *New York Times,* "these included off shore races and marathons for outboard pleasure boats such as the Hudson River Marathon, which he won in 1963."

Champion stock marathoner (and propeller maker) Craig DeWald benefited from Hank and Blake's mentoring. When interviewed for *Vintage Culture,* he had many good things to say about the couple, and remembered Bowman's enthusiasm about OPC events. Set to cover — from the docks — a January 1966 "Nine Hour Endurance Marathon" on Florida's rough Biscayne Bay, "Hank jumped at the chance to run an inboard/outboard catamaran no one else would try in the race." The *New York Times* noted that before hopping into the 310 horse MerCruiser-powered craft, he'd told friends the "race would probably be his last because he was getting too old for the hectic action." Coast Guard reports indicate his boat "flipped on a turn in the choppy waters of the (4.2 mile) course and ran over him."

During the decade and a half (1946-61) of outboarding's most spectacular growth, Hank Bowman was truly its best spokesperson. His prolific life had been so positively intertwined with most every aspect of small powerboating, that, for many buffs, non-Bowman magazine articles on the subject seemed to lack personality and conviction. After all, most *Happy Days*-era folks interested in boats and motors recognized his name and appreciated his straightforward style. Occasionally after his passing, a Bowman reprint would appear in *BoatCraft,* or some other ad hoc periodical, and a new generation got to enjoy his style.

Around 1970, I bought by mail order a new (3rd printing, 1963) copy of his *Encyclopedia of Outboard Motor Boating.* Since then, it has provided me hours of enjoyment — especially the racing section — and served as a catalyst for my *Old Outboard Book,* as well as for *Golden Age, Beautiful Outboards,* and *Vintage Culture.* Every time I open one of his publications, something new often jumps out. For example, in the preparation of this chapter, I reread the *Encyclopedia's* introduction only to recognize an encrypted signal of Bowman's greatest ability... He wrote: "I wish to acknowledge generous cooperation from many sources. In particular I wish to thank Tracey Ogden and Craig Mallery, contributors to *Outboard* magazine and recognized outboarding authorities for carefully checking over the contents of the book prior to its submission to the publisher." Of course, he was Tracey Ogden and Craig Mallery, et al. But that was the genius of Hank Wieand Bowman . . . making a little sport in which pint-sized boats and motors racing for tiny prizes take on qualities that are larger than life.

Chapter Seven

Equal Opportunity Outboarding

"During the turbulent late '60s, when my dad was researching racing
history for the Antique Outboard Motor Club, he'd often notice
decades-old references to an equal opportunity oasis that bra-burning
feminists all over the TV news had apparently missed. It's evident that
from day one, outboard racing has been about the only organized
recreational pursuit to be essentially gender neutral."
—*Accomplished stock outboard racer R. C. Hawie recalling his late
father and first AOMC historian, Richard Hawie.*

*M*Y UNIVERSITY RAN A DIVERSITY ISSUES seminar around the time this
chapter was being written. Enthusiastically, I tried reversing the tide of discrimination horror stories and offered positive words regarding outboard racing's long track
record of integrating women into the sport. But nobody there seemed relieved. It was
like hearing about equal opportunity outboarding had wrecked their perfect storm. And
perhaps that's why this relatively unbiased little oasis remains largely a secret.
Considering that outboard racing has had neither a women's division nor modified physical requirements for females, it might amaze modern sociologists that any woman ever
succeeded in the endeavor. In fact, most who have participated have had fun *and* done
well.

It was a woman who co-founded what became the world's best-known outboard
motor company. Only weeks into the job of running the business side of her family's
fledgling firm, Bess Evinrude understood that attracting females into outboarding would
be imperative if Evinrude Motors wanted a chance to reach more than 50 percent of the
available consumers. That's why she made sure young ladies were often pictured operating the engines in Evinrude ads. Reportedly Mrs. Evinrude selected models who looked
wholesome, but not so knockout pretty that boating buffs might doubt the girl's ability
to adjust the carburetor, snap the flywheel knob to life or robustly pull a starter cord.
When big motors were coming on line in the late 1920s, Bess pushed for the (1930) electric starting feature. Ad copy suggested that top-of-the-line Evinrudes were entirely practical for women to operate.

Loretta Turnbull's effervescent personality made her a fan favorite while her driving acumen earned her tremendous respect from racing colleagues. After winning 48 trophies — in rigorous Class "C" competition primarily with men — Turnbull retired from the sport in 1935 and married her doctor fiancée who'd worked his way through medical school as an outboard mechanic. Many of her hydroplanes came from the California-based Crandall (Comet) Boat Company, and were dubbed Sunkist Kid *in connection with her father's association with the Sunkist Orange Growers group. She passed away in 2001. (Courtesy of the Weston Hook archive.)*

Even to chauvinists' eyes, her advertising said *effortless, reliable, and convenient.* For Mrs. Evinrude's way of thinking, getting females interested in outboard boating was simply a logical move. Her policies on the matter melded into Evinrude/Elto corporate culture and spread through much of the industry. Maybe that's why no one thought it particularly odd when *Power Boating* reported on a 1920 outboard race in which several of the 68 drivers happened to be women. While the magazine did note that the ladies received a five-pound box of candy in addition to their cash prizes, and then pictured two of competitors with the caption "lady putt-putt enthusiasts," male racers were similarly posed and dubbed "enthusiast." Those who'd object to the "lady" prefix should understand that it was an expected, universal protocol of the era.

By the late 1920s, outboard racing rigs had sped well past the 10- to 14-mph putt-putt zone. On their knees, real competitors drove stepped hydroplanes within inches of rival craft at 30 to 40 miles per hour. Especially skilled in this world of high-powered detachables was Loretta Turnbull. Dubbed "queen of the outboard racers" (and yes, there were complementary "kings") she began running tiller-steered craft at age 14, and became a tenacious star favored by Evinrude. Turnbull campaigned one of the venerable firm's unique, tractor lower unit-equipped (thus very torquey) *Speeditwin*s. By the early 1930s, she had switched to the popular Class "C" Johnson mills, in order to be able to continue competing on equal terms with other women and men. The Monrovia, California, resident's first boat got dubbed *Hezy-Tate,* but after upgrading hulls, Turnbull's new boats (12 in all) wore the *Sunkist Kid* name. She authored a feature article in the March 1929 *National Outboard,* which appears to provide her equal billing with male counterparts. Turnbull's "Small Things, What They Mean in Champ Racing," offers competitors empirical advice. There is no hint of some "powder puff derby;" rather she outlines, instead, doing experimental work on sparkplugs and two-cycle engines. She admits to having driven "in thirty regattas and dog-tailing in most of the races until [finding] out that the little things and failure to observe them, lose races. [The day she] had everything right," Turnbull spoke from experience, [she] "won the title of which [she was] so proud." In describing this champion's acumen, one *Power Boating* (March 1929) columnist called her boat "that long, slender nose affair that appears to be so unseaworthy but which Miss Loretta Turnbull puts to such good advantage." She did so all over the world, ostensibly serving as outboard racing's goodwill ambassador. After returning from European racing, she was seriously injured in a 1931 flip at a Hamilton, New York, event. Though out of the action for the National Outboard Championships, Turnbull still received considerable press in the races' coverage.

During the Depression of the 1930s, hydroplane competition got faster and more sophisticated. While such increased seriousness in most other assumedly male sports

closed them to females, racing a small outboard-powered boat was still not necessarily considered unladylike. Perhaps it was the perceived "softness" of water? Maybe society had long accepted women rowing dinghies, going for a sail, handling a simple motorized craft, or paddling a canoe? It also could have been that people fitted with lifejacket, leather helmet and goggles looked rather asexual anyway. Whatever the reasons, outboard racing was one of the first forms of equal

A 1923 Evinrude ad shows a woman (with her bathing stockings partially rolled down!) ready to run her model N Sportwin. Even in outboard promotion's earliest days, it was not uncommon to see females at the engine's controls.

opportunity competition. Any woman able to rope over her motor was welcome to race with the guys.

Ruth Herring's husband, Marion, started a boat business in Fort Worth, Texas. That was during the early 1930s, when advertising money was tough to come by. So, to promote the venture, *Boat Sport* noted, the couple "organized a boat club in which each member agreed to purchase a boat and motor." Marion Herring didn't want to get in the racing craft, but was quick to volunteer Ruth. After flipping that (Flowers-brand) hydro, landing Herring and her nice new 1932 Johnson *KR-55* in the drink, Ruth got the hang of staying right-side up. But another man-sized mishap loomed on the horizon. *Boat Sport* asked her about the 1933 NOA Nationals in Chicago. Going full throttle under a huge bridge, she forgot to take the wind suction into consideration. The wind lifted her rig and slammed it down on top of her head. "The next thing I knew," she recalled, "I was wearing my boat for a necklace. The racer sustained a skull fracture from that tangle that troubled her for the next year and a half." Through 1935, though, Herring set numerous NOA world's records in Class "A." She was so concerned something might happen to the nicely tuned *KR,* that when staying in a hotel the night before a race, the outboard stayed with her. Attention to detail — just as Turnbull had practiced — earned her the honorary title "Grand Lady of speedboat racing."

Other noted pre-World War II outboard racers include Isabel Clark and Helen Henstchel. From 1927 through 1929, Henstchel competed very successfully in Classes "B" and "C." She was the first American woman to do so in Europe. Later, the dynamic Ethel Wiget did

HILDA MUELLER
National Champion, Class A, Division One,
for Two Consecutive Years

National Outboard Championship Regatta

Bay City, Michigan
October, 7·8·9·10
1932

for . . .
Outboard Championships of America and World's Records

Races Sanctioned by
National Outboard Association
American Power Boat Association

Under Auspices of
Bay City Outboard Association
Michigan Boating Association

Sponsored by
National Outboard Championship
Regatta, Incorporated

Souvenir Scoring Program Price 15 Cents

Illustrative of outboard racing's egalitarian culture is this souvenir program from the 1932 Nationals. Because Class "A" (Johnson KR) driver Hilda Mueller racked up an impressive pair of previous national championships, her likeness is on the document's cover.

well throttle squeezing everything from "A" to "C" hydro, as well as "C" Service runabout. This famous racing Wiget (her husband Bud is the other one) even served as "riding mechanic" on a fast "F" runabout when the rules allowed two-person teams. In this class, the rider hung on to deck handles, shifting his or her weight to help steer the zipping boat. Though I've unearthed nothing in the epoch's literature that demonstrates palpable gender bias, the weight issue has popped up occasionally in informal interviews. In fact, the seemingly unrelated fat distribution topic generated faded remnants of the only bias against female outboarders I have ever detected. A couple of male racers hinted that

women's upper body weight and wider hips provides them with an unfair advantage over male racers. It has something to do with the vital balancing act that outboard races really are. "When every second up on plane in a light-as-a-feather seven-foot hydroplane counts," one oldtimer reasoned, "anyone with five or so extra pounds up there able to be quickly distributed over the steering wheel and deck can keep her boat parallel with the water on even the choppiest race course. Plus," he conclud-

Anne Jensen "peels out" of the Albany pits to test her 22-1/2-horse Evinrude Speeditwin and family runabout. On the dock, several others with the impending 1947 Hudson River race to New York City on their minds can't help but react to this competitor's verve. By 1950, she'd traded in the Class "C" Speeditwin for a more powerful "E" Class Speedifour. (Albany Times-Union)

ed, "a few extra pounds of natural padding on the bottom sure doesn't hurt the center of gravity situation or bumpy going during a long marathon. No wonder lots of those gals beat us guys!"

Actually, there was a racing class formed, one might speculate, to take some pressure off male throttle jockeys. Alcohol fuel racer Eleanor Shakeshaft personified the kind of driver Evinrude had in mind when it conceived a Lilliputian class of competition mill. Originally labeled *sub-Class A,* the new category was soon named "M" (for Midget Motor) by its originator. Evinrude/Elto's *Midget Racer* debuted in 1933 with a modest 7 1/2-cubic-inch piston displacement. The tiny, opposed-twin was quickly embraced by kids and petite women. At first, the company predicted its cute kicker might do 20 to 25 miles per hour, but serious alky drivers like Shakeshaft coaxed the mini motors past forty. Though also skilled in Class "A" hydro piloting, the Mt. Kisco, New York resident set an

Ethel Wiget heads for the checkered flag in her Johnson KR-powered Neal hydro. Here, she is competing in a Class "A" alky race.

"M" world record at the 1949 Nationals. She got her minuscule, 7-1/2-cubic inch Evinrude up to 42.303-mph. That level of speed had caught the attention of fellows such as Seattle area outboard accessories manufacturer Len Keller, who started his knee pad career with one of the little powerplants. And Pennsylvania dentist Dr. Frawley decided to drive "M" exclusively, eventually racking up records as impressive as Shakeshaft's. For men to follow women's examples was not an arcane occurrence in outboard racing.

In September 1954, *Speed Age* covered female boat racers and praised their willingness to go beyond the glory of the checkered flag. "Not only do they compete," the magazine noted, "they also serve as officials in regattas. They work in the pits. [As racing family partners] they often go without many little conveniences to help keep a [boat/motor] outfit, worth hundreds [of dollars] in top running order. But those things do not provoke headlines." With that appreciation, *Speed Age* heartily delivered the editors' "considered opinion that we do need women in motorboat racing because there are still too few of them, and with more women, the sport may again acquire that magic called *color* . . . And boat racing can still use it, as exemplified by the colorful racing gals of the past." This sentiment, echoed elsewhere in the sport's literature, was hardly a call for discrimination.

The introduction of stock competition, after World War II, brought a greater number of women onto the racecourse, thus providing for an atypical 1950s feminine experience. When petite Dottie Mayer put on her crash helmet and life jacket, she didn't exactly fit the period's *Father Knows Best* television image of a domesticated mother. Not many other women from suburban College Point, Long Island, admitted to having outboard racing in their blood. Then again, not many could say they'd received a Class "M" Midget hydro outfit as an engagement gift. According to *Boat Sport* (February 1954), Mayer's future husband, Emil, thought the boat and little Evinrude motor might be a good way to explain the joys of his hobby. The soon-to-be bride gave throttle-squeezing a try and, during the 1941 Albany-to-New York Marathon, became the first woman to complete the 130+ mile slog in an alky hydroplane. She continued campaigning her diminutive "M"

Eleanor Shakeshaft's outfit of racing togs, sneakers, sneakers, life vest (with head support), and lightweight crash helmet was standard 1940s-1950s issue for outboarders of either sex. By the early 1960s, though, such headgear was replaced by what is typically termed a "full motorcycle-type" helmet. The older style cap offered no neck protection and its visor "beak" could snap the head if suddenly met with 40+ mph water resistance. Here, Shakeshaft relaxes before a race in her tiny Class "M" hydro dubbed S-P-O-R-T for Shakeshaft Professional Outboard Racing Team.

rig into the 1950s, often enlisting Emil and her primary school-age daughter, Pat, to assist as crew. Mayer proved outboard racing could be a true family affair.

Marilyn Donaldson, too, challenged the stereotypical notion of what a girl was supposed to do in the Cold War era. While her friends might have been playing with their stuffed animals, she was fooling with the high-speed needle on her *Mercury KG-4H Rocket Hurricane.* The Dayton, Ohio, youth began racing (with a *KF-5*) at age 11, after watching her father run big Mercs in "DU" competition. During the racing season, she traveled as much as 500 miles a week to compete in "JU," "AU," "BU," "ASH," as well as "BSH." The 1951 Winnebagoland Marathon gave her resume a lift when at age 14 she won its "AU" event. *Boat Sport* proudly noted that the victory made her the first young woman to ever finish the rugged 92-mile race, and "the first minor to win it." And then just for good measure, Donaldson dug out her little Mercury *KF-5,* shooting it through an APBA five-miles-in-competition mark at 22.026 mph. The well-throttled cruise helped her snag a national "JU" speed record in 1952.

Donaldson's racing relationship with her dad was not particularly unusual, as many outboarding fathers (albeit, often those without sons) encouraged their daughters to round the buoys. After all, there was a rich history of positive role models like Turnbull and Shakeshaft. Engine builder Randolph Hubbell introduced his daughter to the sport. Like other dads, he understood that through his careful mentoring, racing could help instill confidence, planning preparedness, networking, strategy skills, some mechanical know-how, concentration, focus, and a useful degree of nerve. Undoubtedly there were boat racing families that mused — "What parent wouldn't want these strengths developed in a daughter, especially one subsequently heading off to the university and then into the real world?" And finally, as a true testament to outboard racing's history of equality, this book need not segregate women racers into a single chapter. The reader can find other evidence of both genders participating head-to-head throughout the text.

Chapter Eight

Cottage Racers

"Skeeter isn't designed for sanctioned races as she won't make their hairpin turns, but [the 7-foot 10-inch plywood hydro] readily planes with a 5-horse outboard. This nautical punkin' seed will whip the pants off many highly-touted commercial speedboats."
—*1950s* Science and Mechanics *craft print #157 boat plan description.*

*A*DISTANT HUM WAVERED through an open summer cabin window. Jim Bouton's parents didn't wake to the porpoising sound, but it piped him to consciousness. "Who's out on the lake at six?" the teen wondered, reaching for his grandfather's old binoculars. "And what kind of motor is making that whine?" He caught just a glimpse of black, silver, and blue before the bouncing spec disappeared past the purview of his tiny loft window.

Perennially downcast Harry Haylett at the marina didn't remember details. He was just a landlubber begrudgingly pumping gas and selling snacks during college summers at his uncle's small establishment. "I told you, Bouton," he said drowsily, "to me boats and

The author and his cottage racing rig. Although having won the 1953 Stock Outboard Nationals under the driving skills of Dick O'Dea, this Sid Craft runabout was far from seriously competitive when the picture was snapped in the summer of 1971. Before the author acquired it (and a blown-up Merc KG-7Q) for $50, the bottom had been repaired with a heavy patchwork of replacement wood and several coats of fiberglass with wavy resin. For an additional 10 bucks, a casually spray painted Mercury KF-7 powerhead was rescued for the old Sid Craft from a crumbling outbuilding of a bucolic marina. Amazingly the leaky little craft and ratty mill hit 40-mph and could best most other local family pleasure craft equipped the then usual 25 to 60-horse OMC models. What a delight it was to have observers ask, "Did you say your boat only has a 10-hp motor?"

This grainy 1950s photo shows a father and daughter "cottage racing team" in their Minimax hydro. Robert Mills sent the picture to Science and Mechanics *with the* caption, "It's the first boat I ever attempted to make." The Marshalltown, Iowa, man was one of thousands who sent for the magazine's Minimax plans and followed through to enjoy the finished product. Though designed for the docile style of "five-and-change" horsepower fishing outboard that Mills used, more than a few of these eight-footers were over-powered with the likes of a Mercury Mark 25 or better! The now decades-old boat design was amazingly stable and has been resurrected for the 21st Century in an update by a kit boat firm in the Buffalo, New York, area.

motors are all the same. I got other things to worry about besides who's got what smelly eggbeater on what leaky tub." Harry's better-spirited relative caught the end of the conversation, smiled and walked on to the dock. For an old guy, Elton Haylett sure could make lugging a full six-gallon gas can in each hand look like fun. "Jim," he winked, "is tough-break Harry giving you static?" The sour nephew threw up his hands in disgust and bounded toward the little office/store. "Naw, Harry's OK, Mr. Haylett. I was just asking him about a new boat I thought I saw this morning."

"Real early today, son?"

"Right around six, sir."

"Yeah, I heard someone ripping around out there when I first opened up this morning. I'll bet it was that rich kid whose family rented the Delaney place at the end of the lake."

"Rich kid?"

"Sure, they're loaded with dough! The fellow brought his kid in Friday. Had a nice blue Arkansas Traveler 12-footer. Wanted some gas and oil, then asked me to show the kid how to start the outboard. Imagine that, bought a new rig at the boat show, and had no idea what it was or how it worked. Don't them rich folks beat all?!"

"Do you remember the motor, Mr. Haylett?"

"Ah, Jimmy Boy, I wondered when you'd ask me that. Remember when you were in the shop looking through my stack of *Boating Handbook* magazines, and you showed me the picture of that new Martin "200" and racing lower unit?"

"Yes sir, I asked if you'd ever seen one in person."

"Well, son, now I can say I actually have. That rich kid who woke you up on this beautiful day had one of those very same pressure-cooking big Martins. Oooweee, what a racy gearcase on that baby! Mean-lookin' little speed-prop, too."

Lost in wistful momentary reflection, the marina owner recounted the tale about his brief stint as a Martin dealer prior to hitting upon "the deal of a lifetime" when Scott-Atwater came a'callin.' But Jim had enjoyed the story before, so could take a moment to deal with the inevitable possibility that his plywood craft and tire store outboard were no longer sovereigns of the little waterway he called home. For most of the week, that elusive oscillation from the mysterious rich kid's Martin served as the 14-year-old boating buff's alarm clock. Jim resolved to move up his timetable for the next morning to see if he could catch his rival.

The early air was chilly enough to have left dew all over the Sea-Bee outboard. It made the steering grip slippery. Jim gave the tiller a quick dry off with his jacket sleeve. A couple pulls on the cord got the boy's 10-footer underway. He deftly crouched over the craft's "wheel deck" and on the boat's modest front seat, coaxing the craft to plane. It was at this point when Jim felt most at one with his motor. As if mechanically linked to the 12-horse, something ethereal communicated to him every spark, compression, and metering of fuel. A skip unnoticeable by ordinary owners would send a diagnostic signal to Jim comparable to a doctor's electrocardiogram. So far, all was well on his smooth-surfaced kingdom.

There's a spit of land, where anglers like to hide, jutting out from the little lake's otherwise predictable shoreline. Suddenly, from behind a group of pines on that point, Jim spotted his challenger. The two small boats toyed with their territories for a few minutes.

The true satisfaction of cottage racing is having your tiny craft pull ahead of much more powerful boats. That's what's happening in this scene where a 10-foot hull and six-horse Merc overtakes a cruiser pushed by a mill with at least 10 times the output. Ok, so there are a ton of people and gear in the bigger boat, and the big motor is a Mercury, too, but . . .

Then, the sleek blue aluminum craft made a deliberate run toward Jim Bouton. He thought about the approaching Martin while glancing at his Sea Bee's mag lever. For an instant, the puffy-looking private-brander seemed silly, but the thought was cast away as an easy prejudice a "real" brand-name motor like the oncoming "200" can erroneously plant.

Old man Tacker knew his racing. Although his hydro was long gone, he still had an alky Evinrude "M" from the thirties hanging on a set tub in his cabin garage. The sight off his screened porch prompted a competitive grin and enthusiastic swig of steaming cocoa. "Well, Hubbell," he whispered knowingly to his purring cat, "looks like Jimmy-Boy and that new boat are about to give us a little excitement today." Then he turned commentator for the feline audience. "A-hoo, there they go! The newcomer's Martin has got eight horses over Bouton's mill, but they're pretty much even out there. No wonder, with the blue tin boat porpoising like that." He moved through the squeaked-open porch door to get a better look around the huge trees marking his side yard. "Still dead-even, Hub. What a contest! They'll have to turn and head back our way cuz they're running out of lake."

Sure enough, the race continued after both boats rounded an invisible buoy Jim marked in his imagination years ago. The senior citizen transitioned from spectator to participant by grabbing a flag he'd attached to his stairs in early July, and happily made a beeline for the end of his rickety dock. He raised the banner with one lanky hand, while animatedly pointing at it with the other. The kids caught the drift and sped toward the newly established finish. A hundred yards from Tacker it was a certain tossup. "Come on, Jim-Boy!" he yelled with Hubbell suspiciously watching from the beach. "Get down outta the wind resistance."

The Sea-Bee was stressed to its limit and revving higher than the salesman in the Goodyear place, back home, would recommend. Michigan Wheel had promised Dad, though, that the accessory AJ-20 high-speed prop wouldn't harm the engine. Jim had placed the bronze two-blade high on his Christmas list. *TO: Our Motorboat Racer. FROM: Santa's Helpers,"* a tag on the box had read. "Hope this makes your sleigh go faster!"

The Martin kid made two fists around the motor's red plastic fluted steering/throttle grip. An extra 1/4-inch twist didn't seem to make any difference. The big black and silver powerhead sang loudly, playing the jumping boat's bottom like an overeager percussionist. A small rooster tail welled up about three feet aft. Now only 20 yards away from Tacker's flag, the competitors had mere seconds until one would be honored as "champion" by an old man's friendly gossip. Tacker stuck out his arm to eye the crucial demarcation, then marshaled reserve strength onto the flagstaff. It was waved as about a half-dozen inches of nose on Jim's clear-coated runabout painfully crossed the line. Mercifully unvanquished, he immediately began easing the mag lever back to slow and turned for the dock. The rich kid, expressionless, stayed wide open while veering off toward the spit. The boat was gone even before Jim had a chance to tie up. He knew Tack would have something to say.

"Well Kiddo, you're still the number one cottage racer around these parts."

"Barely," the boy admitted.

"Just barely are very important words here," unfolded the veteran's wisdom. Both you kids' motors check in at just under 20-cubes, but that Martin is meant for real Class "B" work. Your Sea-Bee is a good kicker, but it's a fishin' engine. Your dad was the one who picked it out, right? You won because of driving experience. Ain't nothin' wrong with that. And, why did the other kid lose?" he asked expecting a thoughtful answer.

"Probably all the stuff in the boat."

"And?" he waited like a grandfatherly marine sage.

"And, the tilt angle on the Martin was kicked way out."

"Sure was. Out a mile. That's why the kid's boat was bucking so much that a kindly 'ol Sea-Bee 12 could win the race. Plus," Mr. Tacker reminded, "smart driving on your account, Jim. Don't get me wrong, you did well today."

There they were. The veteran racer holding court on the dock, with the boy looking up from his little boat. "Jim, when I was at the sportsman's show last spring, I seen how easy it is to adjust them Martin transom angles. All you gotta do is turn the handle between the clamps."

"I know. I've got a new Martin catalog and read about the easy adjustment, Mr. Tacker. Maybe I should let the other kid know."

"Probably means you'll lose your *fastest boat on the lake* title," he admitted. "When that Arkansas Traveler planes out, it's really gonna go. 'Course, you know the true spirit of cottage racing includes sharing what you know with your competitors. That way, the competition become friends, they give some of their competition secrets with you, and the racing stays fun. Remember, Jimmy-Boy, people are more important than boats and motors. Live like you're in a race to make and keep the most friends. That's one really worth the checkered flag."

During the conversation, Hubbell had walked across the dock and jumped on to the front seat of Jim's craft. "That dang cat," Tack laughed "always nosing into other people's business. Like me, I guess."

"Naw... actually, you've given me something to think about."

At supper, Jim's folks mentioned bumping into the elderly gentleman downtown. "Mr. Tacker mentioned something about you helping someone with motor troubles."

"No Dad, not really. There was nothing actually wrong with the engine. Just needed some adjusting."

"Well, that's nice, honey," Jim's mom smiled, "we're glad you're willing to share your knowledge with others, even with visitors to the lake."

Mr. Bouton agreed, especially since the boy's advice had later allowed that Martin to best his Sea-Bee. "Son, what would you say to trading the old *12* for one of those 16-horse Scotts over at Haylett's?" I hear there's even a racing lower unit accessory available for that model." But the ninth-grader's mind was elsewhere. He even stared silently past his favorite summer supper dish. Mrs. Bouton broke through the odd silence. "Jimmy," she wondered, "is your new motor friend about your age?"

"Uh... yeah, I guess so." he noted quickly, now ready to shield himself behind a long drink of milk. "Or, maybe she said she was fifteen."

There is an art form called cottage racing. Practiced well, even the most impecunious outboarder can use it to transform modest equipment into a new *Swift Big Bee* hydro and bright blue *6N-HR Champion Hot Rod*. Notches in speed depend, most importantly upon emotional dedication to the genre. Magically, the more motors one can identify merely by sound, the faster your dented aluminum rowboat will go. In these craft, imagination equals quality. It's also vital to begin small and think big. Early victories can best be won with a low-power kicker missing enough parts to make it seem really useless and daring to ordinary consumers. "If it's noisy, it must be fast!" And then there's the unwritten rule cottage racers loyally embrace: *No lower cowling or fully intact rewind starting.* Above all, practitioners of this sport understand their endeavors are meant purely for enjoyment. Here, feelings matter. It's agreed that no one ever holds a cottage regatta unless it's sanctioned under the auspices of fun. Anytime that spirit is weakened, the affected cottage racer may head to shore — especially when you're only racing against yourself.

The pursuit got its name from good-natured performance rivalries found on every navigable waterway. Few were the summer cottage folks who didn't know which was the fastest boat around their lake, river, or ocean bay. Speed buffs also kept track of runners-up and new comers out to make a reputation. While the sleekest craft and tallest motors were often much admired by this crowd, their

"The magazine that shows people how" was at its best during the 1950s boating boom. That's when Science and Mechanics *made sure each issue made some reference to building one's own boat. The April 1956 issue is a case in point, as a lively cover illustration of a step-bottomed hydro shared equal billing with a sporty car. The magazine offered hundreds of craft prints, including plans for dozens of cottage racing hulls. Enthusiasts who sent for the prints and construction procedures were usually treated to several concluding paragraphs of "outboard racing hints."*

scuttlebutt might center upon a clever do-it-yourself hull like the "soapbox" boats once popular among penurious skippers on Long Island. These were concocted from a mere sheet of 4 x 8-foot plywood with 2 x 8-inch boards serving as sides, bow, and all-important transom. That's where the captain would hang a mill from the "super bargain" section of the local boat shop's used outboard rack. Motors of 7-1/2-hp or more were coveted for this cottage racing class. One long ago soapbox pilot verified that if the transom board was sturdily nailed into the plywood, one could even dare to use a salty, second-hand 10-horse Merc *Lightning* or *Hurricane*. "But you had to really grip the tiller, and keep looking at the seam between the plywood and transom board," he warned. "If you weren't ready to kill the motor when the soapbox hit some waves and started coming apart, you lost the race *and* your $35 outboard."

There were cottage racers blessed with an erstwhile sanctioned runabout or hydro. Through a member of our church I bought — with $50 painfully scraped-together dollars — an early 1950s Class "A/B" *Sid-Craft* once owned by legendary stock racer Dick O'Dea. Its accompanying *KG-7Q* Merc had blown up and was in a bushel basket under the deck. Consequently, I made a bracket for my 1965 six-horse Mercury, and at least *felt* like a cottage racer for a summer or two. Others were skilled enough to craft nice little racing hulls from magazine plans. Around my dock, there was a perennial argument about how best to finish these projects — with a color scheme of various bright paints, or clear varnish. It was my contention that the latter provided for optimum performance, while many of my compatriots declared that glossy reds and oranges would somehow make such cottage racers notably faster. Regardless of theoretically possible hull choices, flat-bottom wooden rowboats or vee-bottomed aluminum counterparts saw the most cottage racing action. Though a major Coast Guard transgression, the key to victory in this competitive "class" was to violate the horsepower capacity recommendations more vigorously than your rival. Maverick cottage racers laughed at the tiny rectangular Outboard Boating Club *(up to ___ OBC hp)* tags present on the inside of most transoms. If on a patrolled waterway, they'd pry the "10-hp maximum" plate from their featherweight 12-foot aluminum *Lone Star Little Fisherman* before clamping a souped-up 20-horse Merc *Mark 25* to the darn thing. And man, what a ride kneeling between the stern and second seats! A 7-foot 9-inch Arkansas Traveler jon boat now on my shoreline was once partner to a Scott-Atwater over three times more powerful than the craft's suggested limit. That questionable combo survived to remind local folks of the day it was the fastest cottage racer on the river. The fact that it bested several bigger and much more expensive craft put the modest baking pan of a boat (and its Scott *10*) in the local cottage racing hall of fame.

Even if not a structural challenge to the boat, there are motors that can qualify as a cottage racing engine. True devotees to this specialized class understand it is extremely risky to bar any outboard from cottage racer status. Nor should it be considered proper to judge a motor based on operational condition. One of my first cottage races was won with a nonshift six-hp Lauson *Sport King* suffering from horrible ignition coils. It never did start that day. But, neither did my compatriot's corroded forward-only Eska *Golden Jet 5.* We marked the course anyway, agreeing that whoever could continuously pull on their starter cord long enough and fast enough to propel his boat over the finish line would win the "Quicksilver National Championship," . . . or some goofy title we concocted and continued to talk about all that sixth-grade summer.

Vintage Culture's Certified Cottage Racing Engines

Please be advised that outboards on the following alphabetically formatted roster made the cut through careful consideration by a select group of former and current cottage racing drivers. Many are members of the Antique Outboard Motor Club and still compete for fun at various meets. By way of definition, the absolute best examples of this genre of motor:

1. visually and/or audibly impressed kids
2. were missing a few cosmetic parts
3. could suffer a broken rewind starter mechanism and be cranked anyway (preferably by an odd length of abandoned clothesline)
4. could be fitted with an aftermarket *Aqua-Jet* speed prop (from the Michigan Wheel catalog)
5. steered with a tiller, and
6. were available used for "paper route money" (or less than $100).

None were actually designed for out-and-out racing. Those that were, dubbed "factory-built competition engines," are covered in this book's sister volume — *The Golden Age of the Racing Outboard.* This book's cottage racer list represents "regular service" motors that may have been loosely marketed with some aspect of "informal amateur hotrodding" in mind. In no way is it claimed to be exclusive. Nor does the document seek to question youthful competition memories of some imaginative Neptune 1.7-hp *Mighty-Mite* owner who "blew the doors off" an 82-year old neighbor who was paddling a canoe.

CHAMPION
There was a little Mobil gas station in Gloversville, New York, about six miles from the nearest waterway. During the early 1950s, its enthusiastic proprietors decided to branch out to attract local boaters. Amid the grease rack and office, Abbot and Fitzsimmons set up a modest Champion outboard franchise, and even took on a line of aluminum boats. Sunny summer days would find the sawhorse motor display out near the pumps. By 1956, they were able to tell Socony Mobil Oil's publication, *Small Craft News,* that the

Through the early 1960s, few boat and motor shops were the completely bottom line-driven marine mega-marts that dominate pleasure craft retailing today. Many, like this Seattle outboard shop, were staffed by folks who had time to chew the fat about the year's hottest hulls and engines with even the most impecunious enthusiasts, whether adults or kids. Typically the proprietor was the chief boating nut and invited such talk (especially in colder months), as he and his co-proprietor wife lived upstairs and weren't in any particular hurry. "Good" customers made it a point, though, to buy at least a pack of shear pins or maybe a speed prop to go along with the informative conversation and handful of brochures that represented the visit's main purpose. Harland sold Mercury products but his neon sign pointed out "Repairs all makes."

Champs were "easy to sell and that the marine products helped their automotive business." No doubt at least a few of the slender Champion outboards, noticed by dads and sons filling up the family car with high test, were of the 19.94-cubic-inch variety.

First offered for 1953 in *Hydro-Drive* (fluid transmission), or traditional gearshift versions, Champion general-purpose "B" size motors were rated at 15-hp. In 1954, the big *Hydro-Drive* motor was kept at 15, while some stats show the $33 cheaper gearshift model with 14 horses. The novel *Hydro-Drive* feature was discontinued in 1955, but Champion's resulting gearshift capstone outboard was raised to 16.5 horsepower (sometimes called

A nicely restored mid-1950s Champion "B" Hot-Rod with factory open exhaust stack. (It's right behind the top sparkplug wire.) Between events, most racers would stick a clean rag in the assembly's opening so as to prevent foreign matter from getting on the pistons and cylinders.

Catalogued amid smaller sisters like a 7-1/2-horse fishing model was the remarkably compact Champion 15-hp twin. With racy lower unit and high-revving powerhead, this big motor in a little package stood ready to make a cottage racer's dreams come true.

Sweet 16, **Pacemaker**, or **Blue Streak**) where it stayed through the Minneapolis company's 1958 demise.

These were beautiful motors, deceivingly small (just 58 pounds), somewhat busy-sounding, and a rather rare sight on most lakes, even near dealerships like the service station in Gloversville. To be sure, however, on a very light hull with the right prop (allowing for high revving), the 20-cube Champs were fast. After all, they were closely related to the Class "B" Hot-Rods. Also notable cottage racers were the even less common Majestic, and Voyager offshoots. These were Champion's "value-brands," and from 1954-58, came in the 15-hp denomination. An even rarer Sea Flyer 15 was offered through B.F. Goodrich in 1954.

After the factory closed around 1958, racks of leftover Champions (including unsold dealer inventory) sometimes made their way to a deep discounter. Performance outboard buff Rich Yost tells of noticing a 1967 newspaper ad filled with sundry stuff on special. Among the featured items on "closeout" were "real 16.5 horsepower outboards." He drove to the bargain merchandiser to find rows of new 1956 Champions, each with a shiny red remote fuel tank. Yost bought one for $125, and has never run it.

CHRIS-CRAFT

Around the time Eisenhower moved into the White House, boaters were really getting hungry for outboards of all sizes. That's why, in early 1953, a project team at Chris-Craft was excitedly ready to build a prototype 25 horse motor with forward-neutral-reverse. It would have moved the fledgling outboard label into the early 1950s "full-line" (5.5- to 25-hp) club, and given cottage racers something more to talk about.

Alas, by the end of that year, the big boat maker quietly closed its outboard division, leaving the 10-horsepower **Commander** as a legacy to those who appreciate friendly competition. This 19.94 engine is often compared to its "B" class contemporaries from Mercury. A good 10 Chris could make boastful Merc owners eat a few words.

ELGIN

Sears and Roebuck was really pleased with the Elgin outboards that West Bend

Aluminum first designed for them for 1946. The big retailer had no problem selling thousands to people in almost every American and Canadian nook and cranny. From 1950 to 1954, Elgin's biggest was a unique 24-cubic-inch, 16-horse twin. Interesting features included a fiberglass hood and low-mount rewind start (at the bottom front of the cowling). One was sold, in the spring of 1953, to a Central New Yorker who passed away a few months later. I happened upon it in the late 1980s, becoming only the second person to run it. That Elgin 16 allowed me to go back in time, do a little cottage racing against a couple of modern motors, and show off a classic-looking mill. The motor provided a fun ride (on a 14-foot aluminum rowboat), but admittedly wouldn't be a real threat to a good Merc, Chris-Craft 10, or Champion 16 1/2, each of those with 4 fewer cubic inches piston displacement. A few were able to see the checkered flag while a short-lived APBA rule allowed for the circa 25-cubic-inch Class "C-1."

An Elgin that has long impressed some of *Vintage Culture*'s cottage racing panel is the almond-shaped 10.6-cube twin that began life in 1946 as a 5 1/2-horse rope start kicker. Through the 1950s, its block was used on Elgins of 5, 6, and even 7 1/2 horsepower. The best of the genre is the late 40s, pea-soup green version with a little aluminum rope sheave starter pulley (Sears-Elgin was cast onto this piece) peeking above the fuel tank. The motors were well designed, and surprisingly quick on the right hull. Perhaps by coincidence, a significant number of these bargain fishing motors (about $130 new in 1948) have been noted planing *Minimax* hydros. Such craft, made from 25 bucks worth of plywood, required an equal value in pre-owned power. A 1960 used motor guide lists the plentiful Elgin model **571.58611** (a 1947 standard 5.5 hp motor) as having a trade-in value of between $6 and $10. With that size price tag, and nice streamlining, the Elgin 5 1/2 was often just the kind of secondhand outboard an entry-level cottage was looking for. Dealers with mainstream motor franchises always seemed to have at least one on the back motor rack, waiting patiently for a parsimonious cottage racer kid who'd appreciate it.

ELTO (see also: Gale Products)

If we can agree on middle ground that says a good cottage racer should have a sleek, rowboat-length lower unit; steering handle, distinctive exhaust song, telltale cooling water outlet, exhibit speed over power; not be difficult to carry; and have a nicely pitched two-blade bronze prop in its arsenal, then consensus votes the 1928-31 Elto **Service Speedster** (just under 20 cubic inches) as quintessential. Arguably the best utilized of this series are 1928-29 models without underwater exhaust or rudder steering. Amateur water speed buffs not hard hit by the Depression had access to the **# 905 Special Speedster**. Too big to qualify for class "B," but not large enough to fit snugly into "C," this 24.87-cube mill was an amalgamation of parts from other Eltos. Twelve horses and two-blade *High-Speed Speedster* (the factory-built racing *Speedster* version) prop, however, gave it the "guts" to take on a host of competitors. *Special Speedsters* were contemporaries of 1931 through 1933. Those wanting to impress the summer crowd with a big motor could consider any of the following: The 1928-29 **Service Quad** provided its share of Elto cottage racing. [Although the '28 was somewhat faster with a light load.]; 1930-33 **Senior Speedster** 14-hp (which can step lively with a Michigan E-260 speed prop), and standard 21.1 and 25-horse **Super "C"** (1931-33) opposed twins also did the marque proud in informal competition.

EVINRUDE

It wouldn't be too presumptuous to claim that Evinrude helped invent cottage racing. Not that Ole Evinrude thought to promote high-speed outboarding, but his early customers sure did. Informal clamp-on competition began (around 1910-1911) as soon as two or more Evinrude rowboat motors were sold to people on the same lake or river. By 1926, the model *U Speeditwin* represented Evinrude's fastest product, doing the name proud in some 80 different versions into the 1970s. For cottage racers, the favorite **Speeditwin** came with the **6039** designation. This 22.5-horse classic was available from 1939 through 1950 except for the war years. Even then, however, some of these opposed twins were built for military purposes. The long-running 30-cubic inch Evinrude also saw its share of victorious "C" Service racing. Other "certified" Evinrude cottage racers include:

    Lightfour (15-cubic inches, 9.7-hp) 1934-1949. Design-wise, this mill doesn't appear to be a likely racing candidate. Perhaps its four cylinders and nearly 10 full horse power — which was once considered to be the border line into big motordom — put the *Lightfour* in the running.

    Fastwin (19.94-cubic inches, 14-hp) 1950-1952. Truth be told, this motor was euphemistically named. But at least the two-cylinder "twin" statement proved accurate. Upon encountering a Mercury *KG-7 Hurricane Ten,* the wise 1950 *Fastwin* owner quickly took solace in the fact that at least his new 14-hp motor had a F-N-R shift. Oft times, it was put in reverse to back away from such Merc challenges.

The 22.5-horse Evinrude Speeditwin was produced from the late 1930s to 1950. By about 1952, when these large, forward-only motors were made hopelessly out of date by gearshift-equipped outboards, thousands became available on the used market. Many of this legion were picked up for cottage racing duty — as well as for modification in "C" Service competition.

EVINRUDE

EVINRUDE *Super* FASTWIN

15 hp*
67 lbs.

*OBC certified brake
hp at 4000 RPM

A real cottage racing "sleeper," this "average American" Evinrude Super Fastwin delivered 15 legitimate horses from its 20-cubic inch powerhead. Maybe the 1953-56 machine was not an even match for an equivalent Merc, but it was a good compromise between family engine and out-and-out racer. Actually, the Super Fastwin did see a bit of sanctioned 1950s action in the Canadian "BU" category where it competed free of equivalently sized Mercury machines.

Super Fastwin (19.94-cubic inches, 15-hp) 1953-1956. Unlike its predecessor, the completely revamped bearer of *Fastwin* lineage was nicely stated. It commanded 15 legitimate horses, the ability to skim a light hull, and stamina to pull a young water-skier. Plus, the *Super Fastwin* provided the convenience of a full shift. No match for a *Mark 20* contemporary, but a darn good compromise for cottage racers with parents who wouldn't buy "one of those only-good-for-speed" Mercs.

Fleetwin (12.4-cubic inches, 7.5-hp)1950-1954. These blue classics with the top-of-the-tank mounted neutral clutch knob were not especially quick. But there were so many on America's waterways, that batches of evenly matched *Fleetwins* and ubiquitous row-boats saw summers of unofficial stock competition. To aid the sizable fleet of *Fleetwin* cottage racers, Michigan Wheel Company worked up one of its racy *Aqua-Jet* propellers (AJ-420), which was perfect for adding a mile or two per hour over the standard fishing prop.

Speedifour (50-cubic inches, 33.4-hp) 1937-1950 and **Big Four** (59.4-cubic inches, 50-hp) 1946 & 1949. One had to have a good-sized craft to hold either of these giants. While that meant many got pressed into service on houseboats and the new craze, outboard cruisers, the class "E" *Speedifour*, and "F" *Big Four* became instant favorites of marathon competitors. The quads were best capable of pushing a heavy hull through rough waters. In the vernacular of the day, you'd have to have a "screw loose" to attempt hefting one on a small, home-brew racing shingle. Even so, there was always the proverbial guy, fresh out of the service, who built a boxy plywood-looking *Zip,* or *FireFly* boats from *Science & Mechanix* plans. He'd find a cheap, banged-up *Speedifour* in a marina's back room, fix it up, (slop it over with some spare house paint) and be the talk of the local cottage racing community.

GALE PRODUCTS

Johnson's early 1930s purchase of a refrigerator factory in Galesburg, Illinois did little to help the ailing outboard maker. But when Evinrude bought Johnson in 1936, that "Gale"

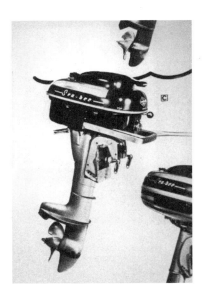

Though incredibly generic, the Gale Products/OMC-based Sea-Bee 12 wore a rear steering bar (for optional wheel steering) and could be quickly fitted with an Aqua-Jet high-speed prop. OMC noticed a large number of their 12-hp engines being drafted into cottage racing, so tendered a page or two of "souping-up" tips for the plain-Jane twin. Sea-Bee motors were sold through Goodyear Tire stores, but the same outboards appeared with different names — like Sea King — for other retailers.

plant figured nicely into the new owner's plans. There in 1949, its line of "value" motors began including the likes of an alternate-firing **Elto "12" Speedster.** "Modern" (post-World War II) Eltos turned out to be one-year American offerings, as the line's name was changed (although Elto continued in Canada through 1958) to **Buccaneer** in 1950. Continued as star of this freebooter marque, however, was the 19.94-cubic inch 12- horse.

Also cranked out by Gale Products (in addition to Elto, Buccaneer, and finally just plain Gale), were private-brand engines for a variety of merchandisers — such as Ward's **Sea King,** Spiegel's **Brooklure,** Fedway's **Saber,** Gamble Stores' **Hiawatha,** Standard Oil's **Royal,** B.F. Goodrich's **Sea Flyer,** as well as the Good Year **Sea-Bee** like Jim Bouton's in our opening story. The best of theses 12-hp cottage racers wore "economy" nonshift lower units. Michigan Wheel took early note of the model's proliferation, and also saw that the typical buyer had at least one kid in the family who wanted an outboard that was a notch above some generic fishing engine. The propeller company's first batches of high performance *Aqua-Jet* bronze two-blades included a racy *AJ-20* for Gale Products' ubiquitous twelves. Oddly, the 12-hp Gale Products powerhead was not dissimilar to Evinrude's logy, 1950-1952 Fastwin. No matter, there was a blip on the stock outboard, outlaw modified, and cottage racing scene when these mills were considered as the poor man's Mercury *Hurricane.* And affordability was built into the design. In 1951, for example, a Merc *KG-7* retailed for $384.50 compared to just $246.75 for the Buccaneer 12. Used, the Gale represented a real bargain basement deal. Even factory officials got word from the hinterlands that their plain Janes were being enlisted for racing purposes and so printed a service bulletin for budget-minded speed demons. The info sheet, *Souping The Elto Speedster,* also applied to other Class "B" non-shift Gale products, and began:

> The Elto (1949) *Speedster* is a fast, well-built motor as it leaves the factory, but where it
> is desirable to squeeze an extra mile or two out of it in racing, some modifications can
> be made. For strictly stock racing, the only permissible changes will be a new propeller,
> and smoothing and polishing the ports, piston heads, and in fact, any surface over

which gas vapor passes. Some additional balancing work can be done. Michigan Wheel Company of Grand Rapids, Michigan, has a two-blade 9 x 10 inch propeller *(AJ-20)* for this motor, which is faster than the standard wheel. However, some who have worked on the Speedster claim the standard wheel is even faster if the rear edge of each blade is trimmed off. It must be trimmed to the point where there is no reverse curve left in the rear edge. This trimming is simply a cut and try proposition.

OMC's tips ventured into the "mod" realm with suggestions of installing a bigger carb and gas line, filing down and polishing the skeg and gearcase, raising compression, and hinting that, if one knew an expert outboard mechanic, he might be employed to convert the Gale Product's motor to burn alcohol fuel. Were any of these suggestions authorized? Well, no. "It must be pointed out," the manufacturer concluded, "that these changes are not recommended by Evinrude Motors, and very definitely void the warranty. They [were] merely presented in answer to definite requests for information" on how to make a garden-variety family outboard into a real neat cottage racer.

JOHNSON

In the midst of the 1930s Depression, Johnson officials knew something in their line would have to be discontinued. That's why for the first time in nearly a decade, the 1935 catalog made no mention of motors over 30 cubic inches. Johnson hoped to move back toward profitability by concentrating on the smaller outboards typically sought by the ubiquitous angler. When Evinrude bought the company in 1936, it promoted Johnson as the dependable fishing engine, leading big-iron buyers straight to the Evinrude dealer. What was left for cottage racers who were loyal to the Sea Horse logo? Many scooted along fine with the 9.8-horse **KA-39** and **KD-15** from 1939 through 1948. By 1949, Johnson replaced these *K* motors with a F-N-R gearshift, remote fuel tank 10- horse **QD.** This was a popular motor that helped define modern (post World War II) out-

Surprising numbers of the Johnson SD outboards showed up in cottage racing circles. That's mostly because their 16-hp rating seemed all powerful to lots of early 1950s boaters, and many of the rather clunky looking 1940-'50 motors had been mercifully relegated to the trade-in rack. What's more, the SD had a rear-mounted steering bar, ample tiller handle/twist grip throttle, and lots of powerhead shrouding that could be taken off for effect.

Arguably, the most ubiquitous OMC cottage racing mill, the Johnson PO (1937-1950) possessed the power to get even weightier wooden boats up on plane. While there were fac-tory-installed eyelets (on the muffler bottom) and rear motor rests (on back of the muffler) drilled to accept a rear steer-ing bar, some PO owners found Johnson's longer accessory tiller/handle/throttle control to be extremely useful when they crouched forward for optimum hull planning/balance. The use of a two-blade speed prop and removal (by four short bolts) of the muffler relief cover could make the 22-horse twin a real mover, and loud, too! Because it had no gearshift, many were traded in (or sold outright quite rea-sonably) for the full-shift OMC models that hit the boating scene around 1951. Some were modified for sanctioned "C-Service" use. A chief cottage racing controversy was whether or not PO was faster than Evinrude's Speeditwin, as both had just about equal horsepower.

boarding. Memory banks are filled with scenes of teens racing Dad's trusty *QD* against lesser kickers. As long as no Mercs were around, the results were typically *Sea Horse* pos-itive. Then there was the 1940-50 **SD** series. Suffice it to say, the bulbous 16-hp, *looked* like it should be fast — if powerhead girth meant anything. For a while, the *SD* even appeared to be highly futuristic, at least in the sense that actors dressed in robot suits in a 1930s sci-fi movie were prescient. Arguably, the *SD* was Waukegan's first shot into com-pletely shrouded "modern" motordom, impressing numerous informal outboard speed buffs. More than a few of the big "round tankers" got their mag levers and throttle han-dles advanced against other-branded foes. Once 1947 rolled around, *SD* owners began picking their battles more carefully, and knew enough to stay away from the darker green challengers bearing a Mercury *Lightning* nameplate. And, some *SD* Johnsons weren't even a cottage racing match for the much smaller Merc *Rocket KE-4* with only 7 1/2 hp to its credit.

Waukegan's five-horse model **TD** (and **TN** with neutral clutch) might seem an unlikely candidate for competition. Still, this kicker's ubiquity made it a natural for nice-ly matched contests among the younger set. Not long after World War II, upstate New York's Fishers Landing Racing Club organized eager junior racers, who owned such fam-ily mills, into the *TD-5-Horse Class*. The docile light green motors provided good clean racing fun, and started a number of future stockers in the sport.

Easiest winner of the *Vintage Culture*'s Johnson cottage racer award is the Class "C" (29.92-cubic inch) **PO** series. They represented the genre well from 1937 through 1950, and placed notably in "C" Service class for decades.

The 22-horse PO was a "cheaper-to-manufacture" version of the complex, external rotary valved *P* Johnsons (the likes of the early 1930s *P-50*). While sharing some parts

with its predecessor, *PO*s used internal valving and wore a boxy Vacturi carb less roman-
tic looking than the older motor's intake air-horned carburetion. But every *PO* had a little aluminum Sea Horse-emblazoned plate on the front of its Vacturi. Serious cottage
racers quickly undid the four screws holding that cover, took it off, and hoped for a little
"ram air" effect. There was also a removable plate on the back of the muffler. Propeller
firms, such as Michigan Wheel, typically counted *PO* people as an important market for
their high-speed two-bladed bronze products. A good prop of this nature gave the *PO*
extra punch. A decent *PO* operator usually held a local waterside reputation for "being
great with motors." Perhaps that was due to the belief that a *PO* in racing trim looked a
bit customized and tinkered with. Then there was the separate lever for spark-and-
Bowden-cabled throttle controls for which not everyone knew the recipe. Here, though,
noise held the key. Sans muffler cover, and on a boat dancing to just a little bit of chop,
the *PO* sang a distinctive song. .

MARTIN

There's a story about an old angler who traded in his trusty 4 1/2-hp Martin on a new
Martin 200. It looked a little big for his needs, but the dealer convinced him he'd come
to appreciate the extra horses required to get to the other end of the lake. The first twist
of the throttle practically stood the senior's wooden fishing boat on end, costing him a
tackle box, lunch, and his lucky pork pie hat.

The *200* was a Martin in the way a Corvette
is a Chevrolet. Its designer, Gilbert "Tex" Sitz,
was thinking more about Class "B" competition
than he was trolling. Although the poppet-
valved biggie could be throttled way down for
hours, a decent example — on a light rowboat
— could best a 16-1/2 Champion, and cause
consternation to *KG-7* Merc owners. Barely a
two-year motor, the "*200*" died young (due to
the mid-1954 demise of its makers), never
enjoying the upgrades needed to correct a few
inherent shortcomings. Those who bought the

Built *by* speed experts, *for* speed lovers, this great
motor with its special Torpedo Lower Unit skims
the waves like a breeze, gives you thrill after thrill
as you show your wake. MARTIN "*Twist*-Grip"
Control, lets you "go ahead as you look ahead"
—a necessary safety feature for high speed operation. Equipped for remote speed and steering controls. Exclusive "big motor" built-in gas ▪tank.
Six-gallon auxiliary tank optional or standard.

*The 1953-54 Martin "200" Silver Streak might be com-
pared to a Chevy Corvette in terms of informal racing characteristics. Both were designed as street legal machines, but
often made local legends of the speed buffs who owned
them. Compared to a Mercury KG-7 or Mark 20, the
Martin "200" possessed a far racier lower unit in standard
"fishing motor" form — just the ticket for a serious cottage
racer.*

1953 or '54 models did get a fast powerhead, as well as the sleekest lower unit of any "standard" service outboard on the market. It marked a package bursting with real possibilities, but only enjoyed an ephemeral heyday. Needless to say, the cottage racer who found one to play with could be a real riparian contender.

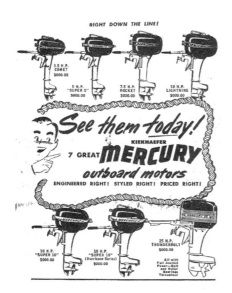

The entire 1950 Mercury line – each a potential cottage racing machine. Those lucky enough to have the 25-hp KF-9 or KG-9 Thunderbolt come their way were in for a wild ride. It actually packed some 40 hp. Notice that three different 10-hp models were available. They ranged in performance from the original KE-7 Lightning to the improved KF-7 Super 10 Lightning, and up to the KG-7 Super 10 in the racy Hurricane series. For most speed enthusiasts, any of them would do.

MERCURY

Having a Merc was like being naturally blond. During the late 1940s through the early 1960s, the Kiekhaefer identity alone carried with it a host of stereotypical expectations. Novice cottage racers had often-heard the news that Mercurys were the fastest. Just saying, "I'm going be getting a Merc next summer," put fear into the hearts of fellow lakeside junior speed buffs who'd still be campaigning with the family Elgin, or some other non-Mercury brand. Selecting a list of Kiekhaefer-esque cottage racers can be an exercise in noting the company's entire run.

Suffice it to say Mercury Marine enjoys preeminent outboard status today because of the ground Kiekhaefer plowed with his "green top" (and other colorful) models of the late 1940s and early 1950s. While all the firm's "B" motors (*KE-7, KF-7, KG-7, KH-7, Mark 20*), handle-steered "C" *Mark 30*, and 40-cube Mercs with tillers (*KF-9, KG-9, Mark 40*) are all especially notable cottage racer candidates, for the purpose of making a commitment, the *Vintage Culture*'s selection committee names the **1956-58** version **Mark 25** as the motor most useful in an informal rowboat speed event. Developing an honest 20+ horses @ 5800 rpm, this healthy 19.8- cuber was 75 pounds of "go!" This engine, along with the 16-hp *Mark 20*, ranks among the company's best 1950s-era sellers. With the *Mark 25*, Kiekhaefer had moved away from a pressure tank system and went with a reliable fuel pump (with single-line tank hose). Like the earlier *Mark 20* (and 1955, 18-horse *Mark 25*), however, our *Mark 25* wielded an aggressively pitched prop with blades the size of garden hoes.

Tiller-steered on a light hull, and with one person aboard, an average *Mark 25* could delight its daring skipper into realizing the rig was downright dangerous. The prop appeared to be the biggest thing about these motors, and so they were typically mismated to 12-foot aluminum fishing boats. Such a combination was often the source of disappointed surprise for owners of "normal-looking" 25-35 hp Evinrudes and Johnsons dependably pushing expensive family runabouts. And then, after a race between the big OMC 25 and tiny *Mark 25* was over, without so much as a smile, the *Mark 25* driver would simply skim away from the OMC man's heartbreak like some cold-hearted blue-eyed starlet in an old "B" movie.

OLIVER

Anyone who'd watched a 10-horse Chris-Craft outboard run against a similarly sized Merc knew there must be something good in that blue 19.94-cubic inch powerhead. When Oliver picked up the famous boating name's two-model line for 1955, it hoped to retain the Chris-Craft lineage, in addition to adding a gearshift, remote fuel tank, and new cowl styling. The venerable farm tractor firm also upped the horsepower of the old Chris 10 Commander to 15. The 19.94- cube Olivers kept the 15-hp rating in1956, and then stepped it up to 16 through 1959 when Oliver started phasing out of the kicker game. Over these various incarnations, the "B" Oliver was dubbed **Commander, Oliver 15, K3, K-4,** and **Lancer.** What kind of cottage racers were these Olivers? They were a rather rare sight, carried primarily by small dealers the likes of F. F. Geary's Mobil filling station in Utica, NY. There, a *15* was displayed right outside the office door (next to the Coke machine) and drew some enthusiastic young skippers looking to get on plane. To be sure, Oliver's F-N-R lower unit was somewhat bulkier than the nonshift Chris gearcase. That slowed the Oliver a bit. Even so, a decent running example could keep up with most of its contemporaries — except maybe a 16 Champion or Merc.

SCOTT-ATWATER

A dinner guest subjected to a tour of my engine collection admitted he was a bit fuzzy on brands of motors. "As kids," he recalled "my brother and I had an old Johnson. . . . I think. We didn't know much about outboards," he noted, "but when we saw people with a Scott, we figured they knew even less."

After reassuring him that the Scott-Atwater brand still had some devoted fans, there was opportunity to summarize the company's speed endeavors. The Scott people had a real chance to become (and stay) major players in the outboard game. They offered one of the industry's first line of F-N-R shift motors (1949), and from 1955 though 1959, marketed bigger horsepower models than did Evinrude and Johnson. When McCulloch bought the business in 1956, it hoped to give Scott a racier public persona. Part of the push resulted in working with the National Outboard Association in the new (OPC) pleasure craft classes. The Scott Custom series (45 and 75-hp) quasi-racers serve as good examples. That's not to say, though, that the smaller motor from the original Scott-Atwater lived life without engaging in friendly competition. Certainly, the brand's 7-1/2, and (perfect "A"-sized 14.82-cube) 10-horse models (especially the 1953 *Gold Pennant* series) were responsible for some rowboat racing work. But, most of the Scott-Atwater's early-to-mid-1950s reputation in this avenue was pinned on the 19.95-cubic-inch 16-horse outboard. Produced in various shapes and colors from 1950 through 1958, the most quintessential Scott Sixteen cottage racers arrived early. For example, the 1950 **Model 509,** and 1951-52's **Model 1-30 Shift** looked big, boxy, and mechanical, had a long twist grip throttle/steering handle, and a remote fuel tank (something Merc didn't offer on its "B" motors until 1953). Making this interesting green and silver package unique, was the **Green Hornet** racing lower unit Scott-Atwater hoped cottage racers would want as an option. Of course, this forward-only accessory defeated the outboard's gearshift function, but, in exchange, added a few coveted mph. The Green Hornet was never very successful in sanctioned Class "B" events, but the ones mated to tiller-steered Scott 16 family fishing engines no doubt set a few informal records. This unit put the 16 on a par with a standard Martin *200*. Probably not as consistently fast, but approaching the same league. Outboarders adhering to the understanding that "variety is the spice of life," were glad the Scott-Atwater 16 (especially with the Green Hornet piece) had a chance to play.

It should be noted that, when wound-out and run on less than its required lube diet of 1/2-pint to a gallon, the center-main needle bearings tended to stick. Today, when one of these motors surfaces, it's typically seized-up internally.

SEA KING

During the 1930s and '40s, Evinrude/Elto had a program of mixing and matching left-over parts to create some interesting private-brand "value motors." One was a revamped Elto *Senior Speedster* sold by Montgomery Ward from 1941-42. Dubbed by Ward as its top-of-the-line **Sea King Giant Twin,** this 15.2-horse opposed-cylinder outboard could move a light boat at speeds up to 25 mph. Appearing rather outdated by the early 1950s, these nonshift motors were frequently fodder for trade-ins. That's where budget-minded kids and cottage racing inevitably came in. I spotted one on a Lake Champlain marina's "clean used motors" rack in the

Not a bad cottage racing mill at a reasonable chain store price. Montgomery-Ward's 1940s Sea King Giant Twin (upper motor) was built by OMC using some early 1930s Elto Senior Speedster parts. With 15.2-hp, a nicely pitched two-blade prop, and a twist grip throttle/tiller, this outboard represented a bargain in what was then considered a pretty big motor.

mid-1960s. Every year the price (scribbled in red magic marker on the gas tank) got a little better, until 1970 when I mercifully acquired it and some other parts for about $15.

WIZARD

The guy who owned the little Western Auto in my town always called Wizards in his window "the poor man's Merc." That's because just about any outboarder with an eye for detail could tell the two brands were linked. Transom clamps, tiller, prop, starter handle, innards, lower unit, etc., were 100 percent instantly recognizable as Kiekhaefer products. And since Wizard was a private brand "value" motor, it had to sell for less than kin kickers displayed in the Mercury dealership. Even so, that didn't mean Western Auto

WIZARD WINS AGAIN! In test after test against other leading outboards in its h.p. class, this mighty Wizard "Ten" consistently beats them all! A terrific package of smoothly harnessed dynamite, with pulse-pounding thrill-a-second speeds up to 35 m.p.h. In official races, it actually outran in a free-for-all ran second only weight, fool-proof for fishing. a bare crawl. Priced up to $90

Western Auto stores never missed a chance to tout its Mercury-produced Wizard outboards to cottage racers. Here is a portion of a typical Wizard ad captioned "WIZARD WINS AGAIN!" For this contest, a bathing suit-clad "test pilot" in a brand-emblazoned aluminum rowboat equipped with a "mighty Wizard 10," blows the doors off a field of similar fishing craft competitors pushed by other makes of outboards. The chain store called their engine "a terrific package of smoothly harnessed dynamite with pulse-pounding thrill-a-second speeds!" No wonder Wizards have long enjoyed hall of fame status with the cottage racing crowd.

versions were required to be slow. Cottage racers on a chain-store budget often aimed to put a Wizard on their home-brew hydros. The biggest was the **Super Power 25 (WA-25)** 30-cubic-inch, four-cylinder in-line. On the drawing board just before its Merc *Mark 30* sister, this tiller-steered Wizard could make quick work of similarly sized motors of non-Mercury lineage. Receiving our cottage racing certification, however, are the Wizard **Super Tens** with direct drive. These 19.8-cube full "B" motors include: the 1955 **WM-7**,

and **WM-7A** offered in 1956-57. The legendary Merc *Mark 20H* racer gave its crankshaft (P/N 401-27), and main bearing race (P/N 21020) to the 1955 Wizard. Even though this nonshift *Super Ten*'s coopted *20H* reed cage only wore half of the reeds of its racier relative, rumors spawned by those exotic, shared components got at least few cottage racers (and their parents) into otherwise modest Western Auto stores.

This owner-modified Wizard Super 10 has been treated to a remote safety throttle hook-up, rear steering bar, back-mounted "single race" fuel tank, and Mercury Quicksilver racing lower unit. The brand's link to Merc made it easy for such mix-n-matching.

Part Four

Racing Collectibles

Evinrude dealers gave out promotional buttons when their brand re-entered organized outboard racing during the 1970s.

Using Dipsy Doodle-type molds, the "BSH" hydro here has a KG-7H Merc with a special rubber band powered lower unit.

The plastic mini Mark 20H Mercury plastic was an updated motor for rubber band-driven hydroplanes originally fitted with an earlier KG-7H. And yes, there were young skippers who spent time on the beach debating which was faster!

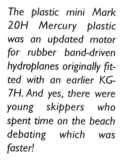

A 1950's Japanese tin toy hydro. Its jack-in-the-box type crank (on deck) makes the outboard go.

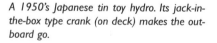

Rendered from a racing photograph showing a field of five "B" Stock Hydros with Merc 20H mills, the picture on this metal lunchbox only has a trio of boats so each craft would appear large enough to make a positive impact on grade school speed buffs. A veteran of many noontimes, it's scratched up, but still wears the original red plastic handle. Some have been noted with an earlier, metal handle.

Chapter Nine

Toys, Publications, and Movies

"You will notice from studying your plastic racing hydroplane model that the driver kneels in the boat when racing. In this manner he can rapidly shift his weight to balance the boat properly. Anyone who has watched outboard hydroplanes racing will agree that this is one of the most thrilling outdoor sports. Order other scale model kits while supply lasts. Only 50-cents with box top!"
—*1950s Kellogg's cereal offer*

COMPARED TO CAR, AIRPLANE, TRAIN, musical, military, baseball, or football fanatics, the young-at-heart outboard racing buff has had to seriously search toy store shelves in order to find models or playthings related to fast boating. Speedboat nuts have always known the toy industry puts most of its efforts into depicting "regular" sports and auto racing. Even so, a surprising number of small companies came through with some trinkets for our minority's tastes. Spotting this stuff in the average hobby shop was a challenge, but well worth the effort. While most were obscure provinces of tiny, short-lived manufacturing concerns, a few of these items were actually widely distributed and therefore at least hazily remembered. For example, during the early 1960s, stock outboarding played into the plans of the Whitman Publishing Company's simple cardboard "spinner" racing game series. Complementing its equestrian and automotive versions, Regatta was essentially a shallow box with card-stock channels in which tiny plastic hydroplanes bounced

The Regatta game was incredibly low tech, but introduced countless folks to outboard racing. Both the boats and motors were generic cartoons and aren't particularly representative of a specific make or model.

upon two-dimensional waves. Flicking the pointer on a ship's wheel motif moved an arrow to the names of tiny racing boats dubbed *Sea Nymph, White Cap, Aloha, Argosy,* or *Dolphin*. If your craft's name came up lucky, it could be nudged about an inch toward the checkered flag. Landlubber players were known to clumsily advance their boat after a spin at the wheel. And handling one's craft in such a manner usually ripped up the course. Along the way, games often lost a hydro or two unless repaired with strips of yellowy cellophane tape. More than a few in this condition became long-ago victims of spring cleaning, making a Regatta game in decent shape rather tough to find today. Originally marketed for around a dollar, Whitman's racing collection found its way to even the most modest 1950s/1960s variety — or five & dime — stores. The self-contained games' low cost and high portability made for perfect distractions during long car trips with bored kids. Some erstwhile Regatta players recall it being their only exposure to stock outboard racing, their impatient moms having selected the colorful cardboard diversion only because Whitman's horse racing and stock car editions were sold out.

Toys

One of the earliest examples of outboard racing toys is Baby, a 1930s cast iron step-bottom runabout with driver and tiller-steered motor. The opposed twin kicker was part of the hull casting and didn't operate. Like a slightly longer (9-1/2-inch) and more detailed metal Hubley-brand step hydro of the same era, power resulted from pushing or pulling this boat on its barely visible wheels. Of course, there were others, but most represented standard service craft rather than pure racers. From time to time, heretofore unknown (or forgotten) outboard racing boat toys from the pre World War II period appear. Some modern reproductions of the antique-looking Baby have surfaced.

In the toy biz, molds to make generic representations of items like cars, rockets, motorcycles, and boats often did lots of traveling. Whenever a manufacturer could market something "new" by making a minor change on existing tooling, profitability on that toy could be easier to reach. And there were plenty of small toy company bankruptcy auc-

tions and outright acquisitions after which molds for plastic models were often reused or revamped. A little Class "B" job reincarnated by various toy firms over the years was the Racing

This circa 1930 metal craft went fastest on a hard surface rather than water. Dubbed "Baby," it rode with three wheels and spawned several imitators from various toy companies.

Speedboat. This three-pointer was best known as _Dipsy Doodle_, a plastic model kit from Monogram. Complete with "Mercury Twin [non-powered] outboard motor and racing driver," it came colorfully boxed with instructions that even included a brief narrative about the Merc _Quicksilver_ racing lower unit. A few years after this circa-1956 incarnation, a clone showed up as a 50-cent premium from breakfast cereal. The plain shipping carton harbored the boat sealed in a crinkly plastic bag. Somewhere along the line, someone used the _Dipsy Doodle_ molds to produce a rubber band driven version. Apparently, this rig was sold preassembled and didn't do justice to the nicely replicated gearcase of the previously mentioned kits.

The Champion Spark Plug people offered clones of these as promotional items. Their version measured 8-1/2 inches in length and was bubble-packed on cardboard. Champion's white hydro with red driver and motor dates from around 1965. Fleet Line was probably the last outfit to adapt a _Dipsy Doodle_-esque mold to toy boat racing. A very similar craft, but with bigger dimensions, became one of the famous model outboard and boat maker's best sellers. Of course, it was fitted only with battery-powered, scaled-down representations of service motors such as an Evinrude or Johnson _40_.

Several race boat makers either authorized someone to build tiny versions of their hulls, or did so themselves. In real life, Speed Liner, a builder of assembled, ready-to-run (full size) sleek outboard hulls, also offered some of these simple, speedy, and reliable craft in kit form. As a promotional venture, Lilliputian-sized Speed Liner racing runabout kits showed up in hobby shops during the 1950s. Likewise, the folks at Southwest Manufacturing Company in Little Rock, Arkansas, thought it would be cute to order a few sheets of lightweight aluminum (as used in soda cans) and make some 17- inch scale models of their marine aluminum Arkansas Traveler _Sportsman_ runabout. This tidy mini-cottage racer was finished in natural aluminum and blue, wore an authentic decal, and could be powered by an electric outboard. Merc featured one with a palm-sized _Mark 55_ in its July 1955 _Mercury Messenger_. The Kiekhaefer dealer newsletter suggested the combo would provide wonderful marketing opportunities. Meanwhile, stock racing buff Art Van Pelt immersed his small Spring Lake,

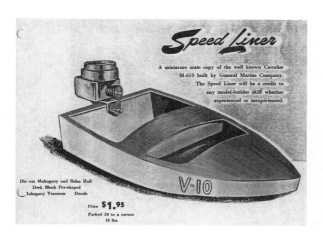

This quickly rendered depiction of a model Speed Liner made its way to a hobby supply catalog. A scale copy of Speed Liner's M-610 Cavalier, it consisted of die-cut mahogany and balsawood pieces, and official Speed Liner logo decals all for $1.95. Dealers were asked to order at least one, 18-pound carton of 24 boats.

Michigan, boat company into all kinds of outboard racing products. In addition to real boats (finished or ready to assemble) Van Pelt marketed authentic racing model kits just the right size for a toy outboard. During the summer of 1955, a three-point hydro and stock utility runabout were offered for three bucks each — or both for $5 postpaid. For promotional purposes, Scott-Atwater gave away (or sold for a nominal charge) the novel, blow-up *Racer* around 1954. Complete with a 16-hp Scott powerhead, the soft vinyl boat could be inflated by mouth via an air mattress type valve. Real imagination was required to play with this toy as it was too small to ride and had no moving parts.

Model airplane engine maker WEN-MAC put one of its .049 mills on water via an outboard gas tank, flywheel and lower unit. While its gearcase wasn't particularly racy, the glow-fuel outboard was meant to be fast. Offered separately — in air or water-cooling, as well as with a rewind start option — it could also be purchased with craft like a plastic Wen-Mac *Corvette Hydro Outboard Speedboat*. The craft had a seven-inch beam and 18-1/2-length. The outfit was generically stylized and didn't really look like any particular runabout or hydro available in real life during Wen-Mac's 1950s run.

Sterling, a prominent Eisenhower-era model maker, contributed to the mini- outboard racing genre through its offerings like *Sea-Dart*. This was a 16-inch long plastic hydroplane kit that could be "assembled in minutes." Of course, such a claim was made kosher by the fact that all amounts of time over 120 seconds contain minutes. No doubt some youngsters — and probably even their parents — took longer than that to put *Sea Dart* together. On the box, Sterling pictured its outboard racer with an Allyn *Sea Fury* single (to be discussed in detail later) on the transom. A cut above most toy or scale outboards using electric power, this diminutive fuel-fired kicker-ette was featured only on the most serious racing models.

Because the glow plug-engined outboards required appreciable acumen to operate, it's likely most toy racers such as *Sea Dart* were mated to battery-powered mills. Toy shoppers with an eye for detail might have even matched this hull with an inexpensive K&O brand electric outboard also labeled *Sea Dart*. While on the subject of battery-powered motors, it need be noted that space won't allow coverage of every toy kicker that might have been used on a model raceboat. While the authentic K&O Mercury *Mark 55*, *Mark 75*, and other "6-cylinder" Mercs, made for

An early edition of the FUJI glow-fuel outboard, this nicely die cast Japanese .049 single didn't really have the Mercury look possessed by one of its more detailed successors, but the lower unit and prop were full-race components.

Van Pelt model racers were just like the real thing because they came from shrunken plans of actual boats and were offered by the big boats' maker. Allyn Sea Fury power was recommended.

great visual speed, they weren't renditions of actual racing engines. Suffice it to say that racy lines are in the eye of the beholder. One could argue that the slightly sleeker than average lower unit on K&O's generic *Hurricane* electric toy outboard defines it as a racer. And there are other examples of gray areas. That's why the watchwords here must be to simply "have fun!" This also applies to fuel outboard miniatures. The Japanese Fuji *Sea Horse .15* comes to mind. One buff clearly sees this glow-plug kicker as a Merc *KG-9* (with exposed, rope-start flywheel) powerhead on a sleek *Mark 55* lower unit, and says that these features are more than enough to pinpoint the beautifully built, hand-sized, red and white mill as *the* toy cottage racer.

Respected plastic kit producer Paul Lindberg digressed from his naval ship focus to offer *Flash* the three-point outboard hydro that "can be motor powered." Ray Gaedke, the artist who painted *Flash*'s box cover, was no doubt influenced by an action *Boat Sport* magazine shot of "C" alky competitor Bud Wiget. But when brush met paper, Gaedke left out Wiget's Johnson *PR*, substituting an Allyn *Sea Fury*, the coveted (by many young racing enthusiasts) glow-plug engine that only existed in modeldom. Allyn outboards (which became K&B-Allyn in May 1955) were the motors that inspired Art Van Pelt to produce his aforementioned model race boat kits.

Los Angeles-based Allyn Sales Company was respon-

"Hey, something about these two pictures looks familiar!" That's because the artist in charge of rendering an exciting box cover for Lindberg model company's FLASH was taken by the action Bud Wiget created with his Neal hydro. The toy version is shown with an Allyn Sea Fury — as opposed to Wiget's Johnson-power. By the way, that is not a racing number on FLASH, it's the price — just $2.57.

After the model airplane engine maker K&B bought Allyn, the little outboards were sold in a generic box bearing both company names, a plane on the cover, and a tiny picture ad for K&B's glow fuel. This box came from a fellow who'd lost his Allyn single during its maiden voyage in a deep Idaho lake. Meanwhile, the motor was built from scrounged parts and is still shy a driveshaft and prop. Even so, the little pair looks happy together.

sible for marketing what is arguably the best toy outboard with an authentic racing gearcase. (At press time, the Alterscale model outboard people announced a beautiful 1:8 scale Mercury Mark *75H,* but *Vintage Culture* covers pre-1970 production.) It is believed *Sea Fury*'s designers worked from drawings of the original "Q-length," long *Quicksilver* lower unit.

First offered in 1954, the tiny powerplants were built by K&B for the Allyn organization. For 1955, a twin was introduced. Piston displacement size "color coding" came in the form of either plain aluminum, blue, or gold cylinder heads. Allyn *Sea Fury* model outboards could be purchased as .049 and .060 (of a cubic inch) singles, as well as .12 (standard) and .15 (racing) twins. Fastidious *Sea Fury* owners might have even asked their Allyn dealers for some *FURY-LUBE.* Sold in a yellow tube, it resembled -in miniature- a container of real outboard lower unit gear grease, and could be used on any *Sea Fury's*

A trio of glow-fuel model outboards including (from left to right) Allyn Sea Fury Twin, Allyn's single, and a Wen-Mac with water-cooled cylinder (note Wen-Mac's water scoop and intake tube). The latter motor was also available with rewind start, and air-cooling.

gears or other moving parts. It appears these outboards were current through 1957, but some hobby shops still had some inventory well into the 1960s. The alternate firing in-line two-cylinder version of standard *Sea Fury* was the featured motor on the box of Ideal Toy Company's 24-inch wooden model kit dubbed *Snappy Speed King*. A bit out of scale for stock or alky representation, this single cockpit runabout was nonetheless a good match for either size Allyn or the previously noted Wen-Mac. Undoubtedly, dozens of other toy outboard racing craft found their way into hobby shops. A large number of them (in plastic, wood, or tin) came from Japan. Some of these (from the Far East as well as American sources) include the 19-inch Allyncraft outboard hydro, Fleet Line's 11-inch *Zephyr* racing runabout, Dumas' 16-inch *Apache*, Cavacraft's 14-inch hydroplane with driver, a three-pointer of 15 1/2-inches in length by Master dubbed *Porpoise*, Ideal Toys' *Speed Demon* as well as *Speed Demon Racer* runabouts (15 1/2-inches and 15-inches respectively), and a 20-inch hydro *Torpedo* from Scientific. With an eight-inch beam, this last boat could handle the largest glow-fuel outboards such as Allyn's feisty twin. The fact that these little mills were advertised in *Boat Sport* especially legitimized them among race fans.

Periodicals

Sometime during the spring of 1933, the *Popular Mechanics* editorial board met to discuss its upcoming covers. Outboard racing had been receiving good newspaper coverage, especially from lively publicity about the lagoon-based boating competition at the 1933 Chicago World's Fair. They decided to commission some outboarding stories and a watercolor showing hydroplanes in action. The resulting painting appeared on the front of the magazine's August issue. A pair of related articles spread the racing bug to many Depression-weary readers. In fact, other outboard racing articles and full magazines

devoted to the hobby predated the above piece. *Popular Science* pulled some positive reader feedback with its September 1928 feature *Outboard Racing Secrets*. At the tail end of the tiller-steered, pioneer racing era, the monthly indicated that "speed — how to get more speed — is the topic of the day with the outboard motor boat owner," and then spent several pages on "how to coax more miles an hour from a

Yes, there were a few dapper gentlemen who raced while wearing a tie, as was depicted on the November 1929 National Outboard Magazine. What makes this issue especially notable, however, is its eyewitness coverage of the first national outboard championships.

light motor."

The late 1920s saw the introduction of a pair of outboard-oriented periodicals with a major focus on racing. The *National Outboard Magazine* came from Napoleon, Ohio's Outboard Publishing Company and appears to have begun in 1928. At about 30 pages (around 10 x 13 inches) per issue, this publication claimed to reach 35,000 readers –though that seems rather hyperbolic for a niche startup. Its table of contents for November 1929 included articles about northern Wisconsin's first outboard race, balloon jousting while operating a motor, the premier national championship races at Peoria, Illinois, and some California racing events. In fact, it was predominantly a racer's resource, even offering speed accessories (tachometers and stabilizer fins) to anybody who signs up some new subscribers. From all appearances, *Outboard Motor Boat* magazine had an easier time netting readers and advertisers. Originated during the spring of 1929, this 9-1/2 x 12-1/2 periodical neared 50 pages by the following year with about a 25 percent ad content. It was published in New York by the Sports Division of National Trade Journals and covered "racing, cruising, commuting, camping, hunting, and fishing" with outboard-powered boats. Content analysis indicates that the racing focus was reduced to a cogent article or two (like the March 1930 "Pep Her Up — some random notes on the art of making a racing motor a bit faster") in favor of more space for cruising and fishing. Still the editor never missed an opportunity to cover big outboard races or new competition record runs.

When the above magazines succumbed to the Great Depression, small boating's strongest publications served as an informational conduit for outboard racing enthusiasts. Majors like *Rudder, Yachting,* and *Motor Boating* nodded to the genre with columns such as the latter's *With the Outboarders*. During the early stock racing era, some of the best of these were penned by longtime racer and outboard company executive Charles D. Strang.

A pivotal year in outboard journalism was 1952, as two notable publications became available then. Without any connection or apparent knowledge of a looming competitor, both *Boat Sport*, and *Speed and Spray* materialized. Each magazine aimed for what it figured to be a lucrative, untapped market. Well before the close of the decade, they'd sadly discover that their target was moving from a close-knit, devoted racing fraternity, to a huge group of pleasure boaters who liked to be on the water, but didn't particularly care to read about others involved in such pursuits. For a few 1950s boat racing seasons, however, these publications chronicled outboard competition like a time capsule.

Boat Sport

"America's First Speedboating Magazine," *Boat Sport* hailed from the East Coast even lthough there was a Los Angeles, West Coast representative listed. Its original owner, Rockley Publications, Inc., was headquartered in Silver Spring, Maryland. Apparently, this

By December 1953, Boat Sport tried attracting a generalized small boating readership by emphasizing cruising — as opposed to just racing — on some of its covers. The dalliance would eventually result in Boat Sport
being swallowed up by sister Aqua Sport. Neither survived the literary transfusion.

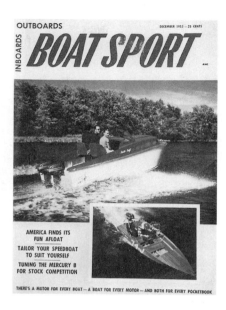

was just where the bimonthly got mailed from. Editorial and Executive offices had a New York City address, which seemed pretty swanky until the fine print got noticed. The entire Manhattan facility was in *Room 1904* at 215 Fourth Avenue. Of course, most of the writing and photography work took place elsewhere, so a Big Apple cubicle was actually adequate. *Boat Sport*'s premier issue, labeled May 1952, was shipped to some mag-

azine distributors and marine retailers on March 31st as a promotional venture. With the free inspection copy was included an introductory letter from Publisher, President and Advertising Manager Joseph J. Hardie. He was actually co-publisher, sharing that respon-sibility with Raymond J. Kelly, a veteran sports editor with the *New York Times*. The idea for the new periodical was an offshoot of racing car publications (*Speed Mechanics*, and *Auto Craftsman*) Hardie had founded. Like many a media strategy today, being able to offer a "boutique" series of related titles theoretically widens one's potential advertising client list. Hardie's announcement notified Boat Shop Dealers:

> The attached copy of the first issue of *Boat Sport* is sent to you with the request that
> you consider the sales possibilities to your customers. If you have a retail trade, it is our
> hope and belief that they will like *Boat Sport* and we urge you to place a trial order with
> us starting with the second issue, which will be dated August 1952 and published about
> the latter part of May. Future issues will be on a bi-monthly frequency. Copies retail for
> 25-cents, the trade price is 20-cents per copy, shipping prepaid to your address. Any
> unsold copies may be returned for full credit upon shipment of the following issue.
> Your customers will find *Boat Sport* increasing their interest in their hobby, which
> should result in increasing the music of your cash register.

At the bottom of this letter was a row of periods signifying where to cut out a mod-est order blank "contract" that simply read: "Put me down for a trial order of _____ copies each issue until further notice, in accordance with the terms of your letter dated March 31, 1952."

Individual subscriptions to this now classic publication ran $1.50 per year. No one at

Boat Sport figured on getting rich from subscribers' money, but with enough loyal readership, advertisers might be better convinced to spend their dollars to reach outboard fans by way of the new magazine. Indeed, advertising therein was quite reasonable, as $300 netted sponsors an entire page of *Boat Sport*. And, if you only needed an inch of space to peddle your marine-related wares, fourteen bucks would do fine.

Many avid *Boat Sport* buffs figured their favorite periodical was owned — at least in part — by its associate editor Hank Wieand Bowman. After all, he wrote most of the articles (either under his own byline, or when the table of contents looked lopsided, using a pen name), shot lots of the pictures, and communicated in a confident, gently authoritative style that greatly satisfied readers. While Bowman never held a share of *Boat Sport* stock, or received more than the going free-lance payment rate for his editorial work, he embodied the magazine and, more than anyone else, power boating competition itself. Suffice it to say, his association with the little publication provided *Boat Sport* with a larger-than-life appearance, and kept it afloat long after lesser literary talents would have abandoned ship for a more lucrative port. During *Boat Sport*'s early years, its cover emphasized "Outboards - Inboards - Hydros: Runabouts, Hop-Ups, Service." From a mass marketing viewpoint, however, such topics were just niches in the broader pleasure boating genre. The racing community had a reputation for being pretty tight with a dollar, and made do with existing gear whenever basement shop wizardry allowed. There was also considerable swapping, hand-me-down transactions, or parsimonious intra-club parts and rig sales. Consequently, the publication was not known for bringing large numbers of free-spending customers to boat and motor showrooms. While companies like Atlanta Boat Works (Aristo-Craft), General Marine (Speed Liner), Kiekhaefer Corporation (Mercury), and occasionally Evinrude as well as Martin used *Boat Sport* as an advertising vehicle, most of the sponsors peddled low-cost "racing secrets" booklets, boat plans, or accessories like $2.98 crash helmets. More than one issue fell into the slow-business category of December 1955's edition. Neither inside nor back cover contained a dime's worth of ad copy. And this at the height of stock outboarding's golden age.

Detail-oriented *Boat Sport* readers noticed that the March-April 1954 edition listed a new publishing name, H-K Publications, Inc. The new name reflected its owners *H*ardie and *K*elly. The old Rockley moniker disappeared from the table of contents page by the next issue. Around this time, H-K started tinkering with their covers. The "OUTBOARDS - INBOARDS" identity which had appeared on most of the previous fronts, was switched to "OUTBOARDS - OUTBOARDS - OUTBOARDS" for June 1954, and later changed back. Cover art, traditionally *Boat Sport*'s rich, colorful calling card, began crossing the line from pure racing to "regular" boating, cruising, and fishing. October 1953's face, for example, showed a man water skiing while a woman on his shoulders played a ukulele and sang. Even though she was pretty, and the duo sported matching designer swim suits, the menagerie must have left at least a few regular racing-focused subscribers asking;

"What the___?" Of course, the pictorial cover experiment was designed to rein in non-racing water enthusiasts along with *Boat Sport's* true believers. Another stab at this was evident on the September 1955 cover. It featured a peaceful shot of an angler in an Evinrude-equipped rowboat casting for bass with a snow-covered mountain in the background.

Sometime in late 1955, H-K must have received feedback causing them to return *Boat Sport* to its racing focus. Beginning in 1956, publication was stepped up from six, to eight times per year (with only January, February, October, and November left out). Gone were the dominant water skiers and peripheral articles like "Late Summer Low-Cost Cruising." Instead, core pieces such as "Inside view of the Merc *30H*," "How to Promote an Outboard Regatta," and "The New '36' Motors Extra Power," backed up the exciting covers depicting outboarders in serious competition.

Boat Sport's long-time editor Harold Hersey died in mid-March 1956. The introduction of Hank Bowman's critically acclaimed *Encyclopedia of Outboard Motor Boating* included words related to Hersey's insightfulness. Bowman credited him with the idea for such a book, and thanked Hersey for successfully advancing the concept to its eventual publishing house. Meanwhile, in their magazine, H-K acknowledged that Hersey's ability to piece together *Boat Sport* would be difficult to duplicate. Following the wise old editor's passing, spelling errors seemed to slip into print more readily. Sid Urytzski, of Sid-Craft boats had his last name written so many ways in *Boat Sport* that few readers would ever know what was correct — "Uretski," "Urytsky," or "Uritski." I'm rather sure the periodical's 1950s typesetter never dreamed somebody living during the next century would be critiquing his work in a historical treatise. Little mistakes were the province of a pulp magazine "factory" trying to turn out a half-dozen shoestring publications each month. That's one of the things that makes tattered old copies of *Boat Sport* so endearing today.

In the June 1956 edition, H-K brass also expressed gratitude for the work their cover-artist, Hal Kelly (no relation to publisher Raymond Kelly) performed with black and white photos. On various occasions, the famous boat builder and racer hand-colored these pictures. A disclaimer would let readers know the spray, water conditions, and boats' beautiful hues were "entirely from his imagination." H-K moved its official address to Canton, Ohio, but kept editorial and executive offices in the New York locale. By early 1957, they were listed as H-K Publications, Inc., based in Detroit, then Minneapolis; still with an ancillary Big Apple mail drop venue. A second new editor since Harold Hersey was giving it a try, and publication was scaled back down to every other month. Yet another editor was in place for the April 1958 *Boat Sport*. No harbinger of the magazine's fate, this 44-pager looked especially healthy. It touted upcoming June and August issues, and contained full-size ads for Merc, Aristo-Craft, and J.C. Whitney. Plus, H-K suddenly boasted other publications, like *Boatcraft*, *Outboarding Guide* and *Water Ski*, not to mention its automotive titles. Such an empire seemed impressive. Behind the scenes, however, the escalating costs for printing and distributing numerous magazines mandated belt tightening. Perhaps an executive and editorial meeting about the dilemma included word that Champion Motors was about to go belly-up, and that Kiekhaefer had discontinued its famed *20H* "B" engine, as it did with the "A" Class *KG4-H*, arguably the cornerstones of easy entry into stock outboard racing. Whatever the reasoning, that session ended with a decision to roll *Boat Sport* into the firm's presumedly better-positioned ("mainstream boater" target audience) *Aqua Sport*. As the newest member of H-K Publications' family of boating magazines, *Aqua Sport* had debuted with a July 1957 cover date even though it was available on newsstands May 21st. A year later, its June-July 1958 edition was retitled *Aqua Sport including Boat Sport*. The amalgamation publication seemed to racing fans satisfied with their old magazine to be top-heavy in the areas of water skiing, skin diving and Cape Cod cruising. Although it did also include some good *Boat Sport*-type articles, and promised more in the next (August-September) issue, this combined *Aqua Sport/Boat Sport* issue represented the end for both. During *Boat Sport*'s (approximately 40 issues) reign as "America's First Speedboat Magazine," the sharply contrasting glossy color covers, and delicate (8-1/2" by 11") pulpy pages made it as much a part of outboard racing's mystique as any winning boat and motor.

Speed and Spray

"International Boat Racing and Water Sports" represented the coverage promise of the Los Angeles area-based, *Speed and Spray* magazine. Its first incarnation appeared in the summer of 1952 published by Marine Publications, Inc., in Newport Beach, California. Green half-tone photos (inside, bright color covers) and attention to detail provided it with an appealing layout. The index page boasted nearly sixty staffers and correspondents from Alaska to New Zealand. Truth be told, this periodical looked a bit more polished than rival *Boat Sport* and seemed to have a good advertising base. (Mercury took some full-color back covers.) Ad prices, though, were probably laughably low. At any rate, this *Speed and Spray* trickled out by

The first incarnations of Speed and Spray were often covered with a patchwork of photos. More than a few, though, were of the 1950s inboard speedboats/ski-boats typically popular in the publication's home state, California. While a small shot of a woman in a stock outboard rig was featured, the August 1953 issue also touted a "hot rod ski-boat with full-house Cadillac [engine]" and a teaser about some hot hull fitted with some souped-up De Soto car mill.

1954. About a year later, the defunct magazine's most notable assets, its name and mailing list, were taken over by C-B Publications, Inc., of Fullerton, California. An explanatory letter about the C-B's hope to revitalize the specialized periodical, as well as a subscription invitation went to every old *S&S* (as the periodical was affectionately dubbed) subscriber. Most met a reception positive enough to be answered with $3.50 for a year's sign-up.

By April 1955, new issues of *Speed and Spray* were rolling off the press. This one billed itself as "The International Magazine of Motorboating," but, understandably, had a bit of a West Coast bias. An informal content analysis reveals the publisher certainly did try including stories from "back East." Like the original, this second *S&S* made for a very pleasing package. The far-flung roster of correspondents and photographers in Hawaii, Alaska (not then American states), the U.S., Canada, England, New Zealand, and Mexico was maintained. Among its technical staff were notable outboarders such as Merc's Charlie Strang, boat builder Ralph DeSilva, motor maker Pep Hubbell, boat designer Ted Jones, Kiekhaefer distributor Elgin Gates, and propeller expert Hi Johnson. There was even an *S&S* cartoonist.

The far-flung staff promised "world coverage of pleasure boating, water skiing, and boat racing." A typical issue ran some 36 to 42 pages (8-1/2 x 11 inches) of rather good quality glossy paper.

Every once in a while, somebody might send them a zinger, but it would usually be a sharp request to return to the early color covers, instead of the latter version's red, white and grays. Operating in the black, however, was something it appears *S&S* had difficulty accomplishing. The last issue in my files is dated May 1956, and rather than a purely race boat theme, its cover showed a woman with matching plaid swimsuit and water skis. It's doubtful the little Golden State boat racing periodical lasted into 1957. Some might have bet *Boat Sport* would fold before the slicker *Speed and Spray*. In the New York magazine's favor, however, was its aforementioned master editor of impecunious pulp. Harold Hersey had an inimitable knack for taking whatever material crossed his desk and crafting it into quintessential ephemera. Among its challenges, *Boat Sport* never even hinted of another stock outboarding chronicle, and seemed to transmit a confidence about boat racing somehow not particularly present in its chief competitor. It also had Hank Bowman. Actually, under one of his many pen names, he'd written a few columns for *Speed and Spray*, but the California magazine just didn't look like home for the venerable boating writer's handle.

Other Publications

Introduced in late 1952, somewhat concurrently with *Speed and Spray* and *Boat Sport*, was "America's only yachting annual." This *U.S. Boats* served as a season's review of all boat racing. While inboarding and sailing competition was the almanac's major focus, it also

In order to qualify its banner bragging about having everything from sailing to racing, Lakeland Yachting would occasionally run some of the latter up the flagpole. Here, the magazine catered to some Mark 55H-powered "D" stock runabout activity for the October 1956 cover.

offered a retrospective chronicle of APBA stock outboard as well as alky events. Understandably, an ad for *U.S. Boats* in APBA's *Propeller* newsletter made no mention of rival National Outboard Association contents, though the publication also covered NOA statistics.

At the close of World War II, the public frenzy towards recreation began spawning seemingly limitless boat and motor sales. The marine pleasure craft pie became large enough for many startup publications to slice. *Lakeland Yachting* put its fork in the piece baked for the millions of boaters who never saw a sea. Subtitled "America's Freshwater Boating Magazine," *Lakeland Yachting* was the official publication of the Inter-Lake Yachting Association, Midwest Collegiate Sailing Association, and the Mississippi Valley Power Boat Association. The latter relationship meant that it had at least one-third of a connection with motor racing. *LY*'s banner promised coverage of "outboarding - sailing - power boating - cruising - racing," but did so with a rather broad brush. Understandably, its racing content pages were few in comparison with those devoted to the wider, more generic pleasure boating market. Perhaps the most curious thing about *LY*'s inboard and outboard competition column was its name, "Speed and Spray." Lakeshore Publications of Sheboygan, Wisconsin, produced *Lakeland Yachting*, with a typical 8-1/2 x 11 inch issue running 60 to 70 pages.

Though never exclusively a boating publication, *Speed Age* of the 1940s and '50s period should be mentioned here. That's because — among articles on hot motorcycles and race cars — the magazine with "everything for motor enthusiasts," did allot laudable editorial space to outboard speed endeavors. The September 1954 issue (82 pages, 8-1/2 x 11 inches) contains pieces like; "Tuning an Outboard," an article on women boat racers, and great outboard coverage of the President's Cup Regatta. Its color cover even managed to squeeze a Mercury outboard into the lower lefthand corner. Enigmatically, this mill is a garden variety 7-1/2-horse (*KE-4* or *Mark 7*) fishing model that someone had repainted maroon.

Around 1958, United Western Enterprises, Inc., (Mrs. J.D. Funk, President) began publishing *American Yachtsman/West Coast Boating News*. Several years later, "the magazine of high performance boating" was just about the only periodical left to witness the fading of stock outboard racing's golden age. In keeping with the times, by 1965, *Boating News* (the name got streamlined) concentrated on inboard drag boats and some offshore outboarding. A letter from a Maine college student, in the January 1965 issue, stated: "Even though yours is a Western magazine, many people in the Northeastern U.S. read [it]. There are many stock regattas in this area that are never heard about. . . . Very little coverage is given [by *Boating News*] to the stocks, just two or three pages once in a while. . . . Could you publish some materials and photos on this topic? If not, what magazine does or will?" The editor promised to try harder, but noted "no boating magazine in the nation exceeds the coverage given by *Boating News* to racing events, stock outboard or otherwise. With a relatively small staff, we cover as much territory as possible. As we grow, we can promise more and more coverage of all the events you and other readers are interested in, but meanwhile we do the best we can." Privately, though, the already overextended magazine manager probably said something like, "If you stock outboarders would just go out to our advertisers, buy boats, motors, and equipment, then mention you heard about the stuff in *Boating News*, maybe we'd be able to hire more correspondents to chronicle your events!" It was a problem common to any ad-based medium trying to serve a niche pastime largely composed of parsimonious do-it-yourselfers.

By the late fifties, after both *Boat Sport* and *Speed and Spray* had sunk, *OUTBOARD* magazine held the distinction of being *the* outboard racing chronicle for a while. The Jacksonville, Florida, monthly began around 1953 as a full- service information source aimed at people who used outboard-powered craft. Produced by the Outboard Publishing Company, Inc., in an 8-1/2 x 11 inch format, *OUTBOARD* was printed on

quality paper and seemed to use a bit of color in just the right spots for true eye appeal. Hank Bowman provided articles and photos for *OUTBOARD*, many of which were pleasure boat oriented. The publishers did recognize his pull with the competition community, and requested an occasional racing piece. Even during *Boat Sport*'s run, Bowman penned an annual *OUTBOARD* feature titled "Winners of the Silver Prop Awards." In it, he'd select

Country singing legend Johnny Cash does one of his top musicians — Marshall Grant — a favor by posing with Grant's Ring of Fire alky racing runabout. The World of Boat Racing's publisher appreciated the shot, too.

The mid-1960s was bereft of periodicals for water speed enthusiasts. For a short while during the era, The World of Boat Racing answered the call, but big advertisers wanting to court its readership were hard to find.

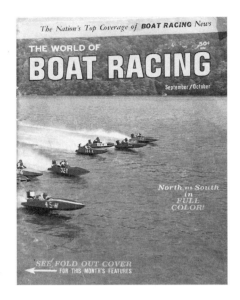

the year's top dozen throttle-squeezers, and outline their achievements. But readers didn't see a Bowman byline. To provide himself with "brand extension," as well to preserve some measure of exclusivity for *Boat Sport*, he used one of his many pen names — Tracy Ogden.

Public popularity of outboard racing was starting to erode at the end of the Eisenhower years. The fifties' real racing magazines disappeared, leaving *OUT-BOARD* the responsibility of picking up some of the pieces. Catering to the niche enabled the publishers to advertise in the 1960 NOA Rule Book (for example) "Enjoy the best racing coverage every month in *OUTBOARD*." By then, that typically equaled a few pages, but was better than what the general yacht periodicals offered. That's a big reason why A. D. LaVelle started up a magazine called *The World of Boat Racing*. When this one appeared in 1964, outboard competition's universe was significantly smaller than it had been just five years earlier. Even so, it needed a newsstand magazine to call its own. A sample table of contents (September-October 1965) featured articles titled: "Launching a 1300cc Hydro," "ER Runabout and 7 Litre Divisionals," "Theory of Hydro Design," "Invitational Boat and Ski Championships," and "Build Ben-Hur." As a 12-year old boating nut, I happened upon a copy of this Minneapolis-based periodical. The colorful action outboard "modifieds" cover drew me to it immediately. Once I began flipping through the pages, it became evident to my grade-school sensibilities that almost nothing within looked like anything I could try or buy at the local marina. Nor were there any ads for motors or boats (except a Hal Kelly plan set mention) to which a beginner might relate. It certainly wasn't the fault of the magazine, though. With Mercury and Speed-Liner then pretty much out of the stock-racing loop, the times just weren't friendly to young, potential stock outboarders — the kind of people required to make such a publication grow. But, at least *The World of Boat Racing* gave it a valiant try.

Although a bit modern for *Vintage Culture*'s first edition, the early 1970s publication, *Hydroplane Quarterly* certainly deserves a mention. Its editor and publisher, Tim Chance, launched the magazine's debut winter 1970 issue with a nod to various predecessors. His interest in boat racing was spawned at the local corner store where he picked up a copy of

While not identified as "publications" in our text, racing event programs such as these deserve this mini-photo essay. Typically, they're rather top-heavy with arcane local advertising (as sponsors' messages helped offset race organizers' costs), but do explain protocols, identify the classes, and have note-taking space for fans who want to record results. Most eye-catching are their front pages as seen here.

Speed and Spray. "Next," the fledgling journalist noted, "I faithfully purchased *Boat Sport* through to the point where it became *Aqua Sport* and disappeared. Next came *Outboard* magazine; then I read the *World of Boat Racing* until my friend Tony LaVelle ceased publication. And now we have another — *Hydroplane Quarterly*. I hope everyone likes it as I plan on putting it out for a long time."

In those pre-word processor/computer desktop publishing days, magazine production represented an especially arduous task. *Hyrdoplane Quarterly* was obviously a labor of love. Most 8 1/2- by 11-inch issues hovered in the dozen, or so, page area, with copy consisting of regular typewriter type. By the summer 1971 edition, Chance apologized for it being "pretty skimpy." The following one was also a bit shy, so he gave subscribers an extra magazine. It was difficult trying to personally attend all the races, write the articles, as well as find new subscribers and new advertisers. A move to Saint Louis, Missouri, was designed to place Chance and his wife, Ann, in a more central coverage locale. Letters to

This 1947 comic book cover illustrates how its publisher figured that outboard racing would register more excitement than a feature on rockets, hence the larger boat and motor picture.

the editor they received were overwhelmingly positive. Most thanked them for keeping *HQ* going, but then wondered when the subscription might run out. Some included four bucks with a note for renewing.

Chance's editorials reflected a nadir in stock outboard racing. The number of participants had shrunk to some the sport's lowest levels. Spectators were also scarce, causing the editor to wonder during the summer of 1971 if it might be due to the fact that "most boat racers look pretty cruddy." He called for a "greater degree of professionalism to impress" anyone watching the race. But the admonitions always ended on a positive note, leading into a bank of articles crafted by one who cared about presenting the era's only periodical "devoted exclusively to the sport of boat racing."

Chance began his project by admitting that he could not do *HQ* alone. "I need the help of the whole racing fraternity," he indicated. "I can't personally cover all of the racing events around the country, so anyone who can be of assistance please write and let me know... either as a subscriber, reporter, or advertiser." Mercury, *Boat Sport's* largest benefactor, was ostensibly out of racing during *HQ's* run, so there were no big corporate ad contributions. Most of the little magazine's sponsors were also small businesses, with modest promotional budgets. By the mid-seventies, *Hydroplane Quarterly* went the way of the legendary publications that originally influenced it. Today, Chance's efforts provide us with an otherwise unavailable window into that era's outboard racing.

How-to Publications, etc.

It's sometimes tough to draw boundaries between garden variety articles and actual pamphlets on our topic. That's because several popularly distributed documents about outboard racing were copied from magazines. "What makes a Speedboat Champion?" came from June 1939's *Popular Mechanics*. The 1937 *Amateur Craftsman's Encyclopedia of Things to Make* offered a treatise on "Pepping Up Your Outboard Motor," and Buffalo, New York's Enterprise Oil Company printed up 25-cent handbooks by Bruno Beckhard, "the outboard motor authority." Beckhard's illustrated *More Power to You* appeared around 1928 with speed stats from the previous racing season, plus the latest competition rules, motor souping tips, boat/motor selection, lubrication/sparkplug information, and how to set up a race course.

In Great Britain, P. Roness Bordewich authored a 72-page *Outboard Motor Manual*. Given out as a promotion for the makers of *Castrol* oil, this passport-sized guide admitted "speed, of course, always attracts [attention]," and concentrated several chapters to preparing an outboard for racing, as well as outlining the late 1920s English outboard motor racing regulations.

Outboard Marine's 1945 decision to stay out of the racing marketplace cut off a major information source for alky-burners. When it had been selling Johnson and Evinrude high performance motors (until about 1942), the industry leader always had at least one factory expert assigned to the occasional job of answering racers' technical questions. After the war, the maker considered engines like a Johnson *KR-80*, Evinrude *Midget Racer*, or *4-60* to be simply passé (though it did reprise a version of the latter into the Evinrude *Big Four*). Manufacturing efforts and customer service were fully focused upon new versions of standard-use models, as well as on research and development of cutting edge models laden with consumer convenience features like gearshifts and remote fuel tanks. Consequently there certainly weren't many manufacturer's representatives eager to, for example, show a novice how to convert an Evinrude (World War II military) P-500 pump into an alcohol-fueled Class "F" racer.

Those who had prior racing outboard experience were generally okay about being on their own, but what about the individual (especially in those pre-stock outboard racing days of 1945-48) wanting to learn how to get into the alky sport? The question was answered by a number of veteran throttle squeezers figuring to share their knowledge with newcomers — and maybe make a few bucks doing it.

Examples of this brand of literature include a booklet by Charles F. Schreiber titled *High Speed Outboard Motor Tuning and Souping Up Methods*. Punched with three holes for a loose-leaf binder, this guide was copyrighted 1946 and 1948, with distribution through Excello Marine Sales of Stratford, Connecticut. Better known because of its long-time inclusion in the Michigan

There was a guy on the local lake who had a homebrew Science & Mechanix-inspired Minimax hydro and ordinary Sears Elgin fishing motor that really whipped past our dock. When asked how he got his rig performing so well, he told us about some "rare secret document" his uncle had sent away for back in the '50s. An entire summer of pestering him never netted a glance at the clandestine paperwork, but my guess is that it looked just like this Van Pelt Secrets of Stock Outboard Motorboat Racing, Book One. Though plain, it offered engine, propeller, and hull tips applicable to most any such equipment.

Wheel catalog, was W. R. Carpenter's *The Outboard Racer's Manual*. Muskegon (Michigan) Outboard Specialties Company also acted as a sales agent for the approximately 100-page volume. The author indicated that his spiral-bound publication served as "a complete manual covering the whats, whys, and hows of racing outboards." In fact, this technical tome was best suited for those with mechanical skills, and a penchant for machine shop work. It remained in the famous propeller maker's flyer through the early 1970s. By then, those placing an order for the 1951 booklet were likely Antique Outboard Motor Club members seeking a souvenir from a bygone boating era.

The early 1950s rise in stock outboard popularity gave rise to do-it-yourself literature for stockers. Boat builder and general all-around outboard speed advocate Art Van Pelt penned one of the genre's best. Titled *Secrets of (stock) Outboard Motor Racing*, this 1954, 30-pager told "how to get the last ounce of speed from your outboard motorboat." It covered everything from the warning signs of poor driving, boat balance, and use of stabilizer fins, to engine compression, motor height, spark plugs, and props. While the $3 booklet's binding — plain old typewriter type on pulp paper, with some line drawings- might seem primitive by today's computerized desktop publishing standards, Van Pelt provided his student readership with a very useful course.

As today's marine magazines are typically on speaking terms with five bucks an issue, it's extra nostalgic to note the 35-cent cover price of what was arguably the neatest little raceboat publication of the 1950s. Hank Wieand Bowman's *Stock Outboard Racing Yearbook* had just over 50 pages and measured only about the size of a *TV Guide*. Even so, it defined stock racing for the novice, showed how to get started, explained closed course, and marathons, then shared photographic and narrative highlights of the 1955 stock racing season. Format and text were nearly identical to Bowman's review of the outboard racing year fitted into various editions of Fawcett Publications' *Outboard Boating Handbook* magazines. No doubt, there were future stockers who spotted *Stock Outboard Racing Yearbook* in their corner drugstore's news rack and enthusiastically picked up a copy. Craig Bowman told me his Dad was hoping the project would sell well enough to attract sufficient sponsors resulting in it becoming an annual. Mercury (touting their *Mark 20H,* new *30H* and *55H*) was the sole advertiser willing to sign, however, causing this 1956 classic to run only once.

Books

If *Vintage Culture* devoted a quarter page to every 20th Century boating book that as much as mentioned racing, there'd be little room for anything else. Several general-purpose outboard titles, however, are considered seminal in their coverage of our topic, so deserve reference herein. Each either introduced outboard racing to readers, nicely massaged an interest for wannabes, or gave immediately useful tips to practitioners. Two appeared in 1930 when outboard racing was initially being embraced by waterside public. Bradford Burnham's *Outboard Motor Boats and Engines* was prepared during 1929 with competition enthusiasts in its proposed target readership. "If you desire to race," Burnham wrote, "you will find plenty of opportunity, usually near at hand. Outboard racing is unquestionably the most popular, exciting, and least expensive form of competitive [motorized] sport to be found today." The lead photo opposite the book's title page came from the Elto Division of Outboard Motor Corporation and showed a field of competition craft near a well-appointed yacht club. Its caption read, "the many entrants in most outboard races increase the excitement for contestants and spectators alike." Along with a nice helping of other racing pictures and fast boat plans exists a chapter devoted to Racing Meets, Rules, and Racing Records. Concurrent with this work, the editor of *Outboard Motorboat* magazine offered *Practical Outboard Motorboat Building and Operation*. It, too, featured publicity shots of racing, as well as three chapters ("Outboard Racing," "Outboard Games and Stunts," and "Staging and Financing a Regatta") devoted to the speed topic.

Author E. C. Schnurmacher began by linking the then new sport with a democracy where every participant has a fighting chance. "Almost every waterway from Maine to California that has witnessed the advent of the outboard motor boat," he states, "has also taken to outboard racing with a great deal of enthusiasm. It certainly is an interesting and exciting spectacle to witness twenty or more little outboards crossing the starting line at the crack of the gun in a race that may be won by any of them. The outboards, due to their number and idiosyncrasies, as well as to the many dark horses in their midst, furnish a type of racing that is, as a rule, more interesting than any other classes of boats." The book ends with a propeller selection chart for motors like the Class "B" Johnson *SR-45* racer, Johnson *TR Giant Twin*, and the *Caille Model 44 Monarch* competition mill, in addition to an outboard glossary (partially reproduced in our companion *Golden Age of the Racing Outboard*) filled with humorously arcane early racing terms.

Volumes defining post-World War II competition include Whittier's *Outboard Motor and Boat Book*. Understandably, the 1949 work's "Outboard Racing" chapter drew largely on prewar graphics and experience, but acknowledged that during the late 1940s "real racing outboards [were] more expensive than [standard-service] stock motors and [were] worth as much or more than when new, due to [OMC's 1942] cessation of [racing motor] production." Consequently, Whittier devoted some copy to reworking stock engines for various levels of competition –from just a bit of hop-up to total alcohol-fire conversion. By 1955, when Hank Bowman's *Encyclopedia of Outboard Motorboating* hit bookstores, stock racing mills (and related hulls) were readily available. No wonder he spent over 70 pages outlining the sport. Bowman's chapters included: "The Outboard in Racing," "Preparing the Stock Motor for Racing," "Grooming the Special Racing Engine, Racing Fuels", "Racing Hulls," and a "Speed Conversion Table" appendix. The content even included plans for making a hand-operated race starting clock, plus a racecourse buoy from an old tire inner tube, some pine boards, and discarded fruit/vegetable basket. For buffs interested in staging a race or even doing some serious cottage competition, *Encyclopedia of Outboard Motorboating* is still a valuable resource.

Movies

One by one, members donned their Lions Club name tags and poured coffee to accompany the civic group's traditional rubber chicken meal. During dinner, somebody routinely commented on the screen near the head table. "Looks like a movie is tonight's special program. Wonder what they're gonna show us." If that meeting took place anytime in the mid-1950s, the flick could have been about an outboard marathon in Wisconsin or upstate New York. Companies like the Kiekhaefer Corporation, and Atlantic Refining often had a film crew at such events, and transformed the resulting footage into a lively bit of free promotion offered to just about anyone with a 16-mm projector. Lots of folks got interested in stock outboard racing through one Mercury promotional movie featuring the Hudson River Marathon. It certainly wasn't any Academy Award winner, but the 1949 short about fighting the Hudson River in tiny outboard boats sure was exciting. Someone in the Kiekhaefer publicity department had liked the way a certain new ABC Radio broadcaster could make even ordinary news sound like a breaking bulletin, and so hired Paul Harvey to narrate the 1949 Albany- to-New York film. Hear his hyperbole that accompanied color action footage of the great race.

> The mighty motors join in a thundering battle hymn as drivers call for all the power they have to give — all making a desperate attempt to break into the lead that means smooth water and top speed. This is the greatest spectacle on water as the huge outboard fleet spreads out to blanket the Hudson in its downriver rush! More than 5000 horsepower is turned loose in a collective blast that rips up the river's surface into a shredded patchwork of foam and spray. One hundred and thirty-six debris and obstacle miles ahead lies the finish line. A real endurance test! Not only for boats and motors, but for the men who drive them as well. Old Man Hudson will take his toll today. There are mudflats waiting for the daredevils who cut the corners too close, driftwood hiding in the waves and wash that can smash in a boat bottom. Two miles below the starting line, they begin to string out like a wolf pack on the run. In groups of twos and threes, they settle down to the grueling game of challenge and pass. And it's a real race to the finish among all the boats in the three big classes ["DU, "EU," and "FU"], for up front, battling the fifty horsepower [Evinrude *Big Four*] jobs on even terms are those remarkable new twenty-five horsepower [*KF-9* and *KF-9HD*] Mercury Thunderbolts, demonstrating, even at this early stage of the race, impressive speed and power for their size... It takes one million, five-hundred thousand motor revolutions to get from Albany to New York. Five thousand RPM at five hours for the course. Hour

after hour that [Mercury] power has to keep paying off at the prop!

Harvey's voice wasn't always in sync with the picture, and one of those darn Evinrudes (a 50-hp *Big Four*) actually had nerve enough to win the race (in terms of being first over-all to the 72nd Street New York checkered flag). Even so, the flick made hay of a 25 Merc taking overall second (ahead of other OMC fifties). The smaller green onions did nicely, too. Here come those "hop, skip, and jump drivers," Harvey announced enthusiastically over views of plywood craft being faithfully pushed to New York City by spunky Merc *Rockets* and *Lightnings*. He smiled while proudly noting, "almost one HALF OF ALL THE MOTORS in the race were MERCURYS!" It was enough to prompt any red-blooded boat buff seeing the movie [perhaps at a Boy Scout or civic group meeting] to exclaim, "WOW! THAT'S REALLY KEEN!" Then chances were just a few miles from the showing, there would be a fledgling Merc dealership with at least one or two of those models on display. Likely it'd even be owned by the guy working the projector, delivering an informal boat-ing safety spiel, and handing out brochures or Mercury souvenirs (maybe a pencil or key chain). No doubt, the grand finale would include an open house invitation to his salesroom after the show — albeit a bit hokey.

A few, authentically Hollywood-quality boat racing movies have entertained theater-goers over the years. The oldest — an early 1930s flick- appears to be lost to time, or at best mired in some corporate ownership rights mumbo-jumbo. Two others — shot about 25 years later — seem to occasionally pop up in the wee hours on cable or sandwiched between raunchy talk show promos and ads for $12.99 compact discs containing every song ever sung, over some lonely UHF-TV channel.

In the early days of sound on film, the busy tune of a marauding outboard motorboat could contribute a sensation of real action. Columbia Pictures commissioned a script about some young outboarders who build a hydro and drive it to victory in a crucial race. The resulting 1932 movie, staring Joan Marsh and William Collier Jr., was titled *Speed Demon*. Most of the action scenes were filmed at the old Long Beach Olympic Marine Stadium. Some of the West Coast's best racers were asked by Columbia to participate in the movie, and to instruct the stars how to get a boat up on plane safely. Depression-era moviegoers who knew their motors recognized Evinrude *4-60* mills, *Speeditwins*, and Johnsons of the *SR* and *PR* persuasions.

Dean Martin and Jerry Lewis were mega-stars in 1955 when they made a picture called *You're Never Too Young*. Somewhere between disguising himself as a 12-year old and stealing jewelry, Lewis gets Martin involved in high-speed boating. Designed to maximize the duo's comedy of errors trademark, their Speed Liner runabout and "B" Merc wind up in a pine tree. Kiekhaefer "loaned" the movie studio its Mercury Jumping Boat Team for the water and airborne sequences. Reportedly, some of the Mercs on camera consisted of *20H* racing powerheads on standard *Mark 25* lower units.

Mercury jumped at the chance to have its outboards featured in the Dean Martin-Jerry Lewis comedy You're Never Too Young. Reportedly, power was in the form of a specially concocted mill – a 20H racing powerhead mated to the standard Mark 20 or Mark 25 lower unit. Movie maven Leonard Maltin says the flick was "fast and funny," awarding it three out of four stars.

Two years later, Pat Boone made the silver screen sing with a musical tale of stock outboard racing titled *Bernardine*. The '50s pop chart topper donned life jacket, knee pads, and helmet to debut as an "ASH" competitor in a craft dubbed *Bernardine Mudd*. Evident was a little bit of outboarding, some rose-colored glimpses into Eisenhower-era teenage life, and tons of Boone tunes. Also starring in the teen idol's film debut were movie veterans like Dean Jagger, and Janet Gaynor. Carl Kiekhaefer made sure fans knew Pat was using a Merc *KG4-H*, and had thousands of *Bernardine* black & white promotional photos printed for dealers to distribute.

One Merc shop set up a motor display right in the local theater lobby, and gave out publicity stills, and entry blanks for a chance to win a new *Mark 30* engine. The Baltimore Mercury dealership gained over 15,000 new names for its mailing list throuh the contest tie-in with the 1957 Twentieth Century-Fox feature. Though today's film critic Leonard Maltin — admittedly a fan of such wholesome fare — can barely manage to give *Bernadine* an anemic two out of four-stars rating and calls it "a very weak look at teen-age life," the full-color, 95-minute, *CinemaScope* presentation probably delighted boat

racing buffs. Some of those seeing the movie during the Saturday matinee might have even made a beeline for a nearby toy shop to search the shelves for a model hydro reminiscent of Boone's craft.

Close observation reveals that consultants were likely employed to give Pat Boone an authentic stock racer look in his first motion picture effort – Bernardine. He's got the kneepads, legal life jacket, helmet, and nice new Mercury Rocket Hurricane KG-4H sans its lower cowls. How else would the Hollywood crew have known that this factory-installed shrouding had to be immediately deep-sixed for one's Merc racer to appear authentic? Of course the true marks of real-ism on this set are the "official" stock outboard racer grease stains applied to Boone's legs. However, they overlooked his hands and arms, which are complete-ly clean.

Chapter Ten

Hop-up Stuff and Racing Outboard Parts

"Early in the [outboard racing] game we found that an extra length shaft produced more speed. The racers who had the extra length ran away from the others."
— *Judge Aaron B. Cohn, 1923*

WHEN JUDGE COHN, the author of our chapter head epigram helped develop outboard racing in the 1910s, he and his fellow enthusiasts immediately began searching for motor hop-up techniques. The reference to extra long lower units seems laughable now, but before the great efficiencies of surfacing propellers (and aerodynamic hulls) were understood, getting a big bite of deep water made sense. In what is believed to be one of the first outboard racing hop-up documents (*Power Boating* September 1923), Cohn recommends fitting your performance "putt-putt" with a tin cup under the mixing valve (to prevent inadvertent water intake), twisting some substantial bailing wire around the water pump hose (so the pipe won't fall off during a big race), custom port the cylinder(s) to yield about 10 percent extra speed, install a large drip-oiler that feeds right to the crankcase, mount a glass sediment bowl in the fuel line between the fuel tank and carburetor, and obtain an accessory telescoping tiller handle to facilitate steering from the center seat.

While the kickers Cohn's pioneers operated in "ye very olden times" were obsolete even before most boaters ever knew there was such a thing as outboard racing, they

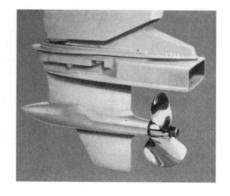

Advertised in a 1960s Chrysler outboard catalog, this racing lower unit was "developed through Chrysler research. Available to all speed-loving boaters [wanting to add it to] the Chrysler 75 and 105 [it] has helped racers chalk up speeds up to 70 mph plus in single installations!"

paved the way for a robust cottage industry — especially in the 1950s — aimed at making motors at least a bit sexier and at least a little faster. For a manufacturer's marketing purposes, hop-up accessories have always had a pair of targets, the sanctioned outboard competitor and the cottage racer. Because the latter, less formal group has always been much larger, makers understood their products must be reasonably priced, easily installed, non-invasive, and quickly reversionary. Ideally, these gizmos should also have a readily noticeable visual, audio, and/or performance effect.

Fancy paint certainly met some of these goals and was, indeed, affordable. Even so, a company in Burley, Idaho, claimed to offer "the cheapest speed you can buy" without any color change. It was Speedwax, "the elixir for racing boats with tired bottoms." An ad in the August 1960 *Propeller*, offered a money back guarantee to any Speedwax user who didn't see a 1-5 mph gain. This product, aimed at hopping-up one's hull, was touted as being "more resistant to surface tension 'pull-down' and water wetting than ordinary waxes." A $10 Speedwax kit was supposed to last 150 to 400 races. The price was right, but, standing on the shore, who could see you were using it? Fortunately, the Vintage Culture's hop-up arsenal also includes high-speed props, sleeker lower units, and, best of all, "dumps," or open exhaust manifolds.

Open Exhaust

Early in the fifties, Cencro-Tone Products saw the sales potential in offering a manifold for the thousands of 10-horse Mercs buzzing America's waterways. The Fort Worth, Texas, concern came out with a grommet-like open outlet that replaced the engines' stock exhaust port cover. When the neighbors started complaining, peace and quiet could be restored in about five minutes by going back to the original equipment. A more cottage community friendly style was introduced around 1953. This one affixed to the same spot, but resembled a stubby stack with a simple cover. When Old Lady Jenkins, who always threatened to call the state police, was away visiting her sister, two small screws were all that stood between that cover and some loud outboard

Cencro-Tone's exhaust "dump" for Mercury's KG-7 Hurricane series.

fun. Cencro-Tone also sold a version for the Martin "*200*," that had more of a "stack" design, promised an extra two miles per hour, and an "exhaust tone resembling larger motors." Not bad for 12 bucks retail.

More widely distributed than the above were similar products from Quincy Welding Works. By 1951, the Quincy, Illinois, company was moving hundreds of its *R-10* series exhaust manifolds and related accessories through mail order and Mercury dealers. Speed

The Quincy exhaust stack for 20-cubic inch Mercs, shown without "courtesy cover."

enthusiasts with a *KE7, KF7,* or *KG7* could install this item like the previously mentioned Cencro-Tone. It too, featured a removable cover affixed by a pair of screws. Quincy's *R-10,* however, was able to be mated with the *R-10A* exhaust stack. This dual pipe accessory used the same screw holes as the removable cover and gave the motor a "Hollywood tune [while] directing exhaust away from passengers." An *R-10Q* exhaust manifold shutter was a more flexible version of the standard *R-10* cover. It had a little lever-activated wheel that opened and closed the exhaust outlet "at the flick of the finger . . . for greater speed or quieter motor. [It could be] turned on or off while running," and gave cottage racers pragmatic options whenever the widow Jenkins shook her fist from the dock.

Also notable in the avenue of Merc exhaust stacks were the beautifully stylized Cyclone headers by Joe Grossman of St. Louis, and Grosse Point Marine Supply's Piper. Both firms made units that fit Kiekhaefer's 20-cubic-inch *KE-7, KF-7, KG-7,* as well as the class "D" *KF-9* or *KG-9.* Grossman once mentioned that the molds, used in making the "B" *Cyclone,* broke rather early on. Consequently, the larger size is a bit more common today. Meanwhile, the *Piper Exhaust* pledged to deliver a "soul-stirring sense of power to the outboard racing enthusi-

The maker of these Piper exhaust pipes said they'd give even the most ordinary KG-9 Merc a beautiful tune of racing motor music.

ast who enjoys the pulsing, deep-throated, staccato rhythm of RACING MOTOR MUSIC." Copy for the Michigan company's ads sounded like it originated in a Southern California movie publicity office, but assured less boisterous boaters that the stacks "can be closed when not in use."

Stacks for non-Merc motors were not quite as prevalent. During the 1950s, Champion marketed the A-600 open

Cyclone exhaust stacks for four-cylinder (left), and twin-cylinder Mercury motors.

An Ohio firm marketed the stack affixed to this late 1940s Mercury KE-7 Lightning. The APBA wouldn't allow open exhausts in its stock races, but some NOA contestants and lots of cottage racers fully approved of the extra "zing" such an accessory would promote.

exhaust chute to owners of its "B" *Hot-Rod*. Hop-up houses like Hubbell cast stacks for the Evinrude *M*, *Speeditwin*, Johnson *SR*, *PR*, and Elto *4-60*. Exhaust deflectors were also available for the *KR* Johnson.

Dual Carbs

Ray Alberty of Bartlesville, Oklahoma, invented a hop-up item sure to appeal to the hundreds of thousands of OMC 35-hp owners wanting a little extra outboarding zing. His dual carburetion accessory, dubbed "Jet-Pac," wasn't really a second carb as much as it was an additional breather, but it was supposed to add about15 percent or five horses to its host mill. During the late 1950s, Alberty made about 2,500 Jet-Pacs, selling most of the inventory within a few years, but never

The light-colored unit mounted on this OMC twin's cylinder block is a Jet-Pac dual carburetion accessory. It was supposed to add at least five-horses to a garden variety Big Twin-style outboard.

restocking. Somewhere in cottage racerdom there was probably a bright white, tiller-steered Johnson Sea Horse 35 fitted with one of the Oklahoman's devices . . . and for good measure, a Hubbell gearcase.

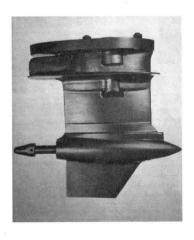

Lower Units

Speaking of Randolph Hubbell, his modest Golden State shop was responsible for more outboard hot-rodding than just about anyone. Though he made everything from reed induction systems for old Johnson *SR* and *PR* mills to external rotary valves for those *Sea Horse* classics, much of the Hubbell mystique was generated with accessory racing lower

This Hubbell model B55C racing lower unit is fitted with an adaptor for mating with OMC alternate-firing twins in the 25 to 40-horse range.

units. Best representative of the South El Monte, California, genre was the B55C. Available through the 1970s, with a 13:16 or 13:19 gear ratio, this streamlined lower unit fit Hubbell's SR and PR replicas, and, with an adapter plate, 25- 40-horse Evinrude/Johnson *Big Twin* motors. Cottage racers with OMC's most mundane family runabout outboard could try for an extra nine-mph (on the right hull) after taking about 15 minutes to attach one of these pieces. Those 36ers running "outlaw" (or non-APBA/NOA sanctioned events) loved the *B55C*, as it was far sleeker than their motor's APBA-legal, stock gearcase. Earlier 1952 Hubbell catalogs listed a 15-1JE Johnson/Evinrude 25-hp racing lower unit for the first *Big Twin* engines. "On and off in five minutes," promised the optimistic little caption, "with gain up to 10-miles per hour." Visually, this version was a bit rounder than the subsequent *B55C*, and probably not quite as fast. For OMC owners wanting to keep their original lower unit's shifting capability, Hubbell's 13:19 "speed gear" set was a nice option. It came in a kit with gears, prop shaft, and related pieces for 25 to 40-horse Johnsons and Evinrudes, as well as for the 25 to 30-hp Gale *Buccaneers* or *Sovereigns*.

Hubbell's brochures also pictured his better-known lower units for pre-World War II Evinrude, Elto, and Johnson racers. Then there was the highly publicized *40-F60* Hubbell Overdrive Racing Lower Unit; well known for helping Hugh Entrop and an Evinrude V-4, 75-horse engine set a world's unlimited hydro speed record of 122.9 mph (to best his earlier Mercury Mark *75H* feat). With a 40-F60, anyone with $300 and a Johnson/Evinrude 50 or 75, vintage Evinrude/Elto *4-60*, four or six cylinder Merc, or even a Scott 60, could be on speaking terms with some pretty fast company. Not only had the just-forward gear unit and adapter plate aided Entrop, but also it was party to an official 1/4-mile 72.4-mph outboard drag and 78.9-mph unlimited runabout records.

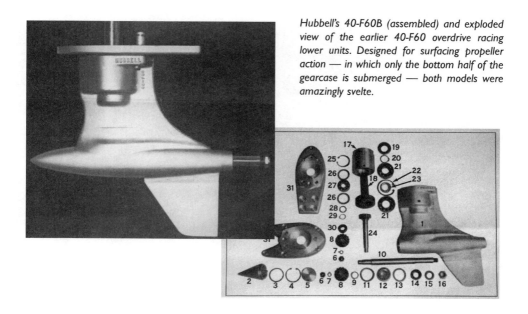

Hubbell's 40-F60B (assembled) and exploded view of the earlier 40-F60 overdrive racing lower units. Designed for surfacing propeller action — in which only the bottom half of the gearcase is submerged — both models were amazingly svelte.

A vintage outboard racing buff in Texas snapped this photo of a couple of "oddball" performance lower units he'd found at some sale. The larger one is a nice example of the early Cornaire-Vrooman gearfoot for the first generation OMC 25-horse twins. There's a little Martin "60" Hi-Speed foot just below it. Not a bad find either!

"Interchangeable with the stock unit in minutes," this piece was not for boaters with sightseeing in mind. It had no water pump, and wouldn't force-feed cooling water to the scorching cylinders until the rig hit 25 mph. With "6250 propeller RPM at a safe 5000 crankshaft RPM," though, that didn't take very long.

Not long after Evinrude shipped its Watertown, New York, dealer some 1951 *Big Twin* motors, plans for another unique lower unit were made. The folks at Vrooman's Marine Sales got to thinking how many high-speed gear feet they might market to the hundreds of new 25 OMC owners just in their upstate area. Multiplying that times all the other Evinrude/Johnson 25 customers the world over, an opportunity for big profits came into view. The Vroomans got together with Watertown machine shop operator John Cornarie, who helped design and produce what has since been logically dubbed the *Cornaire-Vrooman Racing Foot*. Word of a similar piece for the 10-hp Johnson *QD* surfaces occasionally, but so far, none has been seen. All of its components, including a bronze two-blade 11- by 12-inch prop, were the products of tiny local shops. Reportedly, around the time of the hop-up accessory's 1953 introduction, Messers Cornaire and Vrooman went their separate ways.

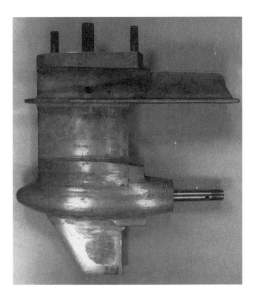

A most interesting result of this conflict/split is that each of their companies subsequently advertised the same item under their respective names. May 1953 *Speed and Spray* ads touted the Vrooman 1:1 lower units as offering "speeds of 60 mph and over" at a price of $100. Across town, Cornaire sold some of his identical units through the December 1953 *Motor Boating* for just 80 bucks. This dichoto-

A GO-MAC lower unit for the Evinrude Speeditwin. The top trailing edge (above the anti-cavitation plate) on another version was angled down towards the rear of the anti-cavitation plate. (Fred Truntz photo)

Check out the tractor gearfoot on this Mercury KG-7Q. That's no standard-issue Quicksilver gearcase! Reportedly propeller maven "Poppa" Smith built it. The story goes that when Merc head Carl Kiekhaefer saw it, he wanted one, too. This item appears to be influenced by a similar-looking Walker-Bauman piece usually associated with large, pre-World War II custom racers?

my ended when Cornaire Machine Company turned its attention elsewhere, leaving Vrooman to be the sole distributor for the lower unit. Enigmatically, neither version never gained acceptance from the APBA. The nicely crafted feet were largely relegated to the cottage racer crowd. The makers recall having produced parts for some 250 of these unnumbered and unlabeled units, many of which were snapped up in North America and abroad by waterway hotrodders. My collection of miscellany includes a nearly finished set of Vrooman or Cornaire (who can tell?) castings, suggesting not all 250 saw action. By 1962, Vrooman ran a modest advertisement for an updated racing lower unit. This one has a slightly different shape — especially the skeg — and included an adapter plate for the later OMC 25- to 40-horse twins.

An equally intriguing and elusive item out of Hot Springs, Arkansas, got snapped up by a number of serious "C-Service" racers. During the early 1960s, Tommy Goslee and his associate Arthur McMeans produced the GO-MAC lower unit just for the Evinrude *6039* Speeditwin. It could quickly replace the stock gearfoot, be class legal, but with a tad more streamlining than the original, provide that commonly sought extra mile per hour or two. By the way, McMeans later served as the first president of the American Outboard Federation upon its 1971 founding. Even before he received this political pull, his lower units pushed some "C-Service" boats to victory.

Before World War II, when tractor lower units found some favor, the Walker-Bauman people developed a few of these pullers for racing use. The most notable was fitted to the rare Draper "X" Class quad of 1937. No doubt, a high priced, hand machined, custom order product, Walker-Bauman units also saw action on motors like Evinrude *Speeditwins*. Most interesting is a tractor lower gearfoot (that certainly appears to be from W-B) found mated to a *KG-7Q* Mercury. Though post-

Scott-Atwater Green Hornet lower unit version #1. Interestingly, this piece actually found a working relationship with a like-branded mate.

Version #2 of Scott-Atwater's Green Hornet lower unit. Earlier models had a longer exhaust snout with rounded end. Few were actually mated to Scott's 16-horse mill. Instead, the majority of this admittedly low production foot got adapted to OMC 25-35 horse twins.

war, it features a Walker-Bauman-like trapezoid skeg.

Allotted several pages in *The Golden Age of the Racing Outboard,* but worthy of mention herein, is the Green Hornet lower unit from Scott-Atwater. This early- to-mid-1950s high-speed foot was designed for hopping-up performance on Scott's 20-cubic-inch 16-horse twin. A long, curved snout exhaust outlet version predated one where the outlet was "sawed off" for greater relief. Neither was actually painted green nor considered very successful on the 16-hp mill, but Green Hornet's latter edition got featured in a *Boat Sport* article where its adaptation to the ubiquitous Evinrude *Big Twin* (25- and 30-hp motors) was suggested.

The universality of Evinrude and Johnson's 60, 75, and 90 hp V-4 outboards gave marine engineers Charles Heston and Walter Peterson a project worth noting. During the 1960s, the duo designed for Universal Projects, Inc., a racing lower unit mountable on any motor in the previously mentioned OMC series. Imagine a cottage racer ripping up the river with a so equipped Gale Sovereign or Sea King 60. On a 16-foot family runabout, the H-P (Hi-Performance, Heston-Peterson) let a stock 75 Johnson experience 60+ mph. The *H-P* was a completely interchangeable lower unit that borrowed the standard, replaced unit's water pump. It's built-in (19:16) overdrive yielding 6000 prop rpm from 5000 at the crankshaft. Being three inches shorter than the stock unit, the H-P didn't

necessitate building up the transom for best prop action. It sold for $296 FOB from Jacksonville, Florida, and the makers noted that spare parts "manufactured so they will fit" were immediately available from stock. The brightly polished H-P and bronze 8-1/2- inch diameter by 18-inch pitch propeller (for hydro) sure could get hot boat nuts to take a second glance at a matronly OMC *V-4.*

Specializing in speedy lower units that made pre-World War II racing motors look extra good were a

H. H. Starnes was a popular alky driver who also manufactured sundry racing outboard parts the likes of this "C" Class lower unit for the Johnson PR and its cognates. (Dave Schell collection)

Many of the racing lower units from tiny manufacturers were built to squeeze an extra fraction of a mph from the long-practiced Johnson PR-based alky "C" Class. This Harden piece — with tiny gearcase and long prop shaft — was just the thing for advancing propeller surfacing tactics and eking out a bit more speed.

number of small but important makers. Randolph Hubbell's work in this field has already been noted. His efforts to keep alky engines going fast years after Evinrude/Elto and Johnson planned were also shared by pros like Clyde Wiseman of Wickliffe, Ohio. Under the Wiseco label, Wiseman offered 1931-type racing gear feet for "C" Service, and *PR* mills. Red Jones (not to be confused with cylinder chroming expert, Wes Jones) from Cardiff, California, specialized in a lower unit suitable for the "A" class Johnson *KR* users. *SR, PR, Speeditwin,* and *4-60* feet could come by way of H. H. Starnes in Hickory, North Carolina.

The December 1954 *Boat Sport* announced the availability of a racing lower unit from Harden Machine Shop from Portsmouth, Virginia. Harden's $175 gear foot was designed to be quickly attached to any external rotary-valved Johnson *PR* or

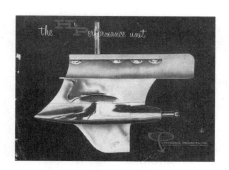

HP Hi Performance lower unit designer Charles Heston had raced outboards in the 1940s and 1950s, and played a major role in the creation of Martin's "60" Hi-Speed gearcase. So, it was only natural that he'd come up with the sleek HP piece in the 1960s. Reportedly, less than 100 were produced.

Evinrude *Speeditwin* Racers. The note also indicated Harden handled "*KR* units, as well as *PR* cylinders and heads, plus a complete line of Wiseco, Hubbell, and Fuller racing parts." Externally, anyway, the Harden "C" unit looked quite similar to the one by Wiseco.

It's possible there was some "badge-engineering" connecting these two neat feet.

Perhaps the most poshly packed high-speed gear foot was produced in late 1953 by the

An Eldridge gearfoot found crudely mated to an Evinrude Big Four/4-60 engine. The installation didn't look very good, but it sure made for a neat cottage racing motor.

Believed to be a Walker-Bauman product, this tractor lower unit was spotted on a 1930s Evinrude Speeditwin. Facing forward, the propeller pulled — rather than pushed — the boat.

Springfield, Massachusetts-based Whitkum Company. Its "C" and "F" compatible item was designed by John Whitehouse, who won the 1948 Albany-to-New York Marathon in "F" stock utility. This "full-surfacing" lower unit was "shipped in a blue, felt-lined hardwood case with built-in racks to hold three propellers." *Boat Sport* for December 1953 noted that Whitkum expected to soon be making props in two diameters and six pitches for the new racing gear foot.

The epitome of low production and high quality was Abbot Machine Shop's racing lower unit for the Johnson PR. It came out of the Jefferson City, Missouri, outboard racing proprietorship around 1954.

And then there's the case of the Montana Champ Clone. Blakney's Glass Shop in Missoula made up a few 6N-HR Champion Hot Rod-style lower units fitted with an adapter plate. *Boat Sport* (June 1957) reported the pieces wore 14:19 gears and were meant to be mated to a Johnson SR. The Blakney foot had a removable water pump, and was designed to "function on a 12 inch hydro transom, thus offering lower than normal center of gravity for . . . better control and three to four miles per hour higher speed than with the original Johnson unit."

Propellers

Even a fast outboard linked to the most svelte gearcase can't accomplish much without its proper propeller. Along with Mickey and Sid, the principals of Sid Craft boats, racer Dick O'Dea knew the

A couple of new-old-stock Michigan Aqua-Jet props wait to be the glass slipper for some seemingly plane-Jane outboards. The results can yield a real Cinderella racing story.

Not to be confused with Johnson out-boards, the Johnson Propeller Company was headquartered in a small San Francisco area facility. From there, it contributed greatly to many a speed record.

value of good props. By 1960, the trio was offering high-pitched wheels bearing the M-S-D label. These props were specially made for them by Vigano of Italy — a firm that attempted to communicate with M-S-D exclusively in Italian. Fortunately, an old tailor near O'Dea's Patterson, New Jersey, home spoke the language. Every time a letter from Vigano arrived, O'Dea would run over to the tailor's little shop for translation. Then the fellow would help him write up another order. He and his partners always breathed a sigh of relief when the resulting overseas shipment actually contained props.

Some racing wheels from Mercury ended up in Italy. They were part of a 1953 package of 12 *KG-7H* motors sold to the Italian navy for training future PT Boat commanders. Merc props were actually labeled Kaminc, which stood for Kiekhaefer Aeromarine, Inc. These high quality propellers were meant to pull the lion's share of the stock outboard accessory marketplace. Much to the chagrin of Fond du Lac, however, most Merc stock racing engine owners instinctively fitted their mills with *Michigan* props or other brands not directly associated with the motor maker.

During stock outboard racing's golden age, Kiekhaefer maintained something of a love/hate relationship with its chief prop rival, Michigan Wheel Company of Grand Rapids. This firm made a major contribution to both organized stock and cottage racing when during the late 1940s it began developing a line of Aqua-Jet hop-up props. Available for all stockers and many service motors in either an AJ (straight through prop hub), or AJC (*Aqua-Jet Cushion* with a rubber "clutch" hub insert), these wheels went through testing so rigorous that they may reliably go from box to race with very satisfactory results.

Some years back, I acquired a Martin "*200*" gear foot from Michigan Wheel's proving site. The poor thing had been banged-up and welded enough times to tell me lots of experimentation went into the firm's 1954 release of its *AJ530* two-blade. Certainly, Michigan Wheel had heard scuttlebutt about Martin's imminent closure, but forged ahead with its new offering for the doomed "*200*" anyhow. The key to acceptance is quality, widespread exposure, and availability for numerous motors. Michigan Wheel has long offered all three.

A few other propeller makers' products often graced the winners' circle and the trailer motor boxes of experienced outboard racers. Oakland-Johnson, or O-J Props of Oakland, California, *DeWald* of Reading, Pennsylvania, Cary Enterprises of New York (importers of an Italian line of props), and Stannus Propeller Company out of Detroit each crafted wheels that were considered among the best in the business. The DeWald name is inexorably linked to stock racing, as this prop company is still owned and operated by Craig DeWald, also famous for his many youthful marathon victories.

Outboard Racing Parts

There's a story about a young fellow who wanted to soup-up his garden variety Johnson KD-15. The guy who helped out at the kid's local marina swore up and down that a KD was almost like a KR racer, "except for the crankcase, or something." Anyway, the youngster sees an ad for a "*Special KR Class 'A' Crankcase,*" and its not too bad, just 15 bucks. Without understanding all the details, he sends his money to Muskegon Outboard Specialties Company. A week or so later, the Muskegon, Michigan, package arrives with a rough casting the kid can't figure out. No matter, that outboard lover has long used it as a paperweight today he wouldn't let leave his desk for 10 times the 1954 price. Back then even if he'd ordered the $50 finished version, it would still have taken considerable expertise to make it go. Largely a province of alky and modified racers, many major engine components were offered from the late 1940s throughout 1960s — and some up to the early Reagan years.

In addition to the aforementioned *KR* piece from Muskegon, crankcases for *SR* and "C" Service could be had via Ezzo Marine in Columbus, Ohio. H. H. Fuller of Independence, Missouri, supplied these parts for *SR* and *PR* motor building. Frank Vincent Marine Company from Tulsa, Oklahoma, made crankcases in *KR*, *SR*, and *PR* sizes. And, of course, the oft-noted Hubbell shop supplied crankcases for the tiny "M" projects clear through to "F" construction. All types of crankshafts were also available from Hubbell, in addition to *PR* cranks from Bill Flannigan in Decatur, Georgia, and *Speeditwin* versions via Clyde Wiseman of Ohio. Wiseman, and Hubbell could supply racing pistons. San

Little ads like this for Muskegon Outboard Specialties Company were mainstays in publications such as Boat Sport. Here, the tiny firm wedged in plugs for a how-to racing booklet and its aftermarket KR crankcase.

Martin Marathon tank. A relatively uncommon Martin accessory is this marathon hand-pumped fuel tank, presumably for the Martin "60 Hi-Speed" or standard "100."

Francisco's Biagio and Huffman made them for *PR*, "C" Service, and *4-60* engines. The folks at Jacoby Boat Works in North Bergen, New Jersey, had high-performance replacement pistons, too. Cylinders and heads were products of Hubbell as well as H. H. Fuller, and Vincent, while cylinder chroming and grinding for alkies and modifieds was the specialty of Westerman Jones of Claymont, Delaware. Jones also produced some of the best replacement PR cylinders that outboard racers have ever known. Cylinder catch-bars could be ordered from H. H. Fuller, or Marshall Eldredge of Lakeland, Florida. These devices prevented high-revving parts from popping off when the throttle was squeezed.

Keller Manufacturing Company of Seattle, and Quincy Welding Works (*V-100 Visu-Matic*) probably sold more safety throttles than any other makers. Over the decades, a host of others like Richardson, Jacoby, Van Pelt, Wiseman's Wiseco, and Kaminc gave stockers the gas, and alkies the fuel.

Fuel

Commercially blended racing fuel for the alcohol burners came with exotic monikers such as *Nitro-X* (Sweney Prosser of Charlotte, North Carolina), Power Mist-Blue Blazer (Francisco Laboratories in Los Angeles), Dynax (from DuPont), Bud Wiget's Super Speed, Experiment, Inc. (Richmond, Virginia) Exol brand, and Chris-Go from Detroit's Christopher Brothers. Most of this rare brew came in five-gallon cans with interesting but strange logos that might not ring a bell for stock or cottage racers.

Racing Throttles

Reportedly packed with some 1953 Mark 40H motors, the KAMINC safety throttles were a low production item. This one was found in unpainted aluminum, but a few others have been noted wearing era-appropriate Mercury green. For the product of a quality outboard maker, this example's lettering casting work is admittedly pretty crude.

Rather ornate for Spartan racing requirements, the B/L Special safety throttle featured a nice competition motif.

Regardless of its potentially long throw (from idle to fast), the Quincy Visu-Matic served as the safety throttle standard and was arguably a part of more racing rigs than any other specific brand of equipment. The little button atop the action lever is a throttle lock. While certainly helpful when both hands were needed to adjust a carburetor, etc., it could defeat the desired safety factor, so was not allowed (by some clubs) to remain intact.

Appendix A

Prop Masters of the Vintage Culture's Hall of Fame

*T*HE BALLROOM AT NEW YORK CITY'S Belmont Plaza Hotel looked pretty classy on a mid-January morning in 1956. Gulf Oil had rented that up-scale facility for a breakfast and awards ceremony honoring boat-racing greats. Oddly, the envelopes on the podium contained no names of outboard drivers. Eighteen years earlier, the Gulf Marine Racing Hall of Fame had been established to honor outstanding speedy inboarders, while keeping Gulf products in the minds of the boating public. After all the certificates, trophies and honorable mentions were delivered, the emcee announced that, during the '56 season, his oil company would be enlarging its Hall of Fame's jurisdiction to include "the popular Stock Outboard and Outboard classes."

Over the years, a number of throttle-squeezers have enjoyed recognition in the Gulf group, by way of other similar industry "halls," *OUTBOARD* magazine's "Silver Prop Award," *Yachting's* "All American Racing Team," as well as through the APBA's Honor Squadron. Yet, many who contributed to the sport go unsung. Herein is an attempt to start an outboard (alky and stock) racing "Hall of Fame" baseline listing. Those noted are <u>some</u> of the personalities who shaped fast outboarding from the 1930s through the 1950s. Several dozen names -that are obvious picks for such a roster- appear in detail elsewhere in this book, therefore are not described on these next pages.

There will, no doubt, be racing greats who are not yet listed herein. That's because this group is *Vintage Culture's* base line, and is designed to become more inclusive. The publisher will forward suggestions readers care to submit. It will be my pleasure to receive your nominating input received through Devereux Books.

Don Baldaccini. APBA Inspectors at the 1954 Nationals thought Don Baldaccini's KG-4H was "too perfect," thus violating the spirit of stock outboarding rules. They never said his winning motor was actually illegal, just so meticulously mechanically manicured that it raised a few red flags. Eventually, though, brass recognized the mill as perfectly legal. That meant the Floridian would get to officially claim the "A" Stock Hydro crown he'd just tentatively won.

Baldaccini got into racing stock motors and boats while a 14 year old with a Merc KE-4 Rocket on a little runabout. The Florida fishing boat class was coming on strong in 1948 for adventurous Sunshine Staters, and with the help of his marine dealer/ stepfather, Baldaccini got into the sport full tilt. By 1950, he'd moved-up to a 10 hp Mercury KF-7 and for '51 competed in runabout and hydro. After high a 1952 school graduation, Don sold off his stock gear and readied for a college career. Not long after classes began, though, an illness forced him out of school. Upon recovery, he went to work managing one of his step-dad's marine outlets and got back into throttle squeezing. Along the way, Baldaccini experienced his share of ups and downs, but in 1956 he displayed a brand of stamina that earned the National High-Point title. In fact, he claimed the honor via the largest score in the history of stock outboarding up to that time.

Back to the 1954 incident . . . A little more than three weeks after the KG-4H disqualification, a letter from the APBA arrived at Baldacinni's Miami home. "Congratulations," it announced. "You are the winner of the "A" Stock Hydro National Championship. Members of the Stock Outboard Commission had considered the young man's case, and found that rather than undermining the spirit of the sport, he embodied its strength in the hey day 1950s.

Hank Bowman. This versatile writer, boat racing advocate, APBA stock outboard official, and sportsman is covered in Chapter Six.

Bob Carver. A Seattle area photographer, Bob Carver lived around racing and possessed a sixth sense for knowing just when to snap the camera shutter, thus capturing exciting split-second images that would otherwise be lost to blur and time. Once, when contracted by Mercury's Carl Kiekhaefer to do a publicity still of a dual-engined outboard runabout making a ramp jump. Carver snagged a crystal clear shot of the twin Mercs upside down in mid air after the boat's transom broke loose. Needless to say, Kiekhaefer was terrified of the picture's power and tried permanently banning its release.

Dean Chenoweth. "In my three years of racing," Dean Chenoweth was quoted in the 1954 Mercury catalog, "I've won 74 trophies and three national titles, but I've never gotten over the thrill that comes with the start of a new race and the chance to pit my driving — and my motor — against top competition. I've used Mercurys exclusively throughout my racing career." Actually, he started outboarding with an Evinrude, but that was only a 1-1/2-horse *Ranger* when Chenoweth was only five. His dad fitted the youngster with a lifejacket, put him in a rowboat, started the kicker and let him putt-putt out in front of the family's Indian Lake (Russells Point, Ohio) cottage. By the time he was 12, Chenoweth had graduated to a Merc 10 and began speeding around the lake.

Coincidentally, in 1950, Kiekhaefer distributor, Merlyn Culver, noticed the youth's rig on the water, and then suggested to Chenoweth's father that the boy looked like he had promise as a throttle-squeezer. After Culver convinced him to enroll in engineering school, Chenoweth seemed to take his place on the racecourse. He certainly was well equipped with the latest gear. As a protégée of the senior Culver, backed by a Mercury distribution network, Chenoweth went through a pair of hydros, seven utilities, as well as five "A" and "B" Mercs in three years. This racing standout dubbed his runabouts *Beedle Bomb* and assigned the tag *Beedle Bomb Kid* to the hydros in his stable. As an adult, Chenoweth moved to inboard hydroplane competition and lost his life in a high-speed mishap while piloting *Miss Budweiser* during the 1980s.

O. F. Christner. During the 1950s and into the 1960s, Christner's Quincy Welding Works employed about a dozen men to convert stock Mercury racing outboards into alcohol burners. Sometimes upwards of 40 powerheads would be on the firm's small production line busy with orders placed by racers throughout North America as well as eager throttle-squeezers from Japan to Africa. Christner's Quincy Loopers set a new standard for alky power via his own racing team and for dozens of Quincy customers.

Doug Creech. Prior to entering the world of outboard racing, this North Carolinian earned a good reputation for his speedy motorcycle competition endeavors. He even owned a Harley franchise. Creech started knee-padding in 1942, and by the conclusion of the 1950 season, had already been APBA highpointer in Classes "A," "B," and "C" for three straight years. In addition to dozens of other kudos, the alky standout netted the Union of International Motorboating's John Ward Trophy in 1953 and '55. That was the first time anyone had been awarded the international outboard hydroplane prize, twice. As in any competitive career, Creech had some trials. The 1956 alky Nationals is a case in point. During a heat — figuratively and literally — his KR mill burst into flames, forcing Creech to abandon the dangerous hydro.

Jon Culver. Winner of many important early stock outboard contests (including firsts at the 1948 Albany to New York Marathon and 1949 APBA Nationals), Jon Culver's youthful determination and dedication to the sport served as a major catalyst in attracting others (especially young people) to the genre. Because his father, Merlyn, worked closely with the Kiekhaefer Corporation, the teen was featured in numerous Mercury ads during the motor maker's seminal years with stock outboarding and the APBA. One could say young Culver began his racing career at age five when his dad put him in a 1936 Bendix single-powered craft, started the kicker from a dock, and sent the boy on his way. When Merlyn Culver — who worked with Johnson, Bendix, and then Mercury — established his Mercury distributorship in Ohio shortly after World War Two, Jon loyally campaigned a succession of Merc stocker models. His last big stock win was a national "CU" title for 1956. By then, Merc was starting to promote its bigger engines, so in 1958 Culver shifted to Powercat-type boats (which developed into the OPC class.) Having long operated his father's inboard racers, he was comfortable with that transition. Inboard or outboard, Culver's secret was to be well practiced and have good equipment — and to get to the first turn before anyone else.

DeSilva brothers. For decades, Bill and Ralph DeSilva built outboard runabouts that consistently showed up in the winners' circle. Sturdy boats with the DeSilva label are still the brand of choice for many an alky racer.

Craig DeWald. 507267Q. Decades after his teenage entrance into stock outboarding, Craig DeWald could still rattle off the serial number of his first "good" competition motor. The KG4Q had almost been forgotten by a local Reading, Pennsylvania, Triumph motorcycle dealership that took on a small Merc franchise for a short time. When the shop decided to stick with two-wheeled motive power, all remaining outboard inventory was fire-saled. But one little mill didn't sell. DeWald's dad had heard about the Quicksilver-equipped "left-over," and first looked it over in storage under the dealer's stairs. That motor helped the youth become one of the 1950s leading Stock Outboard marathon champions. While most other enduro participants didn't want to risk their good rigs in fickle long-range rough water treks, DeWald's strategy called for using his best boat and motor in marathoning. That often gave him the winning edge. He was the 1954 Winnebagoland Marathon's youngest entrant, but that didn't stop him from winning its "AU" title in a real squeaker against a local favorite. The 14-year-old's boat came from a set of Hal Kelly plans and got the name *Flyin' Chips*.

During the winter, the racer worked on his engines, and opponents on the gymnasium mat. As a member of the Reading High School varsity wrestling team, DeWald "turned in a near perfect record of seven wins in eight matches to prove his sports talents [were] not limited just to outboard racing."

Marshall Eldredge. This famed outboarder has done so many notable things in the racing sport that it's difficult to know where to start his resume. A New England native, he regularly headed over to the Empire State for the Albany-to-New York Marathon. In 1937, he won that Hudson grind, but is also remembered for his determination during days he wasn't number one at checkered flag. During one race, Eldredge's boat sank twice in the river water... twice! He bailed it out, got his motor going again... and again . . . , then managed to be counted among the finishers. By the early 1950s, Eldredge relocated to Florida where he precision built -from OMC and his own parts- competition outboards, and was well known for his own line of sleek lower units. At one time, he held the World Outboard Speed Record of 79.685 mph.

Hubert A. Entrop. *OUTBOARD* magazine introduced this Seattleite to a national readership by noting he "made [1955's] biggest racing equipment news with his *monkey-on-a-stick* hydroplane." That's what observers dubbed Entrop's experimental craft that later became known as the *cabover hydro*. Gold Cup designer, Ted Jones, helped him with the concept plans. As the aforementioned publication indicated, "The hull is a true prop rider with a long cockpit which permits the helmsman to sit right out over the forward sponsons. At high speed this design permits the rear planing surface to break free of the water to reduce drag and increase speed." Entrop did a lot of "D" (both stock and alky) work before capturing the world's attention in 1958 when he used one of his unique hulls and Mercury *Mark 75H* to go faster than any outboarder had previously accomplished. That made him the premier outboard driver to enter Gulf Oil's *100 MPH Club*. By the early 1960s, he'd bettered his old Merc record by teaming with OMC and a V-4 Evinrude on an enclosed cockpit hydro.

W. Claude Fox. Chapter Five contains details on this legendary promoter of outboard racing.

Blake Gilpin. Here's an "A" hydro racer who also contributed to the genre through her *Boat Sport* authorship. With husband Hank Bowman, she became the mother of competition boat builders Craig and Shannon Bowman who actively promote APBA stock outboarding in the 21st Century.

Jane Hendrickson. A noted "M" driver, Ms. Herndrickson and her eight-foot Jacoby hydro *Beep* were featured in Camel cigarette's sports stars print advertising campaign. She came to the attention of R. J. Reynolds Tobacco Company after earning APBA Ladies High Point national honors in the 1940s.

Randolph Hubbell. Arguably more than anyone else, Randolph Hubbell helped preserve alky outboard competition for the post-war years. His California shop truly did have — as was often advertised — "the world's largest supply of racing outboard motors."

C. W. "Doc" Jones. This Pacific Northwest/Alaska distributor of Mercury outboards is best known for his role in the late 1950s/early 1960s outboard *world's speed record* race between Mercury and Evinrude. While holding informal racers' koffee klatches at his marine store, Jones helped Hugh Entrop get into the sport. With Jones', and boat designer, Ted Jones' (no relation) encouragement, Entrop later drove legendary hulls for both Kiekhaefer and OMC. Jones sold his Merc interests, and then operated a similar endeavor with Evinrude. Thus, his corporate racing experience truly spanned a wide range.

Ted Jones. Though most associated with inboard-powered hulls, Seattle area speedboat maven Ted Jones has long been recognized as one of racing's all time hydroplane design superstars.

Westerman Jones. This leading alky outboard figure is best known for his high-quality, chrome-treated engine cylinders that showed up in most of the 1950s most successful motors on the pro circuit. At one time, Jones had some seven people working with him in his Delaware shop where the main enterprise was chroming the massive cylinders that the nearby Dupont Corporation used in making plastic film. He notified *Boat Sport* readership (December 1953) that his shop offered Mercury 10 hp owners a hard chrome plating service for their outboards. Included in this service was grinding (of the twin cylinders), chrome processing, and finish grinding. Although, not legal for the era's "B" stockers [as the procedure took the motor out of the "as-factory" realm], the chroming was appreciated by ordinary outboarders seeking "longer wear with better piston ring seal than would be possible with worn stock cylinders."

Len Keller. Remembering this well-liked racer/parts maker, Hugh Entrop noted: "Leonard Keller operated out of a small shop north of Seattle, but it was amazing how good his racing hardware was. We all used it. All of my hulls [including the 75H World's Record breaker] had Keller Hardware . . . from speedometers, steering wheels, hand throttles, etc. And any time your speedometer needed adjusting, he would do it free of charge." Even at boat races where he'd be running "A" Hydro, Keller would be running around the pits adjusting and fixing other people's equipment.

Hal Kelly. Through his many plan-set offerings (*Wetback, Foo-Ling*, et al), this 1950s-era boat designer/builder probably put more racers on the water than anyone else. Kelly was also a painter, photographer, author (*Building Your Boat from Plans & Kits*, Chilton Publishers, 1959), and avid stock outboard competitor. He studied art at the Pratt Institute and several other notable schools. In addition to his seminal *Boat Sport* work, Kelly served as Art Director at Fawcett Publications. He passed away at age 78 in 1997. Observant boat buffs still see his designs offered in the Buffalo, New York area (Clark-Craft) do-it-yourself marine catalog and website.

E. Carl Kiekhaefer. The founder of Mercury never did much safety throttle squeezing, but his mercurially competitive personality opened doors for the aggressive research and development needed to make Mercury the leader in stock outboard motor production. He hired good people, could quickly tell when they were delivering their best, and pushed for more of it.

Homer Kincaid. An outboard great with an especially long racing career, Homer Kincaid enjoyed throttle-jockeying from 1929 through 1971. He started with a home-brew hydro and second-hand motor. During the 1930s, Kincaid drove for others who could better afford top grade equipment. Improved financials following the War allowed him to get back on the water with his own gear. "B" Hydro, "B" Runabout, C-Service Hydro, C-Service Runabout, and "C" Hydro were some of the classes this alky champion mastered. Along the way Kincaid became a V-P in the APBA's Outboard Racing Commission.

Jack Leek. See Chapter Two for an account this west coast boat racer's Class "A" milestone achieved with the Leek combo of mechanical ingenuity and great driving.

Johnny Mann. One the "new NOA's" first Stock Utility star's, Johnny Mann specialized in "B" Stock Runabout. In 1946, the novice boat builder, he got out the hammer and saw for some experimenting that, three hulls later, yielded him a long-nosed, narrow racer for the 1953 season. He drove it to an NOA "B" Stock Runabout five-mile record of 39.709 mph. (It's interesting to note that the NOA rules allowed stockers to run with open exhaust on water bodies with no local noise restrictions.) Mann's craft and associated KG-7 Mercury, might remind Boat Builder's Handbook readers of the "hydro-conic" bottomed Blue Streak that became available in plan form shortly thereafter. *Boat Sport* highlighted Mann for possessing "no previous mechanical skill or boat building experience" and still being able to "top the boys with the big budgets who have work done for them by the pros."

Fred Mathews. The C-Service racing record books were filled with Freddy Mathews' name from 1949 into the 1950s. The Watervliet, New York, racer first snagged impressive titles in '49 with a New England States, as well as the Eastern Divisional Championship in the venerable C-Service class. In 1952, Matthews' season was especially hot -great enough, he figured, to snatch his favorite category's "high-point" honors for a second year in a row. When no notice of high-point achievement arrived, he shot off a letter to the APBA asking who was in charge of headquarters' arithmetic. They said they were sorry for having misfiled his records and goofing up the C-Service high-point awards. He suggested they print an apology in the *Propeller* newsletter. They told him to just leave the big N-1 designation on the sides of his runabout, *"Stardust."*

John Jack Maypole. APBA's 1954 Stock Outboard Nationals yielded one of the genre's most duplicated photos... a shot that caught racing's essence via Jack Maypole's thrilled expression as he negotiated a buoy in his Merc-powered "D" Stock Hydro. He began throttle squeezing around his native Chicagoland and was a mainstay in the big Outboard Club of Chicago. During the 1930s, Maypole was one of the youngest outboarders to claim an NOA national championship. By the 1950s, his name was synonymous with outboard racing. He operated a boat and motor dealership, and even had a sports-oriented program on 50,000 watt WJJD (1160-AM) out of the Windy City. At the 1958 Chicago National Boat Show, Maypole suffered a heart attack, and then died shortly thereafter. At the time of his passing, he'd just been voted to a second term as APBA Vice President.

Stan MacDonald. Stan's Outboard Shop in Ontario, Canada, wasn't a very large establishment, but its proprietor Stan McDonald built-up some of the world's most competitive alky racing outboards. Among his best work were Evinrude-based "C" Service engines for a loyal customer following, as well as for his own expert use. During the early 1990s, when MacDonald came to Fulton, New York, with some racing buddies on the pro-alky US Title Series, I broadcast the races on our family radio station. It was a true testament to "being as young as you feel," as this famous pre-war starter took an opportunity to whip around the buoys at 80+ mph. He passed away a few years later, well into his 90s.

Boots Kaye Morphy. Here's a leading 1950s Class "M" alky driver who also spent time on land in her Hollywood, California, as a movie stuntwoman. One of the petite Evinrude racer's noted 1954 titles came after a record NOA "M" (39.956 mph) straightaway run in her three-point Jacoby hydro.

Dick O'Dea. As one of Stock Outboarding's first stars, the then (early 1950s) teen championed Mercury motors and Sid-Craft boats, and won many important titles, such as the "ASR" crown at the 1953 APBA Nationals. O'Dea approached the endeavor as a science, and as did a few others captivated by racing, worked with competition motors and accessories (like his Jones-O'Dea *Red Head* Mercury cylinder/head replacement) professionally. Photos of his runabout hopping the waves were reproduced in enough Sid-Craft ads to make him well known even to racing buffs who never saw the New Jersey native in person.

Dick Neal. A boat or race-prepared motor wearing the Neal brand was immediately recognizable throughout the racing community as a quality object. The Kansas City, Missouri resident concentrated on alky engines and hydroplanes, but more than a few of his well built hulls saw stock or deluxe cottage racing assignments. A surprising number of these wood and canvas boats survive in collections (with some being actively raced) today.

Gilbert "Gibby" Petermann. If there were such a thing, the "split shift" gold medal for outboard racing would go to this Long Islander. "Gibby" got into the sport in 1936 where he achieved "star" status in "A" and "B" Hydro work. One of *Boat Sport's* most vibrant covers featured him in August '52. He picked up a national championship in "B" Hydro in 1951, "A" Hydro for 1953, then put the Johnson alky motors on a stand and retired the following year. Nearly 25 years later (1978), Peterman got the notion to start throttle-squeezing again... this time in C-Service Hydro and a new (250cc) Class "A" category. And he certainly hadn't forgotten how to win, collecting national championships, straightaway records, and high-point honors. Petermann stayed on the racing circuit until he was 80. The Malverne, New York, water wonder passed away a year later.

(Dick and) **Malcolm Pope.** There's an old racing lexicon that defines the phrase: *To pull a Malcolm Pope,* as any terrific stunt one might be able to achieve in an outboard-powered boat. During the 1920s, he and his brother Dick, "originated the idea of the jumping" outboard racing craft. The duo made numerous action movies involving such thrills. Malcolm pioneered the Cypress Gardens, Florida, shows featuring outboard racing and related antics. After racking up shelves of pre-war alky-burner competition trophies, he returned to serious racing after the hostilities. The 1920s/30s generated star-power made him a longtime draw. Malcolm Pope's pioneering during the sport's early days — when an old-style PR-40 (with standard-service lower unit) made for quite a contrast when he'd take one of his show organization's 1950s hydro and KG-9H for a spin in the Sunshine State.

Billy Schumacher. The youngest driver to be given *OUTBOARD* magazine's 1955 *Silver Prop* award, Billy Schumacher picked up honors for his endeavors in "JU," "AU," and "ASH." The, then 12 year old would have been happy to jump to "B"-size Mercs, but APBA rules indicated he wasn't quite old enough to handle the 20-cubic-inch mills. And there was also the issue of the older stockers not wanting to get passed by a 6th grader! Later, Schumacher got interested in inboards and piloted some unlimited class hydroplanes.

Ralph Scott. A steamfitter from Paducah, Kentucky, Ralph Scott got into NOA action in 1953. Two years later, he'd been crowned NOA's annual high-point champ . . . twice. Scott favored "A" work with both stock and modified-stock classes.

Bill Seebold. Taking a cue from his father (Bill, Sr. who got into boat racing in the late 1930s), this Seebold started with stock outboarding around 1951. Competitors always wondered how he seemed to instinctively know exactly when they were going to make their turns, thus outmaneuvering them. At 25, he was tapped to enter Gulf's Marine Hall of Fame. He spent many of his nearly five decades of boat racing in tunnel hull endeavors, and prompted one of the sport's best known dynasties via mentoring sons who are also noted racers.

R. Allen "Poppa" Smith. An expert in taking an ordinary propeller and crafting it into a real race winner, "Poppa" Smith plied his trade in a humble Shreveport, Louisiana, tarpaper shack. He even had a few layers of the stuff on the floor to provide a soft landing for any props accidentally dropped. Smith began racing in the 1920s and started perfecting his "magic" with propellers in about 1931. By the 1950s, it became the well-liked artisan's vocation. Along the way, he also served as motor inspector for APBA and NOA events. Even while well past normal retirement age, Smith kept on providing throttle-squeezers with wheels that often gave them an all-important extra mile an hour on the race course. Through the years, he maintained that his ability to charm a prop into perfection mystified himself as much as it might amaze a novice.

V. J. Spinner, Jr. On August 9, 1954, Spinner zoomed his 20H-powered hydro through a carefully measured course at 60.482 mph. That made the Mercer Island, Washingtonian the first Class "B" Stock Hydroplane driver to take his rig into the mile-a-minute zone. The feat occurred on the same day and in the same Seattle waters as Jack Leek's 61+ mph Class "A" Merc alky burner record.

Mickey Starego. Half of the team responsible for stock outboard racing's most famous runabout brand — Sid-Craft.

Charles Strang. This father of *"H"* Mercury motors had a notable outboard racing career even before landing a top job at Mercury (and later with OMC). Strang was a leading competitor in the pre-World War II college outboard racing circuit, served as an official with the APBA, and as a respected *Motor Boating* ("With the Outboarders") columnist.

Hershel H. Starnes. An outboard driver everyone liked, H. H. Starnes was most known for a broad smile and racing lower unit company bearing his name. The alky racer proved to be an NOA favorite in "C" Racing Hydro. During the mid-1950s, a heart problem sent Starnes to a specialist who gave him permission to continue with his beloved sport. The Hickory, North Carolinian got in a few more enjoyable throttle-squeezing seasons before succumbing to a heart attack in early January 1958. He was only 38.

William "Rockey" Stone. This Oregonian was best known for his 30-cubic inch work in alky racing. Rockey Stone tasted the sport in 1941, then jumped into full force after World War II. Some of the notable listings on his resume include the 1957 "C" Racing Runabout National Championship, mile-straightaway "C" Racing Runabout for '58, as well as a National Championship in C-Service Runabout the following year. He stayed on the water until 1974, and died in 1992.

Joe Swift. Beginning around 1951, this Floridian's hydroplanes served as the definition of "stock outboard hydro." They were fast, rugged, inexpensive, and plentiful.

Bob Switzer. This "accidental" boat maker got into the business after experimenting with a sailboat and several powered craft. It didn't take long for the boating pastime to consume more of Switzer's focus and earn him a reputation for excellence [as a racer and hull manufacturer] in the fledgling Stock Utility genre. Some of stock's early APBA rules were written (or rewritten) around Switzer's and his family-company partners' inventiveness. Things like power trim for the motor, dagger board-type fin control for negotiating shallow waters in marathoning, and dashboard-mounted carburetion controls all added potential efficiencies to stock outboard racing. Setting up for a boat show, Switzer received a compliment from a fellow manufacturer. "The way you come up with those beautiful sleek hull designs, you're like pioneers," the old marine official remarked. "My company [which sold family-style runabouts in respectable volume] just builds regular *boaty* kind of boats," he lamented. Switzer took a moment to run some numbers in his head, and then exclaimed to his hull-designer, brother Dave, "We should start making some *boaty-boats*, too!" Fortunately, though, the Switzer name has never been associated with mundane hulls.

William Tenney. He liked to show off a jump suit equipped with a big Kiekhaefer Corporation patch under some hand-embroidered script. Bill Tenney was never a Merc man, so it figured that the good-natured competitor's racing garment (a humorous gift from Charlie Strang) noted, "I have not yet moved up to Mercury." During the early 1950s, when the *"move up to Mercury"* slogan was printed on almost every Kiekhaefer catalog, Tenney was still busy moving up speed records with old Johnson iron converted to run on alcohol. As a 10 year old, the native Minnesotan developed a taste for outboard racing during a nine-mph spin around the buoys in a 1925 Lake Minnetonka event. By the time World War II erupted, Tenney was a Yale University graduate who raced on the side. His good looks and pleasant demeanor put an ambassador's touch on the sport wherever he and his hydros (dubbed *Hornet*) toured. Although having logged dozens of races at home and abroad, Tenney first struck National Championship gold with a "C" Racing Runabout in 1952, and then picked up a trophy for earning more points than any other amateur driver that year. "A," "B," and "C" hydro mile-straightaway records came next for him in 1953 . . . a trio of new high marks and all in one day. Through the '57 season [in which he took first in "C" Hydro at the Alky Nationals] Tenney accumulated wins and kudos from others who understood the kind of hard work it took to be successful on and off of the water.

He decided to retire from "formal" outboard racing in 1958. Fourteen years hence, however, I was one of the curious young guys at the Antique Outboard Motor Club's 1st National Meet in Antioch, Illinois, who helped a professorial gentleman put a "B" Neal hydro in the lake. It was quite a shock to see this fellow remove his stylish sport jacket, debonair step into the "I have not yet. . . . " togs, don lifejacket, and football [type] helmet, then fire up the boat's old Johnson SR. One of the other teens who'd assisted with the launch stood there equally incredulous, saying to me, "I sure hope that old guy knows what he's doing." "Yeah," I replied, thinking Tenney was an author or local dignitary who had been offered a "publicity" spin in a real antique racing craft, "Somebody should have warned him this can be dangerous." Noted alky driver Bob Thornton from Virginia was present, too. He'd been in the Antique Outboard club with me for several years, so I knew him. Bob looked at us and chuckled. . . . "Boys, that's the great Bill Tenney. He's been running fast boats since before your parents were born. Nobody needs to explain anything about racing to him!" In addition to throttle squeezing, during the 1950s, Tenney founded a firm called Aeromarine Company which gave him a venue for inventing, engine building, and even importing. Mercs converted to alcohol had begun picking-off vintage OMC racing motors by 1956, convincing him a new brand of alky mill would be needed to battle the Kiekhaefer modified crowd. From 1957 to 1963, his business distributed fast British Anzani racing outboards throughout North America. He sold the shop in 1984 and passed away nine years later while fishing in Siberia.

Orlando Torigiani. A quintessential Class "A" Racing Outboard technician, Torigiani earned APBA as well as NOA national titles in the category for several years in a row (around 1953-54). The famed alky driver hailed from Bakersfield, California.

Seaman "Sid" Urytzski. The co-founder of Sid-Craft Boat Company. After an inexplicably sudden decision to end his business partnership with Mickey Starego and close this firm in the 1960s, Urytzski and a son began Sid-Son Boats and focused on hydroplanes. Be advised that period references show Sid's name spelled in a variety of ways, such as Uretzky, Uretszki, etc. Some direct quotations in this book may use an incorrect spelling.

Frank Vincent. Dubbed the "Tulsa Tornado," he was honored by *Boat Sport* with the recognition that "there probably isn't an alcohol burning outfit running today [1950s] that doesn't include some mechanical advancement, gimmick, or trick that Vincent hasn't has something to do with." In fact, many a vintage racing outboard in contemporary collections (and in use) are equipped with Vincent product — such as cylinder heads. While the Oklahoman began racing homemade hulls, Vincent's 1950s boat of choice was a Neal, and always said that Dick Neal was his toughest racing competitor. During his decades of throttle squeezing, Vincent was hospitalized with racing-related injuries several times, including a stay following a mishap at 75-mph+ with an "X" Class rig. At that speed, *Boat Sport* reported, "a gust of wind caught the [hydro]. The bow rose, got airborne and did a double flip. Somewhere in the melee of whirling boat, motor, and driver, Vincent took a terrific blow on the head. He was hauled from the water unconscious . . . but within a few weeks he was as good as ever [and ready to race]." One of his daughter's married Gar Wood, Jr., and presented Vincent with grandson, Gar Wood III, representing a strong boat racing lineage on both sides of the family.

Jerry Waldman. Mercury and OMC engineering great, Charlie Strang labeled Jerry Waldman (in a 1972 edition of APBA *Propeller*) "probably the most talented powerboat racer of all time." Waldman got into the sport in his native Wisconsin during the 1950 Stock Utility season. There, he quickly established a pair of important new "AU," and "BU" mile straightaway marks. At the Syracuse Stock Nationals, three years later, he grabbed the "DU" crown. Waldman also felt at home in a hydro, demonstrating skill with shingles in "A," "C," "D," and "F" departments. Alky engines also came under his control in APBA and NOA events. Under those sanctioning bodies, Waldman had 26 and 19 titles, respectively. Sadly, he was killed by a hydro that flipped into his boat during a 1972 race.

Paul Wearly. At his first outboard race, Paul Wearly ran fast enough to win a cigarette lighter and a few other pieces of related tobacco equipment. Winning was nice, but the prizes didn't amount to much, since Wearly didn't smoke. That was in Celina, Ohio at one of the old pre-war NOA Division I amateur events. From then on, he ran in pro classes where one had the chance to recoup some of his/her endeavor's expenses. The Hoosier was setting World's Records (Class "C") in 1938 a year before completing an Indiana University degree. During World War II, he worked on government projects with speedboat maker Gar Wood in Detroit. Resuming his outboard racing career at the close of hostilities, Wearly started winning again in "A," "B," and "C" classes to the point where his titles through the 1950s, could be divided up among a half dozen drivers and make each look quite accomplished. He also made stock's first "AU" headlines as non-chalant winner in the '49 Nationals.

During 1955, the consummate alky-burner built-up a 61-cubic-inch outboard racer via Evinrude, Johnson, and Starnes parts and ran it on a Neal hydro to a United States NOA Class "X" record. A couple of years earlier, he formed a small company that built "Wearly" brand hydroplanes. Anytime the Muncie, Indianan wanted to go for a quiet cruise, he could put a small Martin motor on his craft. Wearly had won a race that George Martin sponsored at Eau Claire, Wisconsin, circa 1950. For a prize, Martin gave him the motor, which he liked better than the aforementioned lighter.

John Wehrle. Highly representative of clean-cut, determined young, newcomers to Stock Utility (or Stock Outboard Racing) during the '50s, is Johnny Wehrle. The Hackensack, New Jersey, teen first tried the sport in the summer of 1953, a season during which he and his dad — who served as crew — quickly discovered it was going to take some practice. That summer did include a pair of first place wins, but also netted eight instances where he, his Sid-Craft runabout and Merc ended up drinking river water. Live and learn they did with improvements over the '54 racing calendar. *Boat Sport* noted that during 1955 Wehrle towed his rigs more than 35,000 miles to rack up wins and points in "AU," "ASH," "BU," and "BSH" races spanning from February 6 through December 31, 1955. Twenty-eight events in places as far flung as Lake Alfred, Florida to Delake, Oregon. Although he didn't have much luck at the Nationals, the then twenty year old managed to amass 27,687 points for his many wins, 2nds, and 3rds in 1955. The perseverance those numbers touted netted Wehrle APBA's coveted High-Point ranking, the A.C. Kiekhaefer Trophy (for over-all high point score), plus the John and Flora Bank Trophy symbolizing high-points in any singular class (in this case, "ASH"). His throttle work came at a time when stock outboarding mainstreamed by sizable sponsors, like Mercury, captured the boating public's attention.

Clark "Bud" Wiget. Walnut farming and engineering were just two of this Concord, Californian's professions. Then again, he was also considered to be the consummate alky outboard pro of the 1950s. Wiget earned APBA's Outboard Racing High Point crown in 1953. On August 9th of the following year, he was on the water in Seattle picking up a pair of important American Power Boating Association straightaway mile accomplishments: "C" Runabout (63.581 mph), and "F" Racing Runabout (63.811 mph). Before '54 was through, he amassed two more APBA honors ("F" Racing Runabout in five-mile competition, and another with "C" Runabout). Clark "Bud" Wiget began outboarding with a low-horsepower Caille in 1931. He wasn't racing with that putt-putt, just cruising around in front of a pretty neighbor girl's cottage hoping she'd notice him. Meanwhile some urbane Johnson owner appeared on the lake in a swanky sea sled, and he lost his appeal to the lass. Prior to attending engineering school that fall, Bud started building a boat, then found a cheap, second-hand Johnson *SR-45* "B" racer which proceeded to help him take last place in various Northern California regattas. No matter, he was really into the sport. As finances allowed, he upgraded equipment, improving his competitive record. By 1937-38, things were looking brighter for him in the winners' circle.

At one of the races, he particularly noticed an attractive woman replacing an alky motor's piston rings. She was a recent widow whose spouse, Ernie Millot, had been killed in an "F" Runabout mishap. His marriage to Ethel "Meizzie" Millot formed what *Boat Sport* termed "one of the greatest husband and wife [outboard] racing teams of all time." During their first days together, the couple put $100 down and $30 a month on a . . . battery ignition *ELTO Super C* motor they nicknamed *"Baby."* All Bud's "C" (1941-

1950s) "C" Racing Runabout and "C" Racing Hydro records were set using this family pet.

After a 15-year chemical engineering career with Shell Oil Company, Wiget decided to make a change. He'd inherited a walnut ranch from his parents, so did some farming. The chemical background allowed Bud to produce a line of special oils, nitro and alcohol-based fuels under his own *Super Speed Racing Fuel* banner. He and Ethel also had a shop where they got into the boat business and did special alky engine work. Their custom "C" ignition parts, and "F" cylinder heads were just two of the custom parts in the Wiget catalog beginning in the mid-1950s. Around that time, they sold the ranch, then moved their marine endeavors to Lakeland, Florida. The Wigets and Walt Blankenstein took over the Marshall Eldredge racing outboard shop there in 1955.

Bud's boats of choice were DeSilva runabouts and Neal hydros. When Dick Neal quit making hulls, Wiget started buying Sid-Craft hydroplanes. Those C-Hydros were hitting well into the 80 mph zone by 1963, causing Bud to think he might be getting too old to need such speed in a tiny outboard craft. He sold most of his clamp-on gear and bought an inboard racer that'd go 110+. Bud and Ethel ran those bigger boats until retiring from racing in 1977.

Ethel Wiget. "The best Wiget racing driver," admits her longtime racing/husband partner Bud. -See above (Bud Wiget) listing and Chapter Seven for more details

Ronald Zuback. A noted "BU" Stock marathoner of the 1950s, Zuback hailed from Morgan, New Jersey.

Appendix B

APBA Stock National Champions 1949-60

Note: The lettering code immediately following the engine piston displacement designation indicates boat type. "*U*" = Utility, "*SH*" = Stock Hydro, "*SR*" = Stock Runabout. (example: *JU* = Class J Utility runabout). After the 1951 introduction of *Stock Hydroplanes*, the term *Stock Runabout* began being used in place of the original *Utility* runabout vernacular. Through the early 1960s, however, some publications continued labeling the runabout class as *Utility*. Classes EU and FU typically involved a hull of heavier construction than the other stock runabout categories, and relied upon hefty Evinrude opposed four-cylinder outboards not produced since 1950 and 1949 respectively. Consequently, participation was spotty. The 1956 inclusion of "36" Class seemed to finish off EU/FU Nationals activity, as OMC fans had this new category all to themselves.

1949   **Lake Alfred, Florida**

Class	Winner	Hometown
JU	Roy Ridgell	Gainesville, FL
AU	Paul Wearly	Muncie, IN
BU	Jon Culver	Dayton, OH
CU	Charles Wingo	Baltimore, MD
DU	Jack Maypole	Oak Park, IL
EU	Antonio Stroscio	North Bergen, NJ (Only two boats participated in this "matched race," which did not count as a national championship.)

1950   **Dallas, Texas (White Rock Lake)**

Class	Winner	Hometown
JU	S.H. Winters, Jr.	Paris, TX
AU	Al Montouri	Sherman, TX
BU	Alex Wetherbee, Jr.	Paris, TX
CU	Joe Michelini	Chicago, IL
DU	H.L. "Tex" Flagg	Dennison, TX
EU	Bob Meyer	Kansas City, KS
FU	Roy Buie	Fort Worth, TX

1951   **Knoxville, TN**

Class	Winner	Hometown
JU	Allyn Guerin	Webster, NY
ASH	Emmet Carey	Rochester, NY
ASR	John Krehl	Madison, WI

BSH	Alex Wetherbee	Paris, TX
		(Tommy Haygood finished first but was disqualified.)
BSR	Joe Krupa	Hudson, NY
CSR	Lee Manthei	Green Bay, WI
		(G.G. Slack finished first but was disqualified.)
DSH	Tom Haygood	Orlando, FL
DSR	Jack Force	Akron, OH
EU	Joe Michelini	Chicago, IL
FU	(not enough starters)	

1952 Oakland, CA

Class	Winner	Hometown
JU	Marilyn Donaldson	Dayton, OH
ASH	Dean Chenoweth	Xenia, OH
ASR	Dean Chenoweth	Xenia, OH
BSH	Dean Chenoweth	Xenia, OH
BSR	Ron Zuback	Morgan, NJ
CSR	John Toprahanian	San Diego, CA
DSH	Ivan Harris	Loveland, CO
DSR	Robert Switzer	McHenry, IL
EU	George Churchill	Willamina, OR
FU	(not enough starters)	

1953 Syracuse, NY

Class	Winner	Hometown
JU	Jerry Opperude	Williams Bay, WI
ASH	Don Baldacini	Miami, FL
ASR	Dick O'Dea	Patterson, NJ
BSH	Anthony Lamontia	University, OH
BSR	Gerald Moshier	Phoenix, NY
CSR	Anthony Stroscio	North Bergen, NJ
DSH	Jon Culver	Dayton, OH
DSR	Gerald Waldman	Milwaukee, WI

1954   De Pere, WI

Class	Winner	Hometown
JU	Mike Helm	Thiensville, WI
ASH	Don Baldacini	Miami, FL
ASR	Dick O'Dea	Patterson, NJ
BSH	Bob Parish	Bakersfield, CA
BSR	Eddie West	Berkeley, CA
CSR	Ron Loomis	Santa Barbara, CA
DSH	Frank Huebner	Bay City, MI
DSR	John Jackson	Cincinnati, OH

1955   Devils Lake, OR

Class	Winner	Hometown
JU	Billy Schumacher	Seattle, WA
ASH	Don Benson	Seattle, WA

BSH	Don Baldacini	Miami, FL
BSR	Don Baldacini	Miami, FL
CSR	Ron Loomis	Santa Barbara, CA
DSH	Art Sullivan	Seattle, WA
DSR	Paul Woodroffe	Salem, OR
EU	Dean Mahaffey	Salem, OR

1956   Cambridge, MD

Class	*Winner*	*Hometown*
JU	Billy Schumacher	Seattle, WA
ASH	Dean Chenoweth	Xenia, OH
ASR	Dean Chenoweth	Xenia, OH
BSH	Dave Kough	Hawthorne, NJ
BSR	Dave Kough	Hawthorne, NJ
CSH	William Buck McClung	Portsmouth, VA
CSR	Jon Culver	Dayton, OH
DSH	William Holloway	Monroe, MI
DSR	John Jackson	Cincinnati, OH
"36"	Ed Branding	Lake Villa, IL

1957   Worcester, MA

Class	*Winner*	*Hometown*
JU	Tiger Petrini	Annapolis, MD
ASH	Dave Hoogard	Trenton, MI
ASR	Dean Chenoweth	Xenia, OH
BSH	Chris Erneston	West Palm Beach, FL
BSR	Jack Hall	Pittsburgh, PA
CSH	Frank Goodwin	Hanson, MA
CSR	Johnny Ennenga	Grand Haven, MI
DSH	William Holloway	Tipp City, OH
DSR	Skip Forcier	Grosse Point, MI
"36"	Dan Schartzenbach	Los Angeles, CA

1958   Miami, FL

Class	*Winner*	*Hometown*
JU	Russell Wulf	Amityville, NY
ASH	Dave Hoggard	Trenton, MI
ASR	Dean Chenoweth	Xenia, OH
BSH	Harry Pinner	West Palm Beach, FL
BSR	Paul Kalb	Monroe, MI
CSH	Bob Brown	Miami, FL
CSR	Dick Rees	Pottstown, PA
DSH	Don Baldacini	Miami, FL
DSR	Skip forcier	Grosse Point, MI
"36"	William Kennedy III	Halesite, NY

1959   Seattle, WA

Class	*Winner*	*Hometown*
JU	Jack Holden	Seattle, WA

ASH	Eddie Wulf	Amityville, NY
ASR	Eddie Wulf	Amityville, NY
BSH	Robert Herring	Sheboygan, WI
BSR	Ron Zuback	Morgan, NJ
CSH	Bob Brown	Miami, FL
CSR	Dean Mahaffey	Roseburg, OR
DSH	Dick O'Dea	Patterson, NJ
DSR	John Schedel	Secaucus, NJ
"36"	William Kennedy III	Halesite, NY

1960	Beloit, WI	
Class	*Winner*	*Hometwon*
JU	Russell Wulf	Amityville, NY
ASH	Jack Evans	Denville, NJ
ASR	Gary Stippich	Milwaukee, WI
BSH	Lee Sutter	Seattle, WA
BSR	Ron Hedlund	Wilmette, IL
CSH	Stan Armstrong	Orland Park, Ill
CSR	Keith Stippich	Milwaukee, WI
DSH	Bob Okner	Lake Mohawk, NJ
DSR	Ray Lenk	Detroit, MI
"36"	Bob Moore	Royal Oak, MI

Appendix C

AQUA-JET Quick List

Matching those Michigan Wheel Company Cottage Racer Props by Number and Motor Through 1955

By 1948, post-World War Two boating and baby "booms" jelled to create an eager market for fast propellers that could quickly upgrade the average family fishing outboard into a cottage racer. The folks at Michigan Wheel saw this niche and introduced their line of Aqua-Jet (two-blade) props with impecunious hot rodder in mind. "The tremendous success of this wheel," Michigan's 1950 catalog noted, "which was originally brought out as a semi-custom job for a few of the 7-1/2 and 10-hp motors led to the expansion of sizes (of even more blade pitch options, and for many other engine models) by popular demand." In fact the company's earliest Aqua-Jet offerings were for the garden variety seven-and-a-halves from Sears Elgin, and Scott-Atwater, with an AJ for the sexier Merc Lightning thrown in for good measure.

Most of the AJ propellers listed herein are for non-shift outboards. Where more than one AJ model is listed for the same motor, various pitch options were available. Some motors with forward, neutral and reverse also rated a fast double blade wheel of this ilk. Michigan came out with the Aqua-Jet Cushion with a rubber "slip clutch" hub insert) or AJC series to fit that bill. (e.g. Evinrude's 1951-55 25-horse Big Twin could be fitted with AJC-460 through AJC-464.)

Some of the early Mercuys required a splined adapter ring for mating to an AJ prop. This was offered as a Kiekhaefer option, and replaced the slip-clutch by substituting a pair of shear pins positioned parallel with the propeller shaft. In fact a few Aqua-Jets had hubs cast to fit over a splined prop shaft and related metal slip clutch discs. The classic variety, though, were drilled for a smooth propeller shaft. AJ520 (splined) and AJ521 (smooth) serve as examples for the old 5 and 6-hp Mercs.

It should be noted that this list was compiled using several late 1940s through 1955 Michigan rosters, as well as via a dig through the author's Aqua-Jet box. Some obscure numbers didn't always make Michigan's consumer-reference lists (and appear to be arcane), while other AJ props one may dig up wear a model number not chronicled herein. Post 1955, there was also a trickle of "new" Aqua-Jets released for the 1956-58 Champion 16-1/2, as an example. By that time, though, most motors were shift models and would have required AJC versions, and so the AJ era had ended. Suffice it to say, throughout Aqua-Jet's heyday production run, there were some rather limited production AJ wheels yet to be "discovered," and that this study is admittedly ongoing. Feel free to notify me of any updates, corrections, or nuances connected to the list. In any event, accessorizing one's old cottage racer with an appropriate AJ wheel can be a neat experience.

MICHIGAN #	Motor
AJ8	Corsair, Firestone, Scott-Atwater 7-1/2 hp models
AJ12	Corsair, Firestone, Scott-Atwater 16 hp models
AJ20	Gale Products 12 hp models (including Elto,
AJ22	Hiawatha, Sea Bee, Royal, Buccaneer, Sea-Flyer, Atlas,
AJ23	Brooklure, and Fedway)
AJ34	Martin "60," "66," standard "75"
AJ37	Martin "60" Hi-Speed
AJ39	Martin Twist-Shift "75"
AJ42	Mercury KE-7, Wizard WG7
AJ44	Martin Twist-Shift "100"
AJ45	Mercury KE-7
AJ46	Mercury KE-7, Wizard WG7
AJ47	(same as above)
AJ48	Mercury KF-7, KG-7
AJ49	(same as above)
AJ50	(same as above)
AJ51	Mercury KF-7, KG-7, Wizard WG7A
AJ52	Elgin 7 1/2-hp (1949-55)
AJ53	Wizard WJ7, WM7
AJ55	Mercury KF-7, KG-7, Wizard WG-7
AJ56	Mercury KE-4, Mark 7
AJ57	(same as above)
AJ58	Mercury KG-4
AJ59	(same as above)
AJ80	Mercury KG-9, Mark 40
AJ81	Mercury KG-9 (KF-9)
AJ82	(same as above)
AJ83	(same as above)
AJ84	(same as above)
AJ85	(same as above, and Mark 40)
AJ90	Wizard 6 hp (thru 1954)
AJ125	Champion 4K
AJ130	Champion 4L-HD, and Hot Rod 4KS, 4LS series

MICHIGAN #	Motor
AJ132	Champion (also Majestic/Voyager) 15-hp twin (1954-55)
AJ134	(same as above)
AJ200	Johnson QD (early 10-hp)
AJ201	(same as above)
AJ288	Evinrude 6039-type Speeditwin (w/ 1" shaft)
AJ289	(same as above)
AJ290	Evinrude Speeditwin, Elto Super "C"
AJ301	Evinrude SpeediFour
AJ323	(same as AJ289, and Evinrude SpeediFour)
AJ324	Evinrude SpeediFour, and Big-Four (w/ 1" shaft)
AJ325	(same as above)
AJ326	Evinrude Big-Four
AJ327	(same as above)
AJ332	Evinrude SpeediFour
AJ333	(same as above)
AJ334	(same as above)
AJ335	SpeediQuad, Big-Four, Big Quad
AJ345	Evinrude SportFour
AJ349	Evinrude Lightfour
AJ350	(same as above)
AJ355	Big Quad
AJ400	Neptune Master Twin 16 hp, Johnson S-45, S-65, S-70
AJ410	Evinrude Fastwin circa1950
AJ420	Evinrude Fleetwin 7 1/2-hp (1950-53)
AJ421	(same as above)
AJ430	Chris-Craft Commander 10 hp
AJ431	(same as above)
AJ440	Elgin 16-hp circa 1950
AJ450	Martin "100" (non-neutral)
AJ451	(same as above)
AJ520	Mercury KF-5, Super-5, Mark 5, Mark 6, and Wizard WH6
AJ521	(has smooth bore for 5/6-hp motors without splined Prop shaft)
AJ530	Martin "200"

MICHIGAN #	Motor
AJ615	Evinrude Fleetwin Aquasonic 7 1/2-hp (1954-55)
AJ616	(same as above)
AJ617	(same as above)
AJ1194	Johnson P-50 thru P-80, and Johnson PO series
AJ1195	(same as above)
AJ1196	(same as above)

Index